Nonconformity
in the nineteenth century

Birth of Modern Britain series

General editors:

A. E. Dyson
Senior Lecturer in English Literature,
University of East Anglia

and

R. T. Shannon
Reader in English History,
University of East Anglia

Forthcoming:

Class and Conflict in Nineteenth-Century England
edited by Patricia Hollis

Nonconformity
in the nineteenth century

Edited by
David M. Thompson

Fitzwilliam College,
University of Cambridge

Routledge & Kegan Paul

London and Boston

First published 1972
by Routledge & Kegan Paul Ltd
Broadway House, 68–74 Carter Lane,
London EC4V 5EL
and 9 Park Street,
Boston, Mass. 02108, U.S.A.
Printed in Great Britain by
Butler & Tanner Ltd, Frome and London
© David M. Thompson 1972

ISBN 0 7100 7274 0 (c)
ISBN 0 7100 7275 9 (p)

General editors' preface

The series is concerned to make the central issues and topics of the recent past 'live', in both senses of that word. We hope to appeal to students of history and of literature equally, since each has much to offer, and learn from, the other. The volume editors are encouraged to select documents from the widest range of sources, and to convey the 'feel' of particular controversies when passion ran high. One problem for the modern student is hindsight: often, we fall back on over-simplified visions of history—Whig or Marxist, progressive or conservative—because we fail to imagine events as they were. We hope here to re-create situations through the passions and commitments of participants and contemporary commentators, before the outcome was known. In this way, students are encouraged to avoid both over-simplified judgments and that dull sense that whatever happened was inevitable which can so devitalise our understanding of any period's history, or its art.

We believe that this treatment of the recent past, bringing out the sense of immediacy and conflict, is also the soundest basis for understanding the modern world. Increasingly, we realise that continuity is more striking than discontinuity: nothing could be more naive than a claim for 'modernity' which assumes that the past is 'irrelevant' or dead. It was during the age of Arnold and Gladstone, Disraeli and Tennyson, Darwin and Chamberlain that our most distinctive modern problems defined themselves—the growth of great cities and technology; the battle between individualism and collectivism; the coming of democracy, with all its implications for education, class, vocation and the ordinary expectations of living; the revolutions in travel and communication; the shifting relationships between individuals and the state. Many of the major ideas that shape our world were also born: and in the ferment of day-to-day crises and perplexities, prophetic and widely ranging hopes and fears, we see the birth of modern Britain, the emergence of our world of today. Volume editors have been encouraged in their selection of material from contemporary sources to illuminate that density and complexity of things which is the essence of 'reality'.

Nonconformity was one of the most formative influences on Victorian Britain. Gladstone accorded it the accolade of 'the backbone of Liberalism'; the same might be said for Liberalism's successor, the Labour movement. Its influence was also pervasive in the great educational debates of the century, and in most thinking about the relationship between the state and individual freedom. Though the processes of secularisation have distanced us very considerably from its practices and precepts, its role as a midwife at the birth of modern Britain makes a knowledge of it essential for our generation. This volume treats Nonconformity sympathetically but by no means uncritically. Its author writes from inside, as one of its sons, but also as a historian, who can assess its weaknesses as well as its strengths.

Contents

Preface and Acknowledgments

The history of English Protestant Nonconformity in the twentieth century has been mainly one of decline: nevertheless there can be little doubt about its contribution to the birth of modern Britain. Lord Palmerston's remark that 'in the long run English politics will follow the consciences of the Dissenters' has often been quoted. But a claim for the Nonconformist contribution must rest on a broader and firmer basis than this. That is what this book tries to do.

It is not a substitute for the good modern general history of the Free Churches in the nineteenth century which still remains to be written. For reasons of space it is confined to England, thus omitting the important aspects of Nonconformity in Wales, Scotland and Ireland. As it is a book of extracts the narrative and analysis are necessarily sketchy, being little more than a commentary. But I hope that, by indicating the variety of material available, it will provide a starting point for those who want to explore Nonconformist history.

Something should be said about the principles governing the selection of passages. As always in a book of this kind the main problem is one of length. Some extracts have had to be substantially abbreviated, for example, parliamentary speeches; yet too much abbreviation destroys the flow of argument presented. Other extracts would have been delightful and illuminating; but they were too short to be coherent on their own, whilst to have placed them in context would have introduced much material of marginal relevance. Many extracts are of a similar genre—the description of a place—and it has been very difficult to choose only one or two of these. A similar problem is the temptation to include a number of extracts from one source—the writings of Mark Rutherford, for example. Thus some attractive pieces have been omitted to leave space for less appealing extracts on topics which would otherwise have remained untouched. Other topics were matters of discussion throughout the period, but to avoid repetition one extract from a particular date must suffice. There is a particular problem in the use of fiction. Should extracts be included because they represent attitudes to Dissent, regardless of whether the author had any actual experience of Dissent, or should extracts only be included if we know that the author knew what he was talking about? Generally I have adopted the second alternative, and this may mean that the book under-represents those attitudes critical of Dissent in the nineteenth century. Finally, I have had to omit reference to some topics which are closely related to Nonconformity—the development of free thought, for example. This is an important omission, because it begs the question of how far the 'Nonconformist spirit' is simply Christian; but I can only plead that to tackle this question in detail would have distorted the rest of the book and to raise it superficially would have been a distraction. All this simply reinforces the point that much work remains to be done on nineteenth-century Nonconformity.

I am grateful to all those who made suggestions about material which might be included, particularly the Joint General Editor, Dr R. T. Shannon; responsibility for the selection is, of course, my own. I am also grateful to Mrs C. James and Mrs E. Turner for their help in the preparation of the typescript. Finally, I must thank my wife for her encouragement and help.

I am indebted to the following for permission to reproduce copyright material in the documents indicated:

The Rev. G. W. Rusling, Editor of the *Baptist Quarterly* (10); the Rev. F. Matthewman, Superintendent Minister of the Hinckley Circuit of the Methodist Church (48); William Heinemann for two extracts from *Father and Son* by Edmund Gosse (64) (65); Faber and Faber, for an extract from *Things Past Redress* by Augustine Birrell (66); the London School of Economics and Political Science, for an extract from *My Apprenticeship* by Beatrice Webb (89); Macmillan, for two extracts from *The Life of Joseph Chamberlain*, vol. 4, by Julian Amery (91b) (101); Hodder and Stoughton, for two extracts from *The Life of Hugh Price Hughes* by Dorothea Price Hughes (94) (98).

All possible care has been taken to trace ownership of the selections included and to make full acknowledgment for their use.

David M. Thompson

Fitzwilliam College, Cambridge

Leading Nonconformists
mentioned in the Introduction

Booth, William (1829–1912). Founder of the Salvation Army (1878), which began as the Christian Mission in Whitechapel (1865). Formerly a minister in the Methodist New Connexion.

Bunting, Jabez (1779–1858). Wesleyan Methodist minister; President of the Wesleyan Conference in 1820, 1828, 1836 and 1844; Senior Secretary of the Wesleyan Missionary Society, 1833–51. The leading figure in Wesleyan Methodism in the first half of the century.

Clifford, John (1836–1923). Minister in the New Connexion of General Baptists, at Praed Street (later Westbourne Park) Baptist Church, London, 1858–1915. Leader of Nonconformist opposition to 1902 Education Act.

Dale, Robert William (1829–95). Congregational minister at Carr's Lane Chapel, Birmingham, from 1853 until his death. Friend and supporter of Joseph Chamberlain.

Hughes, Hugh Price (1847–1902). Wesleyan Methodist minister; founded *Methodist Times*, 1885; superintendent of the West London Mission from 1887. First President of the National Council of Evangelical Free Churches, 1896.

Miall, Edward (1809–81). At first a Congregational minister; founded and edited the *Nonconformist*, 1841–81. Member of Parliament for Rochdale, 1852–7, and forBradford, 1869–74. Leader of the disestablishment campaign.

Spurgeon, Charles Haddon (1834–92). Particular Baptist minister. Leading evangelical preacher of later nineteenth century, at New Park Street Chapel, Southwark, from 1854; and then at the Metropolitan Tabernacle from 1861.

Introduction

English Protestant Nonconformity entered the nineteenth century
on the defensive. The older, 'rational' Dissent was under a political
cloud because of its radicalism, and the support of some sections for
the French Revolution; and even the newer, 'enthusiastic' Methodism
was feared because of its unpredictability and its popularity among
the lower classes. Nonconformity left the century on the defensive
too. The Education Bill of Balfour's government in 1902 was seen
as a sinister attempt to reverse the progress of the century and to
eliminate Nonconformity at source by granting State aid to Anglican
propaganda in the nation's schools. The century between is one of
fluctuating fortunes, when Nonconformists constantly expected that
their day would shortly come. But, as Dr Kitson Clark has
observed, 'the Protestant Dissenters have never had their moment at
the centre'.[1] It was expected still in 1902, and many thought that
it had come in 1906 when 157 Nonconformist Members of
Parliament were returned.[2] By then, however, it had passed for ever.

Old and New Dissent

In any period it is a mistake to treat Protestant Nonconformity in
England as though it were uniform. There have always been
important differences within and between the various denominations.
At the beginning of the nineteenth century Nonconformity may be
conveniently divided into two: the Old Dissent of the seventeenth
century, and the New Dissent of the eighteenth-century evangelical
revival. The Old Dissent consisted of four main denominations: the
Presbyterians, the Independents, the Baptists and the Quakers. The
Quakers were the most radical in theology, and by their passive
resistance to those actions of the State with which they disagreed
they soon became a distinct group from the others. The remaining
three were broadly Calvinist in theology, except that the Baptists
were divided into two: General Baptists were Arminian and believed
that the possibility of redemption was 'general', i.e. extended to
all; whilst the more numerous Particular Baptists were orthodox

Calvinists in believing that the possibility of redemption was 'particular', i.e. confined to the elect. Both Independents and Baptists were congregationalist in believing that the essential form of the Church was the local congregation of believers, which was therefore autonomous and not subject to any superior ecclesiastical authority. They differed over baptism. Presbyterians did not believe in the autonomy of the local congregation, but in a Presbyterian form of Church government which consisted of a hierarchy of church courts from the local congregation at the bottom to a national assembly at the top. For all these denominations the eighteenth century was a time of disillusion and decline. The Presbyterians probably suffered most because the exclusion of Dissenters from the universities meant a decline in the supply of educated ministers. It was to meet this need that the Dissenting Academies came into existence. They were also too scattered for effective Presbyterian government, and many congregations became Independent. The other denominations were more frankly sectarian and turned in on themselves.

The New Dissent was the result of the evangelical revival. The best known denomination is the Wesleyan Methodists, but there were others. The followers of George Whitefield, who were Calvinist in theology, formed the Countess of Huntingdon's Connexion in England, and the Calvinistic Methodists in Wales led by Howell Harris were similar. The General Baptists of the New Connexion, led by Dan Taylor, were Arminian in theology like the Wesleyans, but practised believer's baptism. All shared the experience of revival and broke out of the normal confines of the Church (both Anglican and Dissenting) to take their message to the people. They were very successful and grew rapidly.

The Wesleyan Methodists were the most successful, and by 1800 they had caught up and even overtaken the Old Dissent in many counties. They were not, however, without their troubles. After the death of John Wesley in 1791, they were divided between those who wished to remain as a supplementary society to the Church of England, with no sacraments and no service in church hours, and those who wished to recognise that in fact they were now a separate denomination and should have their own sacraments. The Plan of Pacification of 1795 allowed societies to have their own sacraments if the majority of trustees, stewards and leaders agreed, but it was followed by a further dispute over the rights of ministers and laity. Some Wesleyans objected to the fact that the Conference consisted

only of travelling preachers, and in 1797 they broke away to form
the Methodist New Connexion, in which ministers and laymen had
equal representation in the Conference. In the early years of the
new century other groups grew up in the Methodist tradition, but
outside Wesleyanism: the Independent Methodists in 1806, the
Primitive Methodists in 1811 and the Bible Christians in 1815.

There were two new developments in the Old Dissent in the later
eighteenth century. One was the growth of Unitarianism, mainly
among the more educated Presbyterians and Old General Baptists;
but it was strengthened by a number of ex-Anglicans, such as
Theophilus Lindsey, minister of the influential Essex Street church in
London. What usually happened was that the minister of a
congregation became a Unitarian and the congregation followed,
choosing his successor from other Unitarians. Until Unitarianism was
legalised in 1813, there was no separate Unitarian denomination: if
part of a congregation wished to remain orthodox, it usually had to
secede, and most of the new churches so formed were Independent.
Except in the north, Unitarianism was mainly confined to the towns.

The other development was a revival of evangelistic interest
among Baptists and Independents. The old 'high Calvinism', which
had no interest in evangelism because it was believed that God had
already decided who would be saved, was replaced by a more
moderate doctrine that rejected this view. It was under this influence
that William Carey founded the Baptist Missionary Society in 1792,
and Andrew Fuller, first secretary of the B.M.S. and a Baptist
minister at Kettering, was its leading exponent. The evangelical
revival affected all denominations, including even the Quakers, and
its main effect was the increase of Baptists and Independents in the
early nineteenth century.

Denominational organisation and expansion

With this new increase, and possibly stimulated by it, there went the
development of denominational organisation. Wesleyan Methodism
had always been well organised nationally through its Conference,
which stationed the ministers and received regular financial
contributions from the societies. The same form of organisation was
adopted by the various new Methodist groups, the main variable being
the system of representation—the Methodist New Connexion
Conference contained equal numbers of ministers and laymen, the
Primitive Methodist Conference contained two laymen for every

minister. The Quakers also had a well-organised hierarchy of
meetings from the Preparative Meeting at local level to the Yearly
Meeting in London. But the Independents and Baptists by conviction
and the Presbyterians by geography remained loose in their
organisation. Each had local associations covering areas roughly the
size of a county, but these were not very active in the mid-
eighteenth century. It was the Independents and Baptists particularly
who began to strengthen their organisation in the early nineteenth
century, with the foundation or refoundation of many county
associations and the first attempts at a national union.

The reasons behind this development are three: the need to support
the ministry; the urge to foster evangelism; and the development of
publishing work. These features are common to all the main Nonconformist denominations. In the case of Wesleyanism it was Jabez
Bunting's administrative genius that rescued the denomination from
imminent financial collapse in the second decade of the century. The
organisation at the Mission House and the Bookroom was the object
of the Wesleyan Reformers' criticism. Among Baptists and
Independents the main function of the county associations was to
provide financial support for poor ministers and to encourage
evangelism. Nationally, the development of magazine publishing
linked the congregations together and provided the forum for the
suggestions of a national association; and both the Congregational
and the Baptist Unions depended a good deal in their early years on
the profits of publishing work. Both were much slower to employ
full-time staff than the Wesleyans. In all cases the stimulus from the
missionary movement overseas was vital.

The effect of these developments was to increase denominational
self-consciousness, partly at the expense of the old sense of a common
Dissenting interest. This meant a decline in the importance of the
joint committees of the Dissenting Ministers and the Dissenting
Deputies. These bodies were in any case confined to London, so that
they could meet easily and influence Parliament: but with improving
communications a truly national body was preferred. The very
success of Nonconformists in obtaining the redress of some of their
grievances in the 1820s and 1830s reduced the need for common
action: and the divisions caused by the growth of Unitarianism
drew attention to the distinctive theological positions of the various
denominations.

The Nonconformist denominations grew more or less steadily for
most of the century. Growth seems to have been most rapid before

1840 and then in the last quarter of the century, and the absence of reliable statistics for the Congregationalists for the whole century and for the Baptists for the first half makes it difficult to generalise with confidence. The Methodist statistics are more reliable and complete, but the splits in Wesleyan Methodism complicate the picture.[3] The splinter groups which broke away from the Wesleyans in 1827 and 1836 were not numerically large, but the split of 1849 stopped Wesleyan growth altogether for five years, and it took the best part of twenty years to recover the 1849 position: relative to population it never was recovered. Although the reasons are obscure, the 1850s were a trying time for nearly all the Nonconformist denominations. But by the end of the decade growth had begun again. This has sometimes been associated with the 'second evangelical revival' beginning in 1859.[4] Although large mass meetings did take place in the early 'sixties, the increase in the churches is far less than the number of alleged converts; nor is the increase confined to those areas where revival meetings were held, for geographically the impact of the revival was very uneven. It does seem probable, however, that the growth of the second half of the century was mainly urban, whilst the impact of the first half had been rural as well. The pastoral recovery of the Church of England must also have played a part in a slowing Nonconformist growth.

By the 1860s the denominational organisations had passed their first generation difficulties. Meetings were larger, and there was greater formality in debate. More elaborate attempts were made to organise and regulate the finances, particularly those connected with chapel building. Significantly both the Baptist Union and the Congregational Union merged with their respective Home Missionary Societies in the 1870s and 1880s. Old differences were disappearing too. In 1877 the Wesleyan Conference adopted the principle of lay representation, and lay members were admitted for the first time in 1878.

Nonconformity continued to grow in absolute terms into the twentieth century, but it was already declining relative to population. By the time the First World War came it had virtually come to a standstill. The age of triumphant expansion was over.

Worship and theology

The diversity of Nonconformists makes it difficult to generalise about their worship and theology. The most important respect in which they differed from the Church of England was their stress on preaching. Some kept a complete liturgical freedom with extempore prayer; others had a more formal liturgy. The evangelistic preaching service tended to be informal in all denominations. Obviously the Quakers form an exception to this in some ways; but although they did not have formal preaching in the way others did, it could be said that their approach to worship was intended to leave room for that ministry of the Word, of which preaching is an example.

Services tended to be long at the beginning of the century and shorter by the end. The Primitive Methodists laid down a maximum length of one and a half hours in 1850 for normal services,[5] but the Old Dissent seem to have had longer services, largely because of longer sermons. The evening service increased in popularity as the century proceeded. It seems to have begun in the Methodist attempt to avoid church hours, and certainly the Old Dissent clung longer to the traditional pattern of morning and afternoon. By the end of the century morning and evening was the customary pattern in the towns, whilst afternoon and evening remained quite popular in the countryside.

The main theological issue at the beginning of the century was Unitarianism. This had developed from the 'rational theology' of the eighteenth century among the Presbyterians and General Baptists; but it was not confined to those denominations, and both the Church of England and Methodism provided recruits for Unitarianism. It has been suggested that the Biblical emphasis of the evangelical revival was opposed to Unitarianism, but many Unitarians based their beliefs on the lack of Biblical evidence for the doctrine of the Trinity. But the association of Unitarianism with free thought, radicalism in politics and their defence of such people as the publisher, Carlile, who was prosecuted in 1819 for publishing Paine's *Age of Reason* and Palmer's *Principles of Nature*, made orthodox Dissent suspicious: and the bitterness which surrounded many of the orthodox secessions and property disputes drove a deep wedge between orthodox and Unitarian, so that orthodox theology developed with very little contact with the Unitarians.[6]

The theological differences between the Calvinism of the Old Dissent and the Arminianism of the New were still marked in the first half of the century. Jabez Bunting was criticised for taking some part in the management of the *Eclectic Review*, run mainly by Congregationalists.[7] Even moderate Calvinism of the 'Fullerite' variety was some way from Arminianism. Theological differences between the Particular Baptists and the General Baptists of the New

Connexion were still regarded as considerable in the 1860s, though the two branches were both represented in the Baptist Union after 1832, when it changed its doctrinal basis to 'the sentiments usually denominated evangelical', without further amplification.[8] This move was a paradigm of the theological changes of the century, but there were still high Calvinists who stayed out; and the Strict and Particular Baptists, who retained a strict Calvinist position, gathered strength from that time on.

The impact of Biblical criticism, *Essays and Reviews*, and the developments in the natural sciences changed the emphasis of this discussion. Nonconformists were generally hostile to *Essays and Reviews* in public at first, and used it as another stick with which to beat the Church of England. But there were some who grasped the implications of the new thought and accepted them gladly, trying to lead their brethren along the same path: such were John Clifford for the Baptists, and R.W. Dale and A. M. Fairbairn for the Congregationalists. It was not easy: the Congregationalists had been much troubled by the 'Rivulet controversy' in the 1850s, when a book of hymns by T. T. Lynch was criticised for containing pantheism and nature worship. They were troubled again by an unofficial meeting at the time of the Congregational Union Assembly in Leicester in 1877, when a number of ministers were involved in discussions on liberty in religious opinions. The Baptists were torn by the 'Down Grade' controversy in 1887–8, when Spurgeon left the Baptist Union because he thought that they were complacent about lapses from the great Calvinist doctrines. The effect of all this was to create a new dividing line between conservative and liberal evangelicals, which has remained the main theological division in Nonconformity ever since.

Two movements concerning the doctrine of the Church should also be mentioned. The century saw the development of a number of groups who rejected the idea of denominationalism and sought to recreate primitive Christianity on a New Testament basis outside the existing denominations. They included the Brethren, the Churches of Christ and many unknown Gospel and Mission Halls up and down the land. These groups were not all alike, and they were not without some sympathisers in the established denominations, but they represent an interesting byway from the main nineteenth-century road. The other movement was the recovery of a catholic doctrine of the Church among the mainstream Nonconformists that found expression in the movement for Free Church Unity. The unions between Baptists in 1891 and Methodists in 1907, although they did not cross denominational dividing lines, led in the same direction.

That movement was also reflected in the liturgical moves in an Anglican direction that were taking place in the later part of the century. In various denominations experiments were being made with service books, and the compilers of hymn books and books of prayers were becoming more catholic in their collections. There is a useful description of the various styles of Nonconformist service at the end of the century in Charles Booth's *Life and Labour in London: Religious Influences*,[9] and it is worth noting that even evangelistic campaigns were being more highly organised in the days of Moody and Sankey.[10]

Nonconformists and the Church of England

The Nonconformists of 1662 found themselves in that position largely because of disagreements about the nature of the Church, though they did not all share the same beliefs. They represented varieties of anti-episcopalianism. Up to and following 1689 the plea of religious toleration was developed, partly on pragmatic grounds and partly on the grounds of the freedom of religious belief.

The Nonconformists of the eighteenth century were more concerned to make a point about the nature of Christian life and evangelism. They were not essentially anti-episcopalian. Indeed in the case of Wesleyan Methodism it was probably precisely because they believed in bishops that they did not follow the pattern of American Methodism and have their own: 'their' bishops already existed—in the Church of England. For the other elements of evangelical Nonconformity, Church polity was almost irrelevant; they followed the pattern to hand, either Wesleyan connexionalism or traditional independency.

The Wesleyans were reluctant to break with the Church of England. For a long time they had no separate communion services, baptisms, marriages or burials. When they did begin to move away from the Church of England it was mainly because of suspicion of the Puseyite 'Romanising' ritual.

With the Old Dissent it was different. The plea for toleration led to a plea for religious equality: the repeal of the Test and Corporation Acts and then the redress of particular grievances. But it became very difficult to draw a clear line between these grievances. Is the right to be married in one's own chapel the same kind of demand as the right to be admitted to Oxford or Cambridge? Gradually, but inexorably, Dissenters were led to demand the separation of Church and State, as Sir Robert Inglis foresaw in 1828 and as Edward Miall eagerly argued.

Disestablishment only gradually gained support. The Wesleyans, and even some Congregationalists, were against it. The Disruption of the Church of Scotland in 1843, and the formation of a Free Church of Scotland which believed in the principle of establishment but could not accept the way the existing establishment worked, made the Wesleyans think again; and the dispute over the education clauses of the Factory Bill, the developing Puseyism in the Church of England, and the government grant to the Roman Catholic seminary at Maynooth all added further food for thought. But they remained very cautious. The other Nonconformists had no such qualms: they believed that the State should not interfere in religion and that establishment was therefore wrong. They believed in freedom for episcopalianism, but no special privileges. Anglicans had the greatest difficulty in believing Nonconformist assertions that they had no wish to destroy the Church of England, and they insisted on calling this 'political dissent', as though it could not possibly have any theological justification.

A fillip was given to disestablishment by the disestablishment of the Church of Ireland in 1869. But despite the hopes and expectations of Nonconformists no further action followed until the Church in Wales was disestablished in 1914. In neither England nor Scotland did it really reach the stage of being planned seriously.

At a personal level, relations between Anglicans and Nonconformists improved in the last quarter of the century, and still more as the effects of the admission of Nonconformists to Oxford and Cambridge became apparent. Free Church theological colleges moved to each university, and the foundations of the twentieth-century ecumenical dialogue were laid.

Political and social attitudes

There has been a tendency to think of the politics of Nonconformity simply in terms of its alliance with the Radical and Liberal groups in national party politics. There is no doubt that in the history of British Liberalism the Nonconformist contribution has been important, but this does not exhaust the topic. Not only were there various strands within Liberalism, but it is not easy at any point in the nineteenth century to identify the largest group of Nonconformists—the Wesleyan Methodists—totally with the Liberal party at all. Two general points, however, may be made. One is that, on the whole, Nonconformist politics had much in common with, even where they were not directly derived from, the Whig tradition in the 1689 Revolution. The other is that Nonconformist political attitudes were very closely related to their attitude to the Church of England, and therefore that, in so far as the Tory party was closely identified with that Church, this dominated their attitude to the Tory party. Thus Wesleyans, who had an ambivalent relationship to the Church of England, also had a more ambivalent relationship with the Tories than any other Nonconformist group.

At the beginning of the nineteenth century the Old Dissent was clearly identified with the Whigs, and some Unitarians, like Priestley, were more radical still. It was almost inconceivable that anyone brought up in traditional Dissent could be a Tory in view of their dependence on the Whigs for religious toleration itself. For some of those who came to Dissent in the enthusiasm of the evangelical revival, however, this traditional political allegiance had less meaning. The Wesleyans, of course, were much more inclined to support the Tories, and not even Sidmouth's abortive Bill of 1811[11] seriously affected the basis of that support. Nevertheless it was not total. The successful agitation for the repeal of the Test and Corporation Acts in the 1820s did not contain only the traditional Whig Dissenters but some of the newer Dissent as well; and many Wesleyans, including Bunting, supported Catholic Emancipation and the Reform Bill of 1832.[12]

After 1832 it is necessary to emphasise the reverse, that not all Dissenters wanted to go for further reform. The support of Dissenters for the Whig reforms was, of course, important.[13] But many Dissenters, having tasted some measure of political power as a result of the Reform Act and the Municipal Corporations Act of 1835, became less eager for further reform, even though the alliance with the Whigs became politically unproductive after 1837. Nonconformists were not very happy with either Russell's changes in educational policy in 1839 from a Whig government or Graham's educational proposals in 1843 from a Conservative government. Peel's government of 1841-6 is significant in Church history because it was the first Conservative government to recognise that it was impossible any longer to extend the privileges of the Church of England; but this change of attitude did not win Peel many Dissenting votes.

Radical Dissenters were involved in the formation of the Anti-State Church Association in 1844, and many of these were also involved in the Complete Suffrage Union, an attempt to unite middle-class radicals and working-class Chartists. But a greater number, though again not all, supported the Anti-Corn Law League in the 1840s, and some were persuaded that the aims of the League were a direct application of Dissenting principles in the economic sphere. In the 1850s and 1860s and even later there were Nonconformists who gloried in having led the way towards free trade. In terms of party politics, however, repeal of the Corn Laws did not increase Dissenting influence significantly on the Whig-Liberal side of the House of Commons, and by the early 1860s leading Radical Nonconformists like Edward Miall were once again disillusioned with a Whig-Liberal government, as in 1837. It was not until Gladstone's time that Nonconformist voices seem to have a say in Liberal party policy-making, and then only on a modest scale. This lack of Nonconformist influence on national political leadership in the mid-nineteenth century, it should be emphasised, comes at a time when in local politics the Dissenting ministers formed 'a sort of Communist hard core to the popular front'.[14]

If there was a time when there was a fairly simple alliance between Liberalism and Nonconformity that benefited both, then it was between 1868 and 1886; and even then the course of true love did not run smooth. The Nonconformist revolt over the Education Act of 1870 showed how fragile this alliance was: but it also proved decisively to Nonconformists that they could not really turn elsewhere for political support. The reunion of Gladstone and the Nonconformists in the moral crusade against the Turks in the mid-seventies rather disguised this point. There was, however, a new atmosphere of confidence between the two sides, and it was tragic for Nonconformity that this should have been shattered by the Home Rule split.

The Liberal split of 1886 had social as well as political implications for Nonconformity. Politically it divided Nonconformists in a new way, with leading figures on each side. R. W. Dale supported Chamberlain, Hugh Price Hughes supported Gladstone. This division weakened the Nonconformist political impact because it made politics a more controversial subject, and therefore a more delicate one. But it also marks the point at which many of the social ties holding Nonconformists together, which had been gradually weakening over many years, finally broke. In the provincial towns of the early nineteenth century, Nonconformity and the Church of England were almost completely separated social worlds, even where in economic terms people were of the same social class. Segregation in education accentuated this. In 1886 some Nonconformist Liberals found themselves working with Conservatives for the first time, and they realised that the traditional social distinctions were not absolute. From about the same time wealthy Nonconformists begin to send their sons to public schools and become less hesitant about accepting honours. For Liberal Unionists political links become as important as religious links: it becomes possible to be a Nonconformist and a Unionist, if not a Conservative. This also strengthened the class element in political divisions, for the new Unionist recruits were on the whole wealthier than the Wesleyans who had been the main Tory Nonconformists hitherto.[15]

A majority of Nonconformists probably remained Liberal, and the 1890s see the appearance of the 'Nonconformist conscience' as an openly expressed political force. Even so it is difficult to find an instance where the 'Nonconformist conscience' alone caused a Liberal change of policy. Rather more marked is the Nonconformist withdrawal from political commitment, because of its new divisiveness. The education controversy of 1902 therefore is significant because it is exceptional. It reunited many Nonconformists on one political side, as both Chamberlain and Rosebery saw. But the Nonconformist hopes in 1906 were lost in the sands of bitter political strife, and their political influence became that of a steadily declining pressure group.

Radicalism in politics in the nineteenth century did not mean for the most part that Nonconformists had radical social attitudes. They supported the *laissez faire* economics of the Manchester School, though they were concerned about social conditions and some Nonconformists were Chartists. Edward Miall criticised the 'trade spirit' in 1849.[16] But it is unfair to judge Nonconformity by the standards of a later age.

Most Nonconformists supported the Trade Union movement, and Primitive Methodists were particularly involved in the Mining and Agricultural Unions. In the 1870s there were the beginnings of a Christian Socialist movement among Nonconformists, though it is important to distinguish between the Socialism of, for example John

Clifford, and the social concern of, for example, Hugh Price Hughes or William Booth. The commitment to the Labour movement was not, of course, in this period incompatible with support for the Liberal party. Although the Nonconformist contribution to the Labour movement was considerable, there has been a tendency to romanticise it, and it is salutary to recall that there were other influences quite as strong, for example, the secularist tradition in London labour.[17] Nor did the rather restrictive outlook on leisure which was characteristic of Nonconformists endear them to the mass of the working classes. Their agitation against Sunday opening of museums, art galleries and public places, against Sunday rail excursions and Sunday opening of public houses, all hit the working man's main day off more than their concern that there should be no Sunday work benefited him. And their concern to restrict licensing hours and suspicion of music halls and theatres affected his week-night pleasures also. Historians have recognised the moral reformation wrought in much working-class life by Nonconformists; but they have been slower to emphasise its unpopularity.[18] The restrictive Nonconformist social attitudes were weakening as the century drew to a close, but they were still strong.

Social composition

Nonconformity was as diverse in social composition as it was in other respects, though it became more homogeneous as the century progressed. Any national generalisation, moreover, is weakened by the fact that the uneven regional distribution of the various denominations meant that social composition varied from area to area: working-class Unitarians, for example, are mainly confined to the north. Some broad generalisations may, however, be offered as a starting point.

Nonconformity had no aristocrats and very few of the very poor. In this respect it differed from both Anglicans and Roman Catholics, who were represented in each group. The range of Nonconformity was from the respectable working man to the wealthy business man or better professional man.

The Unitarians and the Quakers were probably the wealthiest denominations, the so-called 'aristocracy of Dissent'. They were well represented among merchants, business men, manufacturers and bankers. There were others, of course. The Unitarian Domestic Missions and the Quaker Adult Schools brought many of the

humbler classes within their influence; but these institutions tended
to be separate from the main chapels and meeting houses.

The Congregationalists, Baptists and Wesleyans were the main
middle-class denominations, but there were interesting nuances of
difference. The Congregationalists tended to contain the wealthiest
manufacturers; the Baptists were stronger among small men in
business on their own; the Wesleyans were notoriously strong among
the shopkeepers. The smaller Methodist bodies, the General Baptists
of the New Connexion and the Primitive Methodists reached
farther down the scale with a good representation among artisans,
small craftsmen and other manual workers.

In the countryside Congregationalists and Baptists tended to be
strong among the farmers and independent village craftsmen:
Wesleyan and Primitive Methodists worked among agricultural
labourers. But in the country, even more than in the town, social
composition depended on what else was available: where there was
more than one Nonconformist chapel some social differentiation
took place, but where there was only one its social identity was
really defined in relation to the Church of England, not any one
social group. In Wales all branches of Nonconformity had a greater
social range in countryside and town.

Nonconformists were sensitive to this social differentiation: they
noticed that their appeal was not universal and pondered the reasons
why. Some defined their mission in relation to a particular class.
Congregationalists, for example, felt they had a mission to the
middle class, rather than others: Primitive Methodists felt a
particular mission to the working class. To a greater or lesser extent,
therefore, Nonconformists accepted the class structure and did not
work to change it: all, however, felt guilty about their failures with
the working classes.[19]

As the century proceeded, however, two developments reduced
the social diversity of Nonconformity. At the upper end, the social
discrimination against Nonconformists was gradually eased and
wealthy Nonconformists began to move in wider circles and adopt
the social habits of their class rather than their Church. This process
made it easier for them to join the Church of England, or simply to
stay away, particularly as it was often associated with a move to the
suburbs where their denomination might not be represented. At the
lower end it proved steadily more difficult to hold the allegiance of
the working classes, partly because religious affiliation often went
hand in hand with a mood of self-improvement that led to upward

social mobility, and partly because the movement of population both from countryside to town and within the towns themselves made it difficult for them to retain their religious links. By the end of the century, therefore, Nonconformity was probably more homogeneously middle class than it had been at the beginning. Its ethos had always been particularly suited to the ethic of self-help and self-improvement: it did not satisfy to the same extent those who had achieved their social ambitions.

The Nonconformist contribution

In what ways did Nonconformity contribute to the birth of modern Britain? Assessments of it have tended to come, either from Anglican historians who because of lack of knowledge or lack of understanding have tended to ignore it, or from secular historians who have only been interested in particular aspects and have therefore misunderstood or distorted it. Or they have come from Nonconformist historians who have tended to be hagiographical. Fortunately this is now changing, and a trickle of detailed monographs is beginning to appear. Almost inevitably, however, Nonconformity still comes off badly in the general text books.[20]

It is certainly easy to see its faults. The criticisms of the Arnolds, father and son, that it tended to be narrow in outlook have been true of many local congregations. At the same time, however, many members of those congregations owed even the limited culture that they had to that same Nonconformity, a point too easily overlooked. There has also been an anti-intellectual strain that has run through much Nonconformist life: the virtues of simple faith have been stressed at the expense of the pursuit of knowledge. But this criticism is more fairly made of a particular evangelical outlook that is not confined to Nonconformity; and in each century since the seventeenth there have been Nonconformist scholars of distinction, both in theology and in the sciences. Others have alleged that the moral fervour of Nonconformity has smacked too much of self-righteousness and hypocrisy. This is a more difficult criticism to evaluate as so much depends on the standpoint of the critic. It may be, as Broad Churchmen like F. D. Maurice and Llewellyn Davies argued, that the sectarian element in Nonconformity twisted holiness into being 'holier than thou', but this is a perennial danger for Christians. There has been a hyperbole in Nonconformist rhetoric at times that

the more sophisticated have found distasteful: but it is more difficult
to prove that Nonconformists have deliberately exploited the
passion they have felt in order to mislead and distort. Finally, some
have seen Nonconformity as the aider and abettor of capitalism,
the self-justifying religious ethic behind the worst exploitation in
Victorian England. This opens a large controversy that cannot be
dispatched in a few lines. Despite the views of romantic Tories like
Disraeli, there is no real evidence to suggest that Nonconformist
manufacturers were more hard-faced than those of the Church of
England or no faith at all. Nor can it easily be demonstrated that
such hard-heartedness as there was stemmed specifically from a
particular religious outlook. That nineteenth-century Christianity as
a whole did not attack the roots of the new economic system cannot
be denied, but it was one of the first areas of national life to be
sensitive to its evils.

What then was the Nonconformist contribution? There are four
main elements:

1. Nonconformity was largely responsible for the freedom of
religion and the freedom of thought enjoyed in nineteenth-century
Britain. This established a tradition in which political liberty itself
flourished. Of course, not all Nonconformists showed the same
toleration to their own dissentients as they demanded from the
Church of England for themselves, but at least their arguments were
about the degree of liberty which was permissible, not whether
liberty was permissible at all.

2. Nonconformity provided the means in an age before mass
education for many humble folk to improve themselves and find a
sense of social identity. This is not to say that Nonconformists
educated the working classes. The Church of England built many
more schools than Nonconformity. But the sense of belonging to
a chapel, and having a responsible part to play in its life, meant
quite as much in education as learning to read and write.

3. The existence of a thriving Nonconformity saved England from
anti-clericalism, such as that which developed in the rest of Europe.
There was a Christian alternative to the Church of England which
blurred the sharp distinction between belonging to the established
Church and having no Christian faith. In addition to this rather
negative point, Nonconformity did make a positive religious
contribution. The freedom of its worship and its representative style
of church government have each been absorbed into the Church of
England in the twentieth century. This might be due to the 'spirit of

the age', but Nonconformity demonstrated that change was possible in the Church without disaster.

4. The religion of commitment and action associated with Nonconformity has played an important part in national and religious life. It is practically impossible to be an uncommitted or casual Nonconformist—certainly it was in the nineteenth century. This commitment was also carried over into a commitment to live one's religion in everyday life. For some this meant social action; for others it meant political action.[21] In this way Nonconformity has been the source of much of the idealism in British public life, and has contributed to both the Liberal and the Labour parties. This style of religious commitment has also become much more characteristic of the Church of England in the twentieth century.

In the twentieth century English Protestant Nonconformity has declined in numbers and in prestige. Many believe that its future lies in reunion with the Church of England. Experience suggests that this will not be an easy or a speedy process. If it is possible at all, it will be because the values and ethos of Nonconformity have reached a point of general acceptance where separate existence is not necessary to ensure their survival. In the nineteenth century this was not so; and the variety of Nonconformity, from the room in the village backstreet to the vastness of the city centre Gothic church, bears witness to the depths of men's beliefs. If we ignore them, we ignore a complete dimension of Victorian life.

Notes

1 G. S. R. Kitson Clark, *The Making of Victorian England* (London, 1962), pp. 23–4.
2 They included sixty-five Congregationalists, thirty-seven Wesleyans, eighteen Baptists, eighteen other Methodists, three Presbyterians and ten Unitarians. *Annual Register*, 1906, pp. 12–13.
3 The Methodist figures have been very well analysed by Robert Currie in his book *Methodism Divided* (London, 1968), pp. 85–111, and in an article, 'A Micro-Theory of Methodist Growth', *Proceedings of the Wesley Historical Society*, xxxvi, 1967, pp. 65–73.
4 J. E. Orr, *The Second Evangelical Awakening in Britain* (London, 1949).
5 *The General Consolidated Minutes approved by the 13th (Primitive Methodist) Conference, 1850*, pp. 104–9.
6 U. R. Q. Henriques, *Religious Toleration in England, 1787–1833* (London, 1961), pp. 209–12.
7 J. G. Rogers, *An Autobiography* (London, 1903), pp. 19–20.
8 E. A. Payne, *The Baptist Union* (London, 1959), p. 61.
9 See document 103.
10 For this whole section, see H. Davies, *Worship and Theology in England*, vols iii (Princeton, 1961) and iv (Princeton, 1962).

11 See document 4.
12 The Wesleyan attitude to politics is well discussed in E. R. Taylor, *Methodism and Politics, 1791–1851* (Cambridge, 1935) and in J. Kent, *The Age of Disunity* (London, 1966), pp. 86-102, 127-45.
13 See N. Gash, *Reaction and Reconstruction in English Politics* (Oxford, 1965).
14 J. Vincent, *Pollbooks* (Cambridge, 1967), p. 18. Vincent also says that the traditional belief that Wesleyan ministers were Tory is not borne out by the limited evidence he has examined.
15 For a local example of this, see *The Victoria County History of Leicestershire*, iv (London, 1958), pp. 201–32.
16 In his book, *The British Churches in Relation to the British People* (London, 1849).
17 See S. Mayor, *The Churches and the Labour Movement* (London, 1967). The various books of Dr R. F. Wearmouth (see Bibliography) are the best examples of the romantic tendency.
18 See B. Harrison, 'Religion and Recreation in Nineteenth-Century England', *Past and Present*, 38 (1967), and for a stronger view, E. P. Thompson, *The Making of the English Working Class* (London, 1963).
19 K. S. Inglis, *Churches and the Working Classes in Victorian England* (London, 1963).
20 Examples of the categories cited would be: Anglican, F. Warre Cornish, *History of the English Church in the Nineteenth Century* (2 vols, London, 1910); secular, E. Halevy, *History of the English People in the Nineteenth Century* (6 vols, London, 1924–51); hagiographical, H. S. Skeats and C. S. Miall, *History of the Free Churches of England, 1688–1891* (London, 1891); modern textbook, W. O. Chadwick, *The Victorian Church* (2 vols, London, 1966–70).
21 It also meant missionary service overseas; but the missionary movement, though important, has been excluded from this study.

One   Dissent at the beginning of the nineteenth century

At the beginning of the nineteenth century the initiative in Nonconformity seemed to be passing from the Old to the New Dissent. The Old Dissenting denominations with their roots in the seventeenth century had been declining in numbers and influence for most of the eighteenth century. In many ways the changes which took place among the Quakers (1) were typical of the other denominations also: the many rural congregations dwindled and only the town churches maintained their position; and socially the churches came to consist more of tradesmen than of labourers. Many Nonconformists were involved in the financing of the Industrial Revolution.[1]

By contrast the New Dissent of the evangelical revival was going from strength to strength and also going out to reach the people. Although Wesleyan Methodism had been in the doldrums in the 1790s and troubled by the divisions which led to the secession of the Methodist New Connexion in 1797, the impulse given by John Wesley to open-air evangelism was by no means dead. Because of the suspicion of many of the Wesleyan leaders, however, this impulse after 1800 was to be satisfied outside official Wesleyan Methodism. The first camp meeting (an open-air revival meeting) in England was held at Mow Cop in Staffordshire on 31 May 1807 (2). The style of the meeting was copied from America, and was very much influenced by the American evangelist, Lorenzo Dow, though he had already returned to America when the meeting was held. Other camp meetings followed, but they were condemned by the Wesleyan Conference in 1807 (3), and those who persisted in attending them were expelled. Hugh Bourne and William Clowes, the two founders of Primitive Methodism (as the new movement came to be called) were expelled in 1808 and 1810 respectively.[2] The new movement nevertheless remained firmly Methodist and revived some early Wesleyan practices which had been dropped, for example, the use of women preachers, virtually banned by the Conference of 1803.[3] It is interesting that the enthusiasm of Hugh Bourne was compared by a contemporary to that of the Quaker, George Fox.[4]

The strength of Methodism lay in its organisation, and at the heart of this was the class meeting (16). This was designed to strengthen and uphold the members by an exchange of their religious experience, but it was also the means through which the whole enterprise was financed (8). It was not, of course, completely successful in either respect: Joseph Barker criticised its tendency to hypocrisy and the *de facto* separation of rich and poor within it; the reiteration of the financial rule is a reminder that it was not always observed. But Methodism had here an institution which gave it a greater resilience than the other denominations.

Nationally the strength of Methodist organisation lay in the connexional system and the direct control of the travelling preachers (ministers) by the Conference. The preachers were attached to circuits, i.e. groups of churches, and were expected to travel (14). They were stationed in their circuits by the Conference, and moved every three years. Two or three preachers looked after one circuit.

This forms a striking contrast wiith the Independents and Baptists, who were each in this period makng their first attempts at a national union. The Congregationalists' efforts between 1806 and 1808 came to nought, and it has been pointed out that there was real doubt over the legality of such a move.[5] The Baptists were more successful, and formed a General Union of ministers and churches in 1812 (10).[6] Both denominations, however, recognised the sovereignty of the local church and their unions eschewed any attempt to legislate. They were also chronically short of money.

All Nonconformists shared a discipline of life and behaviour which tended to separate them from their fellows. Plain dress, for example, was common to all, though few went into the detail of the Primitive Methodists (13), apart from the Quakers, who were quite distinctive (9). Reference to the evils of smoking (17) and drink (27) came in due course. It may well be that it was the attack by Primitive Methodists on traditional wakes (village festivals) that led to their hostile reception and persecution in some places (12), but it is also clear that the traditional sources of authority in the countryside, the squire and parson, felt themselves threatened by the new movement.

The government too was suspicious, and Viscount Sidmouth's Bill of 1811 was interpreted by the Methodists as a direct attack on them. For some years it had been known that the government was anxious to impose some new restriction on the qualifications for being able to claim the status of a Dissenting minister, ostensibly because some were using this as a way to escape service in the militia. It was proposed to define a minister as one who was attached to a particular congregation—a definition which would have excluded the whole of the Methodist ministry. The tone of Sidmouth's introductory speech, however, also implied strong disapproval of people with low social status acting as ministers (4). The remarks of William Cobbett in his *Political Register* (5) show that opposition to the Methodists was not confined to one end of the political spectrum, though ironically Cobbett's main objection was to the Methodists' politics. Prompt action by the Methodist Committee of Privileges and the Dissenting Deputies (the London-based committee to protect the interests of the Old Dissent) produced a flood of petitions to Parliament against the Bill. The Archbishop of Canterbury spoke against it and it was defeated in the House of Lords without a division.[7]

In the following year, 1812, Lord Liverpool, the new Prime Minister, secured the passage of a new Toleration Act (6) which is still the basis of Nonconformists' freedom of worship. It was welcomed enthusiastically by the Methodists and the address of the Wesleyan Conference to the societies of 1812 contained a typical affirmation of the loyalty of the Connexion (7). Even so the Act did not grant legal recognition to the Unitarians, who had to wait for the Trinity Act of 1813 (11).

The Nonconformists' ultimate aim, however, was to secure full religious equality, which meant in practice the repeal of the Test and Corporation Acts. These Acts, dating from Charles II's reign, restricted public office to those taking communion in the Church of England. For many years periodic Indemnity Acts had been passed to allow Dissenters to hold office, but this was regarded as unsatisfactory. The last attempt to secure their repeal in 1790 had failed, and after 1800 the whole question was entangled with the larger issue of Roman Catholic relief. Some Dissenters were prepared to grant civil equality to Roman Catholics also, but others, particularly those associated with the Protestant Society (founded in 1811 to protect the interests of the new evangelical Dissent) were strongly anti-Catholic. In 1827 a United Committee of the main Dissenting bodies was formed to campaign for repeal, but even then the Protestant Society waged an independent campaign until 1828. In January of that year the two came together and in February Lord John Russell carried a motion in the House of Commons in favour of repeal (18). The government did not resist the measure, and, though the Dissenters did not achieve everything they wanted, the repeal Bill became law in May 1828 (19). A vital breach had been made in the principle of the 'Anglican constitution' and Nonconformity could no longer be ignored as a force in the nation's life.[8]

The immediate reasons for repeal lay in the political circumstances of the time; but it would have been impossible without the rapid growth of Nonconformity in England and Wales in the first quarter of the century. According to Horace Mann's calculations in 1851 (58) the number of Wesleyan places of worship increased nearly six-fold between 1801 and 1831; the number of Independent places doubled and the number of Baptist places nearly trebled. Membership figures are only available for Methodists: Wesleyans grew from 89,529 in 1801 to 249,119 in 1831; the New Connexion grew from 4,851 to 11,433 in the same period; and Primitive Methodists grew from 16,394 in 1821 to 37,216 a decade later. While Methodist growth was clearly the most spectacular, the Baptists and Independents were growing more quickly after the Napoleonic Wars.[9] The reasons for this growth are complex: social and economic factors cannot be ignored, and, of course, the population was also growing rapidly at this time. But it seems likely that much of the growth was due to the simple evangelical appeal of the Nonconformists at a time when the Church of England was still moribund in many parishes (15). By 1828 a new aggressive confidence was chasing away the last remnants of the defensive quietism of eighteenth-century Nonconformity.

1 Social composition of Quakers, 1806

Extracts from T. Clarkson, *A Portraiture of Quakerism* (1806), ii, pp. 46–8, 53–4, 56–8.

Thomas Clarkson, the great anti-slavery campaigner, here gives some idea of the changes which had taken place in the Society of Friends in the eighteenth century to transform it from a rural movement of lower-class social outcasts to a respectable urban middle-class movement. Similar changes overtook other denominations of Old Dissent, though they did not make such detailed regulations on trade.

In looking among the occupations of the Quakers, we shall find some who are brought up as manufacturers and mechanics. But the number of these is small.

Others, but these are very few, follow the sea. There may be here and there a mate or captain in the coasting employ. In America, where they have great local and other advantages, there may be more in the sea-faring line. But, in general, the Quakers are domestic characters, and prefer home.

There are but few, also, who follow the professions. Their education and their religion exclude them from some of these. Some, however, are to be found in the department of medicine; and others, as conveyancers, in the law.

Several of the Quakers follow agriculture. But these are few, compared with the rest of the Society, or compared with the number of those who formerly followed a rural life. Almost all the Quakers were originally in the country, and but few of them in the towns; but this order of things is reversing fast. They are flocking into the towns, and abandoning agricultural pursuits.

The reasons that may be given for this change may be the following. It is not at all unlikely, but that tithes may have had some influence in producing it. . . . Of later years, as the Society has grown thinner in the country, I believe new reasons have sprung up. For the Quakers have had less opportunity of society with one another. They have been subjected also to greater inconvenience in attending their religious meetings. Their children, also, have been more exposed to improper connections in marriage. To which it may be added, that the large and rapid profits, frequently made in trade, compared with the generally small and slow returns from agricultural concerns, may probably have operated with many, as an inducement to such a change. . . .

. . . I believe, with these few exceptions, that the rest of the Society may be considered as engaged in trade. . . .

The Quakers have thought it their duty, as a religious body, to make several regulations on this subject. In the first place, they have made it a rule, that no person, acknowledged to be in a profession with them, shall have any concern in the slave-trade. . . .

They have forbidden also the trade of privateering in war. The Quakers consider the capture of private vessels by private persons as a robbery committed on the property of others. . . . And upon this motive they forbid it, as well as upon that of their known profession against war.

They forbid also the trade of the manufacturing of gun-powder, and of arms, or weapons of war, such as swords, guns, pistols, bayonets, and the like, that they may stand clear of the charge of having made any instrument, the avowed use of which is the destruction of human life.

They have forbidden also all trade that has for its object the defrauding of the king either of his customs or his excise. They are not only not to smuggle themselves, but they are not to deal in such goods as they know, or such as they even suspect, to be smuggled, nor to buy any article of this description even for their private use. . . .

They discourage also concerns in hazardous enterprises in the way of trade. Such enterprises are apt to disturb the tranquillity of the mind, and to unfit it for religious exercise. They may involve also the parties concerned and their families in ruin. They may deprive them again of the means of paying their just debts, and thus render them injurious to their creditors. Members, therefore, are advised to be rather content with callings which may produce small but certain profits, than to hazard the tranquillity of their minds, and the property of themselves and others.

In the exercise of those callings which are deemed lawful by the Society, two things are insisted upon; first, that their members never raise and circulate 'any fictitious kind of paper-credit with indorsements and acceptances, to give it an appearance of value without an intrinsic reality'. Secondly, that they should pay particular attention to their words, and to the punctual performance of their engagements, and on no account delay their payments beyond the time they have promised. . . .

2   The Mow Cop camp meeting, 1807

An extract from J. Walford, *Memoirs of the Life and Labours of Hugh Bourne* (1855), i, pp. 121–4.

The camp meeting at Mow Cop was the first held in England and is here described by Hugh Bourne, one of the founders of Primitive Methodism. It was estimated that between 2,000 and 4,000 people attended, and the description gives some impression of the atmosphere. Later meetings followed this pattern, though in a more organised fashion (see document 22).

Mow camp meeting was appointed to be held on Sunday, May 31st, 1807. The morning proved rainy and unfavourable, which rather put it back; but about six o'clock, the Lord sent the clouds off, and gave us a very pleasant day.

The meeting was opened by two holy men from Knutsford—Captain Anderson having previously erected a flag on the mountain to direct strangers, and these three, with some pious people from Macclesfield, carried on and sustained the meeting a considerable time, in a most vigorous and lively manner. They conducted it by preaching, prayer, exhortations, relating experiences, etc. The Lord owned their labours, grace descended, and the people of God were greatly quickened. The congregation rapidly increased, and others began to join in holy exercises.

One of the men from Knutsford, a lawyer, and an Irishman (who had been converted under the ministry of Lorenzo Dow) related the troubles he had passed through in Ireland. In the late rebellion in that unhappy land, he had been deprived of thousands, from a state of wealth and affluence, in which he had been brought up, and in which he had lived, he with his family had been reduced. But for this he thanked God, the taking away his substance had been the cause of his gaining the true riches; and he had since given up his profession of an attorney, because he found it too difficult to keep his religion in that profession. This man exhorted all to pray for our gracious king, who was worthy, because he granted liberty of conscience; but he himself had seen a time in Ireland when a protestant knew not at night but his house and family might be burned before morning. . . .

. . . Meanwhile, the people were flocking in from every quarter. The wind was cold, but a large grove of fir trees kept the wind off, and made it very comfortable. So many hundreds now covered the ground that another preaching stand was erected in a distant part of the field, under the cover of a stone wall. Returning over the field, I met a company at a distance from the first stand, praying for a man in distress. I could not get near: but I there found such a measure of the power of God, such a weighty burning of joy and love, that it was beyond description. I should gladly have stopped there, but other matters called me away. I perceived that the Lord was beginning to work mightily. Nearer the first stand was another company praying with mourners. Immediately the man in the other company was praising God, and I found that he had obtained the pardon of his sins, and was born again. I believe this man to have been the first that was born of God at this meeting. Many were afterwards born again or converted in the other company; the number I could not ascertain; but from what information I was able to collect, I suppose about six.

Meantime, preaching went on without intermission at both stands, and about noon, the congregation was so much increased, that we were obliged to erect a third preaching stand; we fixed it a distance below the first, by the side of the fir tree grove. . . .

Many preachers were now upon the ground, from Knutsford, Congleton, Wheelock, Burslem, Macclesfield, and other places; and a most extraordinary variety appeared. The man who was turned from deism had been in the field of war, when the grandees of the earth drew the sword and bid the battle bleed. He had seen death flying in every direction, and men falling slain on every side. He had walked in blood, over fields, covered with mountains of dying and dead. He shewed the happiness of our land, and the gratitude we owed to God for being exempted from being the seat of war. Another, who had seen the horrors of rebellion lately in Ireland, persuaded us to turn to righteousness, because we were exempt from these calamities. E. Anderson related the devotion he had beheld in many parts of the world, which we suppose to be in darkness and superstition, and exhorted us to turn to God, lest they should rise up in judgement against us. All the preachers seemed to be strengthened in the work. Persuasion dwelt upon their tongues, while the multitudes were trembling or rejoicing around.

The congregation increased so rapidly that a fourth preaching stand was called for. The work now became general, and the scene was most awful and interesting. In this glass, any one might have viewed the worth of souls. To see the thousands of people, all (except a few stragglers) in solemn attention; a company near the first stand wrestling in prayer for mourners; and four preachers dealing out their lives at every stroke. These things made an impression on my mind, not soon to be forgotten; this extraordinary scene continued till about four o'clock, when the people began to retire; and before six, they were confined to one stand.

About seven o'clock in the evening, a work began among children; six of whom were converted, or born again, before the meeting broke up; and the power of God seemed to have a great effect upon the people present. At about half past eight o'clock at night, the meeting was finally closed. A meeting, such as our eyes had never beheld! a meeting, for which many will praise God in time and eternity! such a day as this we never before enjoyed! a day spent in the active service of the living God! a Sabbath in which Jesus Christ made glad the hearts of his saints, and sent his arrows to the hearts of sinners. The propriety and great utility of camp meetings appeared to every one; so great was the work, that the people were ready to say, 'We have seen strange things to-day'. O may the Lord carry on his work, till righteousness cover the earth, for Jesus' sake. Amen.

3   The Wesleyan Conference condemns camp meetings, 1807

Minutes of the Wesleyan Conference, 1807: collected edition, ii, p. 403.

The Wesleyan Conference was suspicious of those who were
enthusiastic for camp meetings, and also feared that they would give
the government an excuse for invoking the Conventicle Act against
them. They therefore disowned them, and those who persisted in
supporting them were expelled.

Q. 20   What is the judgement of the Conference concerning what
are called Camp-Meetings?
A.   It is our judgement, that even supposing such meetings to be
allowable in America, they are highly improper in England, and likely
to be productive of considerable mischief. And we disclaim all connexion with them.
Q. 21   Have our people been sufficiently cautious respecting the
permission of strangers to preach to our congregations?
A.   We fear not: and we, therefore, again direct, that no stranger,
from America or elsewhere, be suffered to preach in any of our places,
unless he come fully accredited; if an Itinerant Preacher, by having his
name entered on the Minutes of the Conference of which he is a
member; and if a Local Preacher, by a recommendatory note from his
Superintendant.

4 Debate on Sidmouth's Protestant Dissenting Ministers' Bill, 1811

Extract from *Parliamentary Debates* (first series), xix, cols. 1128–33.

The Bill was designed to exercise closer supervision over the registration of Dissenting Ministers, and was aimed particularly at Methodist Ministers who were not attached to separate congregations. These extracts are from the debate in the House of Lords on the first reading on 9 May 1811. Viscount Sidmouth (a) explains his reasons for introducing the Bill: Lord Holland (b) defends the right to freedom of religious opinion. The Bill was later defeated without a division.

a.

Viscount *Sidmouth* . . . said, it was his intention at this time to bring under their consideration the abuses which had arisen in the interpretation and the execution of two statutes, the 1st of William and Mary, and the 19th of George 3rd, so far as the same related to Protestant Dissenting Ministers. . . . If their lordships would turn their attention to the terms of these two acts, they would find that the appointments of ministers and teachers of religion were made contrary to the spirit and true intent of those statutes. He should ever consider the present mode of appointment as injurious to society, and such as he was sure was condemned by every worthy and enlightened Dissenter. It was a matter of importance to society, that not every person, without regard to his moral character or his intellectual faculties, should assume to himself the office of instructing his fellow-creatures in their duty to God. It could never be the wish of the Dissenters; indeed, from the communication he had had with that respectable class of men, he knew it was contrary to their ideas that a person should thus take upon himself the assumption that he was competent to become the religious instructor of others. On this subject he had gained extensive information, and had been made acquainted with facts, which shewed that abuses existed to a considerable degree in the self-appointment of improper individuals. For such was the mode generally pursued on this occasion, that if any person, however depraved, however ignorant and illiterate, whether descending from a chimney or a pillory, if he appeared at the quarter sessions, and claimed to take the oath of allegiance to his Sovereign and that against Popery, and made the necessary declaration provided by the 19th of Geo. III, he was entitled to, and could demand a certificate, although there was no proof of his fitness to preach, or of his having any congregation requiring his ministerial services. Thus it resulted that the immunities granted by these acts were in a number of instances claimed and enjoyed by individuals, to the greater burden of the rest of their fellow-subjects. Down to 1802, one of those immunities was an exemption from military services; and, to this time, from serving on juries, and other civil duties, which were forced upon other members of society. . . . With respect to the mode of rectifying such abuses, he now meant to present a Bill to their lordships, and then should desire that it be read a first time. The object of this measure was, in the first place to procure a clear declaration of the law, to remove the erroneous interpretation adopted by magistrates in general, and to prevent improper persons from their own assumption taking upon them an office of all others the most important to a well-regulated community. He should be sorry if it were thought that he cast any imputation upon the different orders and classes of men; but in the account of abuses he had received, and the individuals described, though he would forbear to mention any name, there were persons claiming those certificates, who were cobblers, tailors, pig-drovers, and chimney-sweepers. . . . It would also be understood, that he was not wishing to alter the Act of Toleration, but to provide that persons applying should not be entitled to their certificate, unless they had one signed by six reputable housekeepers of the persuasion to which he belonged. The noble viscount read the provisions of the two Acts, and inferred from them that the intention of the legislature was not to grant the certificate to any but such as were in holy orders, or were the teachers of a congregation. . . .

b.

Lord *Holland* said, he would not act so irregularly as to oppose the first reading of a Bill, but he thought it right, in candour, to state, that he could not agree with the noble viscount in the object proposed.

The noble viscount founded his measure upon an opinion, that it was only by the permission of government that persons were entitled to preach those religious doctrines which they held. Now, he on the contrary, was of opinion, that every person had a right to preach those religious opinions which he conscientiously believed. He regretted that the noble viscount had spoken invidiously of persons in inferior situations of life becoming preachers, for surely they were fully entitled to preach those religious opinions which they conscientiously believed, as those who received the advantages of the rich endowments of the church. He regretted also, that his noble friend should have at all touched upon the subject, as in his opinion it could only tend to excite dissentions. No case had been made out which called for the interference of Parliament. The exemptions from civil duties, of which the noble viscount complained, could only apply to a few persons, and it was better that those few persons should have their exemptions, than that Parliament should run the risk of exciting those dissentions which must be caused by meddling with the Toleration Act. . . .

5 William Cobbett on Dissenters, 1811

Two extracts from Cobbett's *Political Register*, May 1811, in J. M. and J. P. Cobbett, *Selections from Cobbett's Political Works*, iv, pp. 52-3, 59-60.

These passages were written at the time of the agitation over Sidmouth's Bill, and include an attack on the Methodists for their political support of Pitt and the government. They show that not all radicals opposed an established religion, and that anti-Methodist prejudice was slow to die.

a.
That men, that *all* men, should be allowed to worship their Maker in their *own way*, is I think, not to be doubted; but, if the government once begins to meddle, it must establish somewhat of an *uniform creed*, and that this creed will not suit all men is very certain. Whether the

government *ought ever to meddle* with religion is a question that I will not now attempt to discuss; but this I am not at all afraid to assert; that, without *a state religion*, a kingly government and an aristocracy will never long exist, in any country upon earth; therefore, when the Dissenters, as in the present case, come forward and volunteer their praises of kingly government, and boast so loudly, and so perfectly gratuitously, of their 'ardent loyalty' to their venerable Sovereign', whose goodness to them 'has made an indelible impression upon their hearts'; when they do this, they do, in effect, acknowledge the utility and the excellence of a state religion; because, as I said before, and as all history will clearly prove, *without a state religion a kingly government cannot exist.*

If this be the case, it must be allowed that the government is bound to protect its own religion, which is to be done only by *keeping down others* as much as is necessary to secure a predominance to that of the state. And, then, we come to the question; whether it ought not, for this purpose, now to do something to lessen the number of Dissenting Ministers, who are daily increasing, and whose influence increases in proportion beyond that of their number. Indeed, *if we allow that a state religion is necessary*, this is no question at all; for, in proportion as these Dissenting Ministers increase, the Church of England must lose its power. . . .

Now, as to the moral benefit arising from the teaching of Dissenting Ministers, it is sometimes very great, and I believe it is sometimes very small indeed, and, in many cases, I believe, their teaching tends to immorality and to misery.

Amongst the Ministers of some of the sects there are many truly learned and most excellent men, and such there always have been amongst them; and, even amongst the sects called Methodistical, there have been, and, doubtless, are, many men of the same description. But, on the other hand, it must be allowed that there are many of the Methodistical Preachers, who are fit for anything rather than *teaching* the people *morality*. I am willing to give the most of them full credit for sincerity of motive, but to believe, that the Creator of the Universe can be gratified with the ranting and raving and howling that are heard in some of the Meeting-Houses, is really as preposterous as any part of the Mahommedan Creed; and, if possible, it is still more absurd to suppose, that such incoherent sounds should have a tendency to mend the *morals* of the people, to make them more honest, industrious and public-spirited, for this last is a sort of morality by no means to be left out of the account

I have heard it observed by very sensible and acute persons, that even these ranters *do more good than harm*; but, if they do any harm at all, the question is, I think, at once decided against them; for, that they can do any *good* appears to me utterly impossible.

I am clearly of opinion, that, to lessen the number of this description of Ministers (for so they are called) would be a benefit to the country, provided it could be done without creating *a new source of political influence*. And, as to the politics of the whole sect of the Methodists, they are very bad. Never has anything been done by them, which be-spoke an attachment to *public liberty*. 'Their kingdom', they tell us, is '*not of this world;*' but, they do, nevertheless, *not neglect the good things of it*; and, some of them are to be found amongst the rankest jobbers in the country. Indeed, it is well known, that that set of politicians, ironically called THE SAINTS, who have been the main prop of the PITT system; it is well known, that under the garb of sanctity, they have been aiding and abetting in all the worst things that have been done during the last twenty years. . . .

b.

In short, they are *Dissenters* merely because they have *no tithes*, and in that name only do they resemble the Dissenters of the times before the Revolution; they are as much like the Dissenters of old times as a *horse-dung* is like an *apple*. Those were fanatics, but they were honest and just men, full of courage and full of talent; they understood well the rights and liberties of Englishmen, and upon the maintenance of them they staked their lives. The mongrel 'SAINTS' of our days are as keen for places, pensions, contracts, and jobs, as the inhabitants of any perjured borough in the kingdom; and indeed, if I were to be put to it to find out the most consummate knaves in all England, I should most assuredly set to work amongst those who are ironically denominated 'SAINTS'. They were the great corps of scouts in the famous times of *No Popery*, and did more with that base and hypocritical cry than all others put together. One of the bawling brutes in my neighbourhood told the people, that 'the King, Lord bless him! had saved them all from being burnt by the *papishes*'. Was it for a service like this that he was to be exempted from Lord Castlereagh's Local Militia? A congregation of these '*Saints*', in a neighbouring county, *cashiered their Minister* because he spoke at a town meeting, against the clamorous outcry of '*No Popery*'; and, in consequence thereof, a gentleman gave him a living in the Church.

Many, very many, instances of their base time-serving in politics might here be mentioned; but, enough has, I think, been said to show, that the increase of their members cannot be expected to be attended with any good effect. I would let them alone; but, I would give them *no encouragement*. There are persons who like them, because they look upon them as hostile to *the Church*. Their hostility is for the *tithes*, which they would exact with as much rigour as the present Clergy, and would, if possible, deserve them less. But, *my* great dislike to them is grounded on their *politics*, which are the very worst in the country; and, though I am aware, that there are many very honourable exceptions amongst them, I must speak of them as *a body*; and, as a body I know of none so decidedly hostile to public liberty. This is an age of *cant*. The country has been ruined by cant; and they have been the principal instruments in the work, and have had their full share of the profit.

6   Toleration Act, 1812

Public General Acts, 52 Geo. III, *c.* 155.

After the defeat of Sidmouth's Bill, Lord Liverpool's government introduced a new Toleration Act, which repealed the Conventicle Act and consolidated the legislation affecting Nonconformists' freedom to worship, and the conditions for registration of ministers and meeting houses.

An Act to repeal certain Acts, and amend other Acts relating to Religious Worship and Assemblies, and Persons teaching or preaching therein. (29 July 1812)

Whereas it is expedient that certain Acts of Parliament, made in the Reign of His late Majesty King Charles the Second, relating to Nonconformists and Conventicles, and refusing to take Oaths, should be repealed, and that the Laws relating to certain Congregations and Assemblies for Religious Worship, and Persons teaching, preaching, or officiating therein, and resorting thereto, should be amended; [13 & 14 Car. II, *c.* 1, 17 Car. II, *c.* 2, 22 Car. II, *c.* 1 repealed.]

II   And be it further enacted, That from and after the passing of this Act no Congregation or Assembly for Religious Worship of Protestants (at which there shall be present more than Twenty Persons besides the immediate Family and Servants of the Person in whose House or upon whose Premises such Meeting, Congregation, or Assembly shall be had) shall be permitted or allowed, unless and until the Place of such Meeting . . . shall have been or shall be certified to the Bishop of the Diocese, or to the Archdeacon of the Archdeaconry, or to the Justices of the Peace at the General or Quarter Sessions for the County, Riding, Division, City, Town, or Place in which such Meeting shall be held; . . . and all such Places shall be registered in the said Bishop's or Archdeacon's Court respectively, and recorded at the said General or Quarter Sessions; the Registrar or Clerk of the Peace whereof respectively is hereby required to register and record the same; and the Bishop or Registrar or Clerk of the Peace to whom any such Place of Meeting shall be certified under this Act shall give a Certificate thereof to such Person or Persons as shall request or demand the same, for which there shall be no greater Fee nor Reward taken than Two Shillings and Sixpence; and every Person who shall knowingly permit or suffer any such Congregation or Assembly as aforesaid to meet in any Place occupied by him, until the same shall have been so certified as aforesaid, shall forfeit for every Time any such Congregation or Assembly shall meet contrary to the Provisions of this Act, a Sum not exceeding Twenty Pounds, nor less than Twenty Shillings, at the Discretion of the Justices who shall convict for such Offence.

III   [Penalty on Persons teaching or preaching without Consent of Occupiers.]

IV   [Preachers in and Persons resorting to Religious Assemblies certified under this Act, exempt from same Penalties as Persons taking Oaths under the Toleration Act, 1689.]

V   [Oaths and Declaration to be taken by all Preachers, etc., when required thereto by a Magistrate.]

VI   [No Person to be compelled to go more than Five Miles to take such Oaths.]

VII   [Any Person may require a Justice of Peace, etc., to administer the Oaths, etc., under this Act.]

VIII   [Justices shall give the Parties a Certificate of having made such Oath.]

IX   And be it further enacted, That every Person who shall teach or preach in any such Congregation or Assembly, or Congregations or Assemblies as aforesaid, who shall employ himself solely in the Duties of a Teacher or Preacher, and not follow or engage in any Trade or Business, or other Profession, Occupation, or Employment, for his Livelihood, except that of a Schoolmaster, and who shall produce a Certificate of some Justice of the Peace, of his having taken and made and subscribed the Oaths and Declaration aforesaid, shall be exempt from the Civil Services and Offices specified in the said recited Act passed in the First Year of King *William* and Queen *Mary* [the Toleration Act], and from being ballotted to serve and from serving in the Militia or Local Militia of any County, Town, Parish, or Place in any Part of the United Kingdom.

X   [Penalty on producing false Certificate.]

XI   And be it further enacted, That no Meeting, Assembly, or Congregation of Persons for Religious Worship, shall be had in any Place with the Door locked, bolted, or barred, or otherwise fastened, so as to prevent any Persons entering therein during the Time of any such Meeting, Assembly, or Congregation; and the Person teaching or preaching at such Meeting, Assembly, or Congregation shall forfeit for every Time any such Meeting, Assembly, or Congregation shall be held with the Door locked, bolted, barred, or otherwise fastened as aforesaid, any Sum not exceeding Twenty Pounds, nor less than Forty Shillings, at the Discretion of the Justices convicting for such Offence.

XII   And be it further enacted, That if any Person or Persons, at any Time after the passing of this Act, do and shall wilfully and maliciously or contemptuously disquiet or disturb any Meeting, Assembly or Congregation of Persons assembled for Religious Worship, permitted or authorized by this Act, or any former Act or Acts of Parliament, or shall in any Way disturb, molest, or misuse any Preacher, Teacher, or Person officiating at such Meeting, Assembly, or Congregation, or any Person or Persons there assembled, such Person or Persons so offending, upon Proof thereof before any Justice of the Peace by Two or more credible Witnesses, shall find Two Sureties to be bound by Recognizances in the penal Sum of Fifty Pounds to answer for such Offence, and in default of such Sureties shall be committed to Prison, there to remain till the next General or Quarter Sessions; and upon Conviction of the said Offence at the said General or Quarter Sessions, shall suffer the Pain and Penalty of Forty Pounds.

XIII   Provided always, and be it further enacted, That nothing in this Act contained shall affect or be construed to affect the Celebration of Divine Service according to the Rites and Ceremonies of the United Church of *England* and *Ireland,* by Ministers of the said Church, in any Place hitherto used for such Purpose, or being now or hereafter duly consecrated or licensed by any Archbishop or Bishop or other Person lawfully authorized to consecrate or license the same, or to affect the Jurisdiction of the Archbishops or Bishops or other Persons exercising lawful Authority in the Church of the United Kingdom over the said Church, according to the Rules and Discipline of the same, and to the Laws and Statutes of the Realm; but such Jurisdiction shall remain and continue as if this Act had not passed.

XIV   Provided also, and be it further enacted, That nothing in this Act contained shall extend or be construed to extend to the People usually called *Quakers*, nor to any Meetings or Assemblies for Religious Worship held or convened by such Persons; or in any Manner to alter or repeal or affect any Act, other than and except the Acts passed in the Reign of King *Charles* the Second herein-before repealed, relating to the People called *Quakers*, or relating to any Assemblies or Meetings for Religious Worship held by them.

XV   [Offenders to be convicted before Two or more Justices. Forfeitures to be levied by Distress.]

XVI   [Appeal after Conviction to General Quarter Sessions.]

XVII   [Penalties to be sued for and prosecuted within Six Months.]

XVIII   [Limitations of Actions.]

XIX   [Public Act.]

7   The loyalty of Wesleyans, 1812

An extract from the Address to the Societies, *Minutes of the Wesleyan Conference, 1812*, collected edition, iii, pp. 304–5.

Wesleyan Methodists made a regular habit of reaffirming their loyalty to king and country, so that there should be no danger of being suspected of radicalism. This extract from the Conference address after the passage of the Toleration Act is typical.

. . . [Our] religious privileges appear of late to have been in considerable danger, but, in consequence of a timely application to the Legislature, sanctioned and supported by his Majesty's Government, we have the satisfaction to inform you, that an Act of Parliament has passed which fully secures them to us, and will enable us to worship God and promote his Glory without fear, in that manner which we all so highly value. . . .

In contemplating this measure we cannot but adore the goodness of God, who hath remembered us in our time of need, for His Mercy endureth for ever. But while we give the sole glory to that God, who is wonderful in counsel, and who maketh even the wrath of man to praise Him, we cannot but feel a debt of Gratitude due to those through whom such benefits have been dispensed; and we therefore most heartily concur in the sentiments which have been expressed by the General Committee of Privileges, relative to his Majesty's Ministers, and to those other exalted persons of both Houses of Parliament, whose liberality and enlightened policy have been so greatly manifested upon this important occasion. To them we doubt not you will feel the same gratitude, and we trust you will join with us in ardent Prayers for the welfare of those distinguished Characters and their Families, and for that Government by whose conciliating concurrence, and active exertions, this great measure has been produced. But this event calls for more than gratitude. If it does not impose fresh moral obligations, at any rate it strengthens our motives for obedience, and it should increase our alacrity in the path of duty. The well-known loyalty of our Societies, their dutiful attachment to their King and Country, and the simplicity and purity of their object in promoting their own salvation, and that of others, are certainly to be reckoned amongst the secondary causes which have produced such a favourable result. Let us then walk by the same rule; let us mind the same thing. And while we participate in the extension of our religious privileges with delight, let our advantages be improved in the cultivation of those loyal, humble, and pious dispositions, which inspire confidence in our principles, and at once make us happy in ourselves and useful amongst men. . . .

8   The financial rule in Methodism, 1812

Minutes of the Wesleyan Conference, 1812: collected edition, iii, p. 295.

From its beginning Methodism was based on regular contributions from class members of a penny a week. But from time to time it proved necessary to repeat the rule to secure its observance, as here at the time of the financial crisis of 1812.

Q. 18 A. 6   We once more recommend most earnestly to all our Societies, a strict compliance with that original Rule, which Mr Wesley established at the first institution of Methodism; and which requires, that, upon an average, each member shall pay, for the support of the work, one penny per week in the classes; and one shilling per quarter, in addition to the weekly contribution, at each renewal of the tickets. . . .

9   A Quaker's conversion, 1812

An extract from J. B. Braithwaite, *Memoirs of Joseph John Gurney* (1854), i, pp. 84–5.

Joseph John Gurney (of the famous Norwich banking family) was one of the leading evangelical Quakers of the first half of the nineteenth century. This description of his conversion shows the implications of accepting the 'peculiarities'.

I am not sure of the precise time, but I think it was very soon after my father's decease, and after a visit from my dearest sister Fry to our family and meeting, that as I lay in bed one night, light from above seemed to beam upon me and point out in a very explicit manner, the duty of submitting to decided Quakerism, more particularly to the humbling sacrifice of 'plainness of speech, behaviour, and apparel'. The visitation was strong, but my will was stronger; I would not, I did not comply; putting off what appeared to me almost unbearable, to a more 'convenient season'. . . .

Soon after my return home (from Yearly Meeting), I was engaged to a dinner party at the house of one of our first county gentlemen. Three weeks before the time was I engaged, and three weeks was my young mind in agitation, from the apprehension, of which I could not dispossess myself, that I must enter his drawing room with my hat on. From this sacrifice, strange and unaccountable as it may appear, I could not escape. In a Friend's attire, and with my hat on, I entered the drawing room at the dreaded moment, shook hands with the mistress of the house, went back into the hall, deposited my hat, spent a rather comfortable evening, and returned home in some degree of peace. I had afterwards the same thing to do at the Bishop's; the result was, that I found myself the decided Quaker, was perfectly understood to have assumed that character, and to dinner parties, except in the family circle, was asked no more.

10   The first Baptist Union, 1812

Reprinted in *Baptist Quarterly* (new series), iv (1928–9), pp. 124–6.

In 1812 a General Union of Baptist ministers and churches was formed—the first national union for the denomination. The most important principles are indicated in the extracts from the resolutions of the meeting. The doctrinal statement in resolution 1 is typical of Particular Baptist churches of the time: when the Union was reorganised in 1832 'the sentiments usually denominated evangelical' became the only doctrinal standard apart from Believer's Baptism.

1   That this Society of ministers and churches be designated 'The General Union of Baptist ministers and churches' maintaining the important doctrines of 'three equal persons in the Godhead; eternal and personal election; original sin; particular redemption; free justification by the imputed righteousness of Christ; efficacious grace in regeneration; the final perseverance of real believers; the resurrection of the dead; the future judgement; the eternal happiness of the righteous, and the eternal misery of such as die in impenitence, with the congregational order of the churches inviolably'.

2   That ministers and churches, who may hereafter be desirous of uniting with this Society, be admitted, with the consent of the whole body, at the annual meeting.

3   That the formation of this Union be for the purpose of affording to the ministers and churches of the denomination the names of becoming better acquainted with each other, with a view to excite brotherly love, and to furnish a stimulus for a zealous co-operation in promoting the cause of Christ in general, and particularly in our own denomination, and especially to encourage and support our missions.

10   That this Society disclaims all manner of superiority and superintendence over the churches; or any authority or power, to impose anything upon their faith and practice; their sole intention is to be helpers together one of another, in promoting the common cause of

Christianity, and the interests of the several churches of the denomination to which they belong. . . .

11   Trinity Act, 1813

Public General Acts, 53 Geo. III, *c.* 160.

Unitarians had been disappointed that the Toleration Act of 1812
did nothing to legalise Unitarianism, and in the following year
William Smith, a Unitarian Member of Parliament, promoted this
Act to remedy the position.

An Act to relieve Persons who impugn the Doctrine of the *Holy
Trinity* from certain Penalties. (21 July 1813)

Whereas, in the Nineteenth Year of His present Majesty an Act was
passed, intituled *An Act for the further Relief of Protestant Dissenting
Ministers and Schoolmasters*; and it is expedient to enact as herein-after
provided: Be it therefore enacted by the King's most Excellent Majesty,
by and with the Advice and Consent of the Lords Spiritual and
Temporal, and Commons, in this present Parliament assembled, and
by the Authority of the same, That so much of an Act passed in the
First Year of the Reign of King *William* and Queen *Mary*, intituled
*An Act for exempting His Majesty's Protestant Subjects dissenting from the
Church of* England, *from the Penalties of certain Laws*, as provides that that
Act or any Thing therein contained should not extend or be construed
to extend to give any Ease, Benefit, or Advantage to Persons denying
the *Trinity* as therein mentioned, be and the same is hereby repealed.
II   And be it further enacted, That the Provisions of another Act
passed in the Ninth and Tenth Years of the Reign of King *William*,
intituled *An Act for the more effectual suppressing Blasphemy and Pro-
faneness*, so far as the same relate to Persons denying as therein mentioned, respecting the *Holy Trinity*, be and the same are hereby
repealed.
III   [Acts passed in Scotland against Blasphemy repealed.]
IV   [Public Act.]

12 Persecution of Primitive Methodists, 1818–19

Extracts from (a) J. Davison, *The Life of William Clowes* (1854), pp. 86–7, 89, and (b) H. B. Kendall, *The Origin and History of the Primitive Methodist Church* (n.d.) i, pp. 342–3.

The early Primitive Methodists met with some of the ill-treatment that had befallen the early Wesleyan preachers three-quarters of a century before. Both these extracts relate to experiences in the Midlands revival of 1818–19—William Clowes in Nottinghamshire and Leicestershire, and John Garner in Warwickshire. Violence, economic sanctions and noisy distractions were all tried.

a. *William Clowes*

At Shelford a gracious work broke out, but it was bitterly opposed by the persecuting hosts. A steward of the proprietor of the village hurled his anathema against us, and those that should have the temerity to harbour us. One man, however, mustered courage to brave the storm, and opened his house for preaching. He was therefore served with a notice to quit. He, however, owned his house, although built on the land of the proprietor. The steward determined to eject him, but the man stood firm, and the opposition was not persevered in. Another persecuting character was taken away by a premature death, and thus the way was made more smooth, and hindrances to our progress removed. . . .

At Bottesford the banner of the cross was unfurled, amidst rampant opposition. A band of music was hired to annoy us, and occasionally the scene was very dramatic. The preacher and people were singing, the band playing, the dogs barking, and some of the persecutors grinning; but partial deliverance arrived when the drummer was convicted by the truth preached; and a place was obtained for regular services. . . .

b. *John Garner*

At this place [Sow] we had preached several times, but to little purpose, the inhabitants being vile persecutors, and the parish clergyman conducting himself towards us in so vile a manner that prudence forbids it being published. No sooner had I entered the village than stones were flying in every direction. I made haste to the house of Mr – where a few people were assembled to hear the word of life. The mob followed me, surrounded the house, broke the windows, and compelled me to stop the meeting. Seeing no probability of the persecution abating, I was necessitated to expose myself to the malicious rage of the wicked, by whom I was furiously driven out of the village with stones, rotten eggs, sludge, or whatever came first to hand. The friends who accompanied me seeing the madness of the mob, became afraid, and endeavoured to effect their escape by taking a footpath. The rebels followed me out of the village, and some of them seized me; others propped my mouth open with stones, while some were engaged in attempting to pour sludge down my throat. The cry was raised, 'Kill the devil! d— him!' Immediately a man knocked me down, and after I had been shamefully beaten with the hands and feet of my enemies, and with divers weapons, I was dragged to a pond, around which they gathered, hoping soon to be gratified with my death. At this juncture of time I had not even a faint hope of ever being rescued from them alive; hence I committed my body and soul into the hands of the Lord, and most earnestly wished for death to put an end to my sufferings, which were almost insupportable. However, 'the thoughts of the Lord are not as our thoughts, neither are His ways as our ways', for, contrary to my expectations, He made a way for my escape. One of the vilest persecutors rescued me from the fury of his companions; and some of them pursued my friends, who had at first escaped. Then the rebels were withdrawn from me. After having walked a few hundred yards, I perceived a woman much affected, tears were rolling down her cheeks; she kindly invited me into her house, and then assisted in washing my head and face. Being somewhat recovered, through the hospitality of my hostess, I returned, with the assistance of a friend, to walk to Bell Green, a distance of perhaps two miles, and by my kind friends at this place I was cordially entertained and taken care of. They lent me what clothes I wanted; for my persecutors had also torn my clothes, of a portion of which they afterwards made a scarecrow. After being carefully nursed at Bell Green a few days, I was enabled to attend to my usual labour.

13   Plain dress for Methodist preachers, 1819

Minutes of the Primitive Methodist Conference, 1819, p. 5.

Like the Quakers, the Methodists laid great stress on plainness of dress. The practice was beginning to break down in Wesleyan Methodism before John Wesley's death, but the newer Methodist denominations stressed the same point.

Q. 17   In what dress shall our Travelling Preachers appear in public? A. In a plain one: the men to wear single breasted coats, single breasted waistcoats, and their hair in its natural form; and not to be allowed to wear pantalooks, trousers, nor white hats; and that our Female Preachers be patterns of plainness in all their dress.

NOTE. We strongly recommend it to our brethren, the Stewards, Local Preachers, Leaders and private Members, both Male and Female, in our societies to be plain in their dress.

14   A Methodist preacher's week, 1819

An extract from *An Account of the Religious and Literary Life of Adam Clarke, Ll.D., F.A.S.* (by a member of his family) (1833), ii, pp. 367–8.

Many diaries and journals survive from the early Methodist preachers, and it is impossible to provide even a typical selection. This brief extract from one of the most distinguished Methodists of his day, Adam Clarke, illustrates the packed nature of his programme and some of its hazards.

Oct. 16—Tuesday night, I preached at *Hayle,* to an immense crowd.

Wednesday, I preached at *Helston,* after travelling twenty miles; the crowd was vast, and the chapel suffocating.

Thursday, I preached at *Redruth,* to another of these overwhelming crowds.

Friday, I preached at *Falmouth.* The people came here from all quarters, both by sea and land. This place is situated on a bay; one of the finest and safest I have ever seen.

Saturday, I have preached in this town (*Truro*) at seven o'clock this morning; and although the hour was so early, yet we had the large chapel nearly full, above and below. To-morrow morning I am to preach at *St. Austell,* about fourteen miles from this place, and then my *Cornish* work will be ended. You will enquire how I have stood so much work? I have not stood it, for it has nearly killed me; I have almost totally lost my appetite; am constantly feverish, and afflicted with a dry mouth; my strength is prostrated. All these consequences I foresaw; but I found I must either go through all this labor, or have instantly left the county.

Oct. 22—I am just come in after preaching here (*St. Austell*). The crowd was immense. They had just been enlarging the chapel, building a new end and gallery to it. When I was about to take my text, the gallery gave way: the timbers fairly came out of the walls, yet it did not fall down; but the confusion was awful. I was close to the gallery, and distinctly saw the peril; and had it come down, I knew I must have been the first victim; but at least 200 others would also have been killed. I stood in my place; for had I moved, universal terror would have taken place, and many must have fallen victims to an impetuous rush out. The chapel was soon nearly emptied, and no one was hurt. Many came back again, and I preached; but I knew not till the end of the service, all the miracle it required to save us! Then it was found that, owing to the pressure in the gallery, the timbers being too short, had started out from the walls two feet, and the gallery actually shook to its centre, having nothing but its pillars to support it. Our son John being beneath, could see this plainer than I could at the time; and he saw also, that if it fell, he must be killed if he kept his place, which was immediately before the pulpit; but as he knew his father must be the first victim, he resolutely kept his situation, expecting eternity every moment. But enough of this; it makes one's blood run chill. This is the last crowd I ever wish to see.

15   Nonconformist origins, c. 1820

An extract from J. Guinness Rogers, *An Autobiography* (1903), pp. 2–3.

Many of the new recruits to Nonconformity in the early nineteenth century came from nominal Anglican homes, and were impressed by the evangelical preaching they found among Nonconformists at a time when there was still much neglect in their own Church. The Rev. J. Guinness Rogers was a leading Congregational minister in the second half of the century.

I am a son, therefore, of a father and mother both of whom had, without any previous communication with each other, passed out of the Anglican Church into a humble Dissenting community. The change was a typical one. Like numbers besides, they became Dissenters, not because of any abstract preference for Dissent, but simply because they were attracted to the churches where they had received spiritual benefit. I never heard my mother speak of the reasons which led her to take this step; but my belief is that she and her mother, in whom the change was still more remarkable, had simply become Dissenters because it was from a Dissenting minister and in a Dissenting chapel that they had felt the converting power which had led them to Christ.

16   A Methodist class meeting, c. 1822

An extract from *The Life of Joseph Barker written by himself* (1880), pp. 44–6, 51–2.

The class meeting was at the heart of Methodist life. Here the theory and one view of the practice are described by Joseph Barker. Barker was brought up a Wesleyan, became a travelling preacher for the Methodist New Connexion, was expelled in 1841 and became a Unitarian and then a sceptic, but ended by returning to Christianity as a Primitive Methodist local preacher. His view is thus that of both an insider and an outsider.

The class-meetings are held weekly. The classes ought, according to rule, to consist of ten or twelve members; but they sometimes contain as many as thirty, forty, or fifty, and at other times not more than three or four. Each member kneels down as soon as he enters, to pray a little by himself. The leader then begins the meeting by giving out a hymn, and the members stand up to sing. Then the leader prays, gives out another hymn, and then tells his experience. Sometimes he tells what trials he has met with, and what deliverances he has experienced through the week, what joys and sorrows he has had, how he felt at the love-feast, the prayer-meeting, or the fellowship-meeting, what liberty he had in secret prayer, how he felt while reading the Scriptures, or hearing sermons, or while busy at his work, what passages have come to his mind, or what promises have been applied to his soul. At other times he simply tells how he feels at that moment; while at other times he says nothing about his experience or feelings, but just gives thanks to God for what He has done for him, in a general way, or offers a few words of exhortation or preaching to the members. He then asks each member in turn the state of his mind. A very common form of the question is, 'Well, brother, or well, sister, how do you feel the state of your mind to-night?' At other times it will be, 'Well, brother, will you tell us what the Lord is doing for you?' Different leaders have different ways of proposing the question, and the same leader varies it at times. When the question is put, the member answers. Some of the members tell a long and flaming story; others say little, or next to nothing. Some speak loud, and even shout; others speak so low that they cannot be heard, either by the leaders or the rest of the members. Some are always happy, according to their story; others are always doubtful and fearful, and can never say much either about their feelings or performances. One tells you he has been on the sunny side of the hill all the week; another says he has been on the mount of transfiguration, and that he could say with one of old, 'Master, it is good to be here.' . . .

It was to one of those classes I went. The leader was a draper of Bramley, called G— B—. He was a ready talker and a zealous Methodist. He was loud in his praying, rather bold in his manner, but very ignorant; and willing, for anything I could ever see, to remain so. He was a great preacher's man, and fond of little honours and would do anything to be well thought of or favoured by the preachers. He knew, too, that to be on good terms with the preachers was the way to get customers to his shop; and he was very fond of gain. He had no scruples against laying up treasure on earth, though he read over Wesley's rules to us every quarter. He was a great respector of persons; and though he seemed to have sense enough to know that it was wrong, he had not virtue or shame enough to keep him from practising it even in the face of the whole class. He had abundance of respect for the richer members of his class, or at least he was abundantly ready to show respect to them; but, with the poorer members he could use as much freedom as you like. He would tell the poorer members to speak up; but he never told the richer ones to do so, though the richer ones were generally most prone to speak low. The rich members used generally to get into one corner by themselves, while the poor ones sat anywhere about the room. When he came to the rich members' corner, and found that scarce one of them could speak loud enough to be heard, either by himself or us, he used to feel rather at a loss sometimes what to do, especially when he had just before been urging some of the poorer members to speak; but he durst not complain, not he. Then how did he do? He did just like himself. When he knew that some would be thinking, Why does he not ask them to speak up? he would exclaim, 'Glory be to God! They are as happy as queens here in the corner.' I wonder how we could bear with such a shallow, worthless person for a leader; but we knew no better, I suppose, then?

17   The 'no smoking' rule in Primitive Methodism, 1823

Minutes of the Primitive Methodist Conference, 1823, pp. 2–3.

The Primitive Methodists were one of the first denominations to make any pronouncement on smoking.

1 That none of our travelling preachers shall smoke tobacco, except it be recommended by a physician, in and by a written document, stating to what extent it is necessary.
2 That it be recommended to all our members to be sparing in smoking tobacco.

18 Debates on the repeal of the Test and Corporation Acts, 1828

Extracts from *Parliamentary Debates* (new series), xviii, cols. 677–9, 686–93, 714–15, 733–4, 751–7, xix, cols. 129–30.

Extracts (a) to (d) come from the debate in the House of Commons on Lord John Russell's motion for repeal on 26 February 1828, and extract (e) comes from the debate in the House of Lords on the third reading of the Bill on 25 April.

The debate on Lord John Russell's motion resulted in the unexpected approval of the motion by 237 votes to 193, and a Bill to give effect to it followed. The extracts have been selected to illustrate the main arguments put forward: Russell's considered case for repeal (from which the long historical discussion has been omitted); Sir Robert Inglis's statement of a high Tory position defending the Acts as the inevitable consequence of an established Church; Huskisson's view that repeal would prejudice the question of Roman Catholic relief; and Peel's cool and moderate Tory arguments for doing nothing. The extract from Lord Eldon, who spoke thirty-five times on the Bill, illustrates the fear of 'liberalism' with which the Bill was associated.

a.
Lord *John Russell*: . . . So great has been the improvement in knowledge and liberality, particularly among the middle classes, that the successors of those who most warmly opposed the motion of 1790 are, in 1828, its most zealous supporters. For instance, let us look to what has taken place in the common-council of London. It is notorious, as has been mentioned by an hon. alderman, that in the year 1790, the corporation passed some strong resolutions against the repeal of the Test and Corporation acts, and voted thanks to those members of the city who had opposed the repeal in this House; but so great has been

o

the change in men's minds on the subject since that time, that the corporation has recently agreed to resolutions declaring those acts hostile to the principles of religious liberty. Another circumstance which I look upon as favourable to my motion is, that the powerful antagonist of Mr Fox, in 1790, Mr Pitt, as is now well known, did in a few years after his opposition to the measure, completely change his mind on the subject, and express a wish that the Test and Corporation acts should be repealed. He saw, as every man of enlarged and enlightened mind must have seen, that all things around him were changed since the passing of those acts; that the religious questions which had been the subject of the world's debate at the time of their enactment had given place to divisions purely political; that the dispute for power no longer lay between Catholic, Lutheran, and Calvinist, but between the adherents, of despotism, representative monarchy, and democracy; that he could only defend the constitution by rallying round it the victims of an extinct quarrel, and calling on men of different religious opinions to defend the same form of political government. There is only one word more which I would add by way of preface. It may be asked, if I remove these securities, what other tests would I propose? My answer is, that I am opposed to religious tests of every kind. . . . I would wish to see applied to persons taking seats in parliament, and all the offices of government or corporations, a simple provision, that they should be called upon only to swear allegiance to the king.

I now come to the great principle involved in the numerous petitions before the House; petitions signed by the whole body of Dissenters, by Roman Catholics, and by many members of the established church. That principle is, that every man ought to be allowed to form his religious opinions by the impressions on his own mind, and that, when so formed, he should be at liberty to worship God according to the dictates of his conscience, without being subjected to any penalty or disqualification whatever; that every restraint or restriction imposed on any man on account of his religious creed is in the nature of persecution, and is at once an offence to God, and an injury to man. This is the just and noble principle on which the Dissenters claim the repeal of the Test laws. But I will fairly admit, that there may be an exception to its application . . . : if the religion of any body of men be found to contain political principles hostile to the state, or militating against that allegiance which is due from every subject of the Crown, in that case the question ceases to be a religious question; and you have a right to interfere and impose such restrictions as you may deem necessary, because you do not impose them on religious opinions; you impose them only on political doctrines [hear, hear!]. . . .

You enacted [these acts] to guard against a particular danger; does that danger now exist? If danger were apprehended from Dissenters, why pass acts from year to year pardoning those who by law are excluded from taking office for taking office? I can easily imagine the necessity of pursuing such a course for five, ten, or fifteen years. Government may have said, 'Wait a little, we are not assured of the loyalty of these persons; do not give them freedom all at once, but see first how they will act.' But that parliament should go on with acts of indemnity for eighty-five years—that they should not, at this time of day be satisfied of the loyalty of the Dissenters, is a thing against all rules of justice, of policy, and of prudence.

The next objection is to the nature of the Tests required, which are of a very serious and solemn character. The Sacrament of the Lord's Supper is held by the Church to be most sacred, and it is declared that those who receive it unworthily 'eat and drink their own damnation'. . . . When men are told that if they take the sacrament, they will be fit to hold office, and not without, it is in fact holding out to them a temptation to abuse the sacrament, and to pervert the most holy of God's ordinances to purposes of the most paltry ambition. . . .

It is said, however, 'after all, the grievances of which you complain are only theoretical—they no longer exist in practice—Dissenters are not in fact kept out of office'. I will say, in the first place, that if the case be so, that is not a sufficient argument in support of these acts. Statutes imposing penalties and restrictions on men on account of religious belief can be justified on no other ground than that of necessity. When that ground is taken away, the acts remain exposed in all their naked deformity of principle, and that principle is religious persecution. But it is not a fact that no practical grievance is suffered by the Dissenters. Indeed the fact is far otherwise—the real practical grievance is a great deal more than the legal grievances which appear on the face of the statute. Though it be true that by later statutes indemnity was given to those who omitted to qualify, yet that indemnity was given on the ground that omission was occasioned by ignorance, absence, or unavoidable accident. Those words evidently do not apply to those persons who had omitted to qualify from grounds of religious scruple. . . .

Not only this; it should also be recollected that it is in the power of any corporation, actuated by bigotry, or personal animosity, to carry the Corporation act into effect against Dissenters. I have in my possession a statement of cases which have occurred in the course of the last few years, in which persons who had a minority of votes in elections for corporation offices have been declared duly elected, because a previous notice had been given that the individuals who had the majorities could not act from being Dissenters. . . . More than this; persons admitted to office ought, under the Test act, to produce their certificates. Dissenters do not like to expose themselves to the chance of those certificates being demanded. Rather than that, they will consent to forego office. The consequence is, that not one tenth part of the Dissenters who ought, in proportion to their numbers, at present hold office.

I have now stated, Sir, some of the practical grievances under which the Dissenters labour, but I am aware, whilst I am proving that these acts operate to the exclusion of Dissenters, I am only confirming many persons in the belief that it is necessary to continue them. I allude to those persons who use the argument of the security of the Church, and who think that in proportion as the number of Dissenters excluded is large it is so much the better for the Church, that the establishment is so much the safer. I, however, cannot admit that the security of the Church is founded on any such exclusion. I think with bishop Kennet, and I believe the security of the establishment consists in its moderation, its fair temper, and in its decent worship being conformable to the wishes, sentiments, and consciences of the majority of the people; and if it were not so—if it were not agreeable to the people—can it be imagined that any Test, any exclusive laws, will save the Church, and prevent its being destroyed by the overwhelming mass of its enemies? . . . If the security of the Church of England be founded solely on the Test and Corporation acts, I will ask what is the security for the Church of Scotland? By the articles of Union, the Presbyterian is declared the true religion—it is the established Church of that country, and yet no Test or Corporation acts exist there. . . .

But their case is still stronger.—In order to diminish still further the security of our northern Church, persons of the Church of Scotland cannot come to this country and take office without being liable to the penalties of these acts, although being of the church established by law in another part of the kingdom. Then, with respect to Ireland: if the Corporation and Test acts be necessary to the security of the Church in England, it would be supposed that they must necessarily exist in Ireland. That, however, is not the fact. The Corporation act never, I believe, existed in Ireland. The Test act was introduced there in the reign of Anne, and was abolished some forty-eight or forty-nine years ago. . . .

I have shown that history will not justify you in maintaining these acts. The first of them was raised as a barrier to the throne against a party who had recently overturned it. But whatever the Dissenters of that day might feel towards the House of Stuart, the Dissenters of the present feel nothing but loyalty towards the House of Hanover. The Test act, again, was intended as a barrier against the king, who was a converted Papist; you have now a sovereign who is firmly attached to the established religion. For a long period these acts were maintained for fear of driving the Church into the arms of the Jacobites: there is now no fear that the clergy will look for promotion or favour through any other than the legitimate channel of his majesty's Treasury and Chancery. I have shown you that all ground of necessity fails, the acts having been suspended for more than three quarters of a century. I have proved, I trust, that they violate the sacred rights of conscience, and are of the nature of religious persecution—I have shown that, so far from not inflicting any hardship on the body upon whom they operate, they are fraught with great mischief, irritation, and injustice. I have shown, that they are totally at variance with our own policy in Scotland and Ireland, as well as with the enlightened legislation of all Christian countries of Europe. If I am asked what advantage the country is to derive from the abrogation of such laws, I answer, that the obvious tendency of the measure, independently of its justice, will be, to render the Dissenters better affected to the government, to inspire them with disposition to bear the heavy burdens imposed on them by the necessities of the state with cheerfulness, or, at least, with resignation; and, above all, it will be more consonant to the tone and spirit of the age than the existence of those angry yet inefficient and impracticable laws which are a disgrace to the Statute-book. I have heard with considerable pain, that it is the intention of the new ministry to make this what is called a government question, to array all the power which their influence can muster against it. I am sorry to learn this; not on account of the question itself, whose progress they may retard, but never can prevent—I am sorry to hear it, because it is an indication on the part of government, of a determination to resist the liberality which is daily gaining ground in the great mass of society. . . .

b.

Sir R. H. Inglis: . . . The Dissenters of the present day enjoy the fullest rights of conscience: and I am willing to admit that there is nothing in their overt acts from which I apprehend any danger. With some of them I am intimate, for many more I have the highest respect; but it is perfectly clear, that the principles of Dissenters conscientiously opposed to the Church, can never give the same undivided allegiance to the constitution in church and state which a churchman does. The principles, if carried to the same extent as formerly, would produce the same results. The laws which restrain Dissenters are, and will ever be, left inoperative, so long as those principles slumber also; but I think that they should be retained for the purpose of being exerted in extreme cases, if such should ever arise. In fact, a richly-endowed Church, with all its privileges and immunities, will always be an object of jealousy to those who differ from it: but, connected as it is with the constitution, the state is found to protect it against any dangers from any quarters. Dangers will always exist: and, if the present disabilities were removed, and Dissenters placed on the fullest equality as to power with the Church, some new question, perhaps of property, would immediately be started, on which new struggles and new dangers would arise. The question of tythes would probably come: and, as we should have followed the example of America in giving no preference to any Church, we should be called upon to follow it further, and to enact that no man should pay any thing to any pastor but his own [hear, hear]. . . .

c.

Mr Secretary *Huskisson* said: . . . that the principle which the question then before the House involved, appeared to him to be this—that, whereas, up to the present hour, as the law stood—he would not say, in its practice, but certainly in its principle—the rule of this country was to render conformity to the established church the condition of holding civil offices; but now an attempt was made to remove those laws, leaving others in existence, which bore upon a different part of the population. If, then, they repealed those laws which were the object of the noble lord's motion, and left other laws which were considered by many of an oppressive nature untouched, what became of that general rule? He contended, that from the moment such a course was adopted, the rule was entirely changed, and they created an exception. And who formed that exception? The Roman Catholics alone. . . . He was not abstractedly unfriendly to the proposition of the noble lord; but he could not assent to it, because he was sure that with reference to the Catholic claims, it would make a bad impression. . . .

d.

Mr Secretary *Peel* said: I am not prepared, I confess, to argue that this question is essentially interwoven with the protection of the Church of England. I do not think that the two are so connected, that the Church of England must fall if the Test and Corporation acts are repealed. . . . I think that my right hon. friend's principle is a right one: is there that great practical grievance, that insult resulting to the Dissenters from these acts, which calls upon the House to repeal them? Is there any thing so absurd in these tests as to make the repeal of them necessary? Or are they of such a nature that, if repealed, the Dissenters will be in a better situation? Nothing, in the whole course of this debate, has surprised me more than the enlarged, and I think, aggravated account of the practical grievance which these acts impose upon the Dissenters. I can only say, that so great is my respect for that large and respectable body denominated Protestant Dissenters, that if I could be satisfied that they really labour under such grievances as have been described, I should be very strongly induced to vote for the repeal of the acts complained of. But I do not think that the great body of Dissenters look at them, together with the Indemnity act, as so great an evil as hon. gentlemen have described.

We have been told, Sir, to look at the number of petitions that have been presented to the House. Now, if I were sure that these petitions had been quite spontaneous, and not set in motion by any external influence, I candidly declare that I should be disposed to pay much more attention to them. . . . It had been said, 'Look at the thousand petitions presented last year, and the six hundred this year'—and I am therefore tempted to ask, how many were presented at former periods? . . . In 1824, there were four petitions presented; in 1825, one; in 1820, one; in 1817, not one; in 1818, not one; in 1819, not one; in 1821, not one; in 1822, not one; in 1823, not one; in 1826, not one. The whole number, therefore, in these ten years amounted only to six. . . .

An hon. member opposite (Mr. Fergusson) has described, in very powerful and affecting terms, the distressing effect of these acts upon a country towards which no man can feel more cordially than I do—Scotland. . . . The hon. member speaks of 'horrid penalties', and 'proscription'. What are the feelings of Scotchmen generally now upon the subject? Where are the petitions from that country? From the whole of Scotland? There has not been, I believe, a single petition for the repeal of these acts. . . .

In the same way a noble lord on the other side has intimated that the parties interested in this question were not generally in the highest rank of life; and that from the mediocrity of their station, their rights are likely to be overlooked or to be forgotten. Perhaps the noble lord has properly described the Dissenters as belonging chiefly to the middle class; but, nevertheless, many persons of that persuasion move in a very exalted situation; and I fully agree with the noble lord, that the corporate privileges and honours to which those not immediately in that class aspire are fit and laudable objects of ambition for persons of their condition; such as it is a grievance to be excluded from, and which it is the duty of the legislature to uphold and sanction, rather than to make light of or offend. But, Sir, what is the fact as to the corporate honours? Are the Dissenters practically excluded from corporations? I believe that they are not. . . .

But the next question is this—can it be made at all apparent, what will be the effect of an alteration in the law? Under the existing system, there has, perhaps been less of religious difference in England, for the last forty years, than in the same extent of time at any period of our history. Now, that fact, which an hon. member has treated as a reason for repealing the laws complained of, seems to me to be quite as capable of being made an argument the other way. An hon. alderman informed us, the other night, that thirty-nine years ago, in the city of London, a few persons only had the resolution to stand up for a repeal of these acts; while at present there were not more than six or seven who venture to support them. Is not this a proof of the good under-standing which has grown up between the Dissenters and the members of the Church of England? . . . And it is not at all clear to me, that the Dissenters would gain what they expect by the repeal of these acts. If they excite suspicion and dislike, will they not, as far as the alteration goes, do mischief? The fact is, that the existing law merely gives a nominal predominance to the Protestant established church. A pre-dominance of some sort will be admitted, on all hands, to be necessary, and the present is as slight a one as can well be imagined. Therefore, Sir, I confess I am sorry that I am called upon to vote upon the ques-tion, and heartily wish it had been allowed to remain quiescent; practically offensive as I am convinced it is to no one. . . .

e.

Lord *Eldon* . . . repeated, that he considered this bill a most pernicious measure [a laugh]. Noble lords treated this with a laugh. He was glad to find that he was able to give noble lords some entertainment. He would again assert, that the present measure went to destroy the unity established, by the constitution of the country, between the Church and the State. The measure was nothing more nor less than an attack upon the constitution of the country. It had been one of the consequences of that 'march of intellect', and that 'liberality' of which they had heard so much; and sure he was, that in the progress of time this and similar marches would succeed in uprooting the foundations of all that constituted the happiness and glory of this country. Much praise had been bestowed, by the supporters of this bill, upon the clergy and the members of the Established Church, on account of the small number of petitions presented from them against it. He did not know that they were to be praised for resting upon their oars. If restless activity on the one side was only to be met by dormant apathy on the other, let the consequences rest upon them, and not upon him. No individual could entertain a higher respect for the bench of bishops, than he did . . . but they must pardon him for saying, that he did not conceive that their support of this measure was calculated to strengthen the Established Church. . . .

19   The repeal of the Test and Corporation Acts, 1828

Public General Acts, 9 Geo. IV, *c*. 17.

Most of the discussion in the passage of the Bill concentrated on the declaration (clause II) which was inserted as a safeguard for the Church of England. It was abolished in 1866 (29 Vict., *c*. 22).

An Act for repealing so much of several Acts as imposes the Necessity of receiving the Sacrament of the Lord's Supper as a Qualification for certain Offices and Employments. (9 May 1828)

[Recites the Acts 13 Car. II, st. 2, *c*. 1, 25 Car. II, *c*. 2, and 16 Geo. II, *c*. 30] . . . And whereas it is expedient that so much of the said several Acts of Parliament as imposes the Necessity of taking the Sacrament of the Lord's Supper according to the Rites or Usage of the Church of *England*, for the Purposes therein respectively mentioned, should be repealed; be it therefore enacted . . . That so much and such Parts of the said several Acts . . . as require the Person or Persons in the said Acts respectively described to take or receive the Sacrament . . . for the several Purposes therein expressed, or to deliver a Certificate or make Proof of the Truth of such his or their receiving the said Sacrament in manner aforesaid, or as impose upon any such Person or Persons any Penalty, Forfeiture, Incapacity, or Disability whatsoever for or by reason of any Neglect or Omission to take or receive the said Sacrament . . . are hereby repealed.

II   And whereas the Protestant Episcopal Church of *England* and Ireland, and the Doctrine, Discipline, and Government thereof, and the Protestant Presbyterian Church of *Scotland*, and the Doctrine, Discipline, and Government thereof, are by the Laws of this Realm severally established, permanently and inviolably: And whereas it is just and fitting, that on the Repeal of such Parts of the said Acts as impose the Necessity of taking the Sacrament of the Lord's Supper according to the Rites or Usage of the Church of *England*, as a Qualification for Office, a Declaration to the following Effect should be substituted in lieu thereof; be it therefore enacted, That every Person who shall hereafter be placed, elected, or chosen in or to the Office of Mayor, Alderman, Recorder, Bailiff, Town Clerk, or Common Councilman, or in or to any Office of Magistracy, or Place, Trust, or Employment relating to the Government of any City, Corporation, Borough, or Cinque Port within *England* and *Wales* or the Town of *Berwick-upon-Tweed*, shall, within One Calendar Month next before or upon his Admission into any of the aforesaid Offices or Trusts, make and subscribe the Declaration following:

'I A.B. do solemnly and sincerely, in the Presence of God, profess, testify, and declare, upon the true Faith of a Christian, That I will never exercise any Power, Authority, or Influence which I may possess by virtue of the Office of   to injure or weaken the Protestant Church as it is by Law established in *England*, or to disturb the said Church, or the Bishops and Clergy of the said Church, in the Possession of any Rights or Privileges to which such Church, or the said Bishops and Clergy, are or may be by Law entitled.'

III   [Declaration to be subscribed before two Magistrates.]

IV   [In case of neglect to make the declaration, the election to be void.]

V   [Persons admitted into any Office which heretofore required the taking of the Sacrament, shall make the Declaration within Six Months, or the Appointment be void.]

VI [Declaration to be made in the Court of Chancery or King's Bench, or at the Quarter Sessions.]

VII [Naval Officers below the rank of Rear-Admiral, Military Officers below the rank of Major-General, or of Colonel in the Militia, Commissioners of Customs, Excise, Stamps and Taxes, and all Officers concerned in the Collection, Management and Receipt of the Revenues are not to be required to make the Declaration.]

VIII [Persons now in Possession of any Office which heretofore required the taking of the Sacrament, confirmed in such Possession and indemnified from Penalties.]

IX [Omissions of Persons to make the Declaration not to affect others not privy thereto.]

Notes

1 Care should, however, be taken not to exaggerate the role of Nonconformists, as some economic historians have done. See K. Samuelson, *Religion and Economic Action* (London, 1961).

2 H. B. Kendall, *The Origin and History of the Primitive Methodist Church* (2 vols, London, n. d.), i, pp. 84–5, 99–102. Bourne was actually expelled for absence from class.

3 *Minutes of the Wesleyan Conference, 1803*, collected edition (1813), ii, pp. 188–9. See the Epilogue of G. Eliot, *Adam Bede.*

4 Kendall, op. cit., i, pp. 58–9.

5 A. Peel, *These Hundred Years* (London, 1931), p. 37.

6 E. A. Payne, *The Baptist Union* (London, 1959), pp. 15–27.

7 *Parliamentary Debates*, first series, xx, cols. 233–55. The text of the Bill is in *Parliamentary Debates*, first series, xix, cols. 1133–40. See also B. L. Manning, *The Protestant Dissenting Deputies* (Cambridge, 1952), pp. 130–43.

8 R. W. Davis, 'The Strategy of "Dissent" in the Repeal Campaign, 1820–8', *Journal of Modern History*, xxxviii (1966), pp. 374–93; N. Gash, *Mr Secretary Peel* (London, 1961), pp. 460–5.

9 R. Currie, *Methodism Divided* (London, 1968), p. 87; D. Bogue and J. Bennett, *History of Dissenters* (London, 1812), iv, pp. 327–32, and J. Bennett, *The History of the Dissenters* (London, 1839), pp. 264–7 say there were 532 Baptist and 799 Independent congregations in 1812 and 750 Baptist and 1,203 Independent in 1827 in England. Figures for Wales are not available for 1827, but increase there was faster than in England.

Two   Growing confidence

From the repeal of the Test and Corporation Acts
to factory education, 1828–43

Many of the most well-known descriptions of Dissent in English
fiction date from the period around 1830—just before the Reform
Bill and the coming of the railways. It is interesting that this date
should be taken as the starting point for change. Most of these
descriptions, however, are of the position in the country towns of
the Midlands and southern counties. Mark Rutherford describes
Cowfold (Bedford) (23), a town very little affected by the Industrial
Revolution in its early stages. For this reason George Eliot's
descriptions of the Midlands (28) are more interesting, because she
does describe the effects of the new industries. Both may be compared
with the Rev. J. Guinness Rogers's description of Prescot near
Liverpool (38), but even Prescot was not a new industrial town.
Beatrice Webb's impressions of Bacup (89) are more interesting but
date from half a century later. For this reason, although these
pictures are well-known and important, it is essential not to treat
them as pictures of a timeless and universal Dissent: they show but
a part. It is also well to remember that Dissent was often unpopular,
particularly where the influence of the Church of England was
dominant.[1]

   These pictures of Dissenting life are difficult to fit into a
narrative, but they do provide a living context for it. It is
impossible to understand Nonconformity without knowing something
about the kind of people who were Nonconformists. Joseph
Barker's picture of ordinary chapel folk in County Durham (30) is
a good example. The atmosphere of the Nonconformist Sunday
(even though not all Nonconformists approved (53)) 'with all forms
of reasonable recreation forbidden' provides the necessary background
to Nonconformist worship (24).[2] The routine of week-night
services and prayer meetings was the secular Nonconformist's
equivalent of the monk's daily office, and to see it in that light, even
taking account of its deficiencies (16), helps to explain why
Nonconformists so repeatedly bemoaned the social changes of the
second half of the century which were destroying it (79).[3] But it is
also important to remember that many of those who described this

life did so in order to criticise it. It is useful therefore to compare a book like *The Autobiography of Mark Rutherford* with the memoirs of Nonconformist ministers who did not lose their faith: Newman Hall's description of theological college (39) may be compared with White's description in *The Autobiography*, chapter 2.

All the descriptions indicate the divide which existed between Methodism and the Old Dissent in the 1830s. But there was also a division between those who favoured 'revivalism' and those who did not. It is not clear how far the early Wesleyan and Primitive Methodist revivals can be regarded as 'organised': but it is clear that they were free from the extreme techniques now being tried by some (35). What contemporaries called 'an incessant craving for sensation' should be distinguished from the fervour and warmth of normal evangelical preaching. Even the Primitive Methodists took care to regulate their camp meetings (22), but it was not always easy to draw the line between a proper fervour and artificial excitement.[4]

The 1830s were also the years of the beginning of the total abstinence movement. The Primitive Methodists had been the first denomination to express official approval of temperance societies in 1832 (27). Later that year on 1 September the Pledge of the Seven Men of Preston to abstain from *all* intoxicating liquors was signed, and the temperance movement entered a new stage. (Previously the emphasis had been on abstaining from spirits.) Many Nonconformists were suspicious of this new and more radical movement, as the debate in the Wesleyan Conference of 1841 showed (41). It was only after the foundation of the United Kingdom Alliance in 1853 that the teetotal movement really began to make an impact on Nonconformity as a whole.[5]

Among the Old Dissent, the 1830s saw a hardening of denominational dividing lines with the re-formation of the Baptist and Congregational Unions and the final separation of Unitarians from Trinitarians. In May 1831 three meetings of Congregational ministers and church officers were held, which decided that it was desirable to form a Union of Congregational churches and approved the principles for its constitution (26). The Union was formed on 11 May 1832.[6] At the same time the General Union of Baptist ministers and churches (10) was reorganised on a broader doctrinal basis, which made it easier for the General Baptists of the New Connexion to join their Particular Baptist brethren.[7] Thus the division between Congregationalists and Baptists was more sharply defined as the two groups separated into their own unions: only in one or two places, such as Bedfordshire, was an attempt made to retain the old local union which had included churches of both denominations.

Sharper still was the separation of Unitarians. After the legalisation of Unitarianism in 1813 (11) their dependence on close association with the Trinitarian Dissenters was reduced. In the next few years several legal battles were fought in various parts of the country between Unitarians and Trinitarians to establish which had the right to ancient endowments. The most famous case was that of Lady Hewley's Charity. This endowment dated from 1704 and formed a fund for the support of Dissenting ministers and similar objects. By 1830 all the trustees were Unitarian, and their right to be so was challenged by a group of Congregationalists. Judgment was given in 1833 in favour of the Trinitarians (31) and this decision was upheld on appeal in 1836 and in the House of Lords in 1842. This immediately exposed the property of any Unitarian congregation founded before 1813 to similar legal action, and to forestall this the Dissenters' Chapels Act of 1844 was passed, which laid down that unless the trust deed explicitly restricted the property to Trinitarians the usage of the last twenty-five years established title. The acrimony of these legal actions, however, led to the withdrawal of the Unitarians from the Dissenting Deputies in 1836, and the establishment of the (Trinitarian) Presbyterian Church in England in the same year.[8] From the 1830s the Unitarians ceased to take an active part in the life and politics of Dissent, and as they had previously provided many of the leaders this had important consequences. There was a gradual change in the emphasis of Nonconformist political activity.

No Nonconformist had ever doubted the validity of political agitation if his own interests had been threatened: the Methodist response to Sidmouth's Bill of 1811 had shown that. To a lesser extent the same had been true of the agitation to repeal the Test and Corporation Acts. When the question was more remote, such as Catholic emancipation, a distinction between individual and collective action, such as that made by Joseph Entwisle (20), was more likely to be drawn. Where the issue was a moral one, such as slavery, Methodists (and others) did not hesitate to urge those with the vote to exercise their political power as in 1830 (21). The view of the Quaker, J. J. Gurney, that Christians ought to be involved in politics where 'humanity, justice, virtue, and moral and religious

improvement are concerned' would have been echoed by most
Nonconformists.[9] The problem, of course, was to draw the line
between moral and political issues.

It is quite clear that the 1832 Reform Act did increase the political
consciousness and the political power of Dissenters, as George Eliot
and the Duke of Wellington observed (28, 29). One of the first
actions of the Reformed Parliament was the abolition of slavery in
1833. After this, Dissenters turned to the redress of five specific
grievances: payment of Church Rates (for the support of the parish
church); the fact that marriages had to take place in the Church of
England; the lack of a general registration of births, marriages and
deaths; the exclusion of Dissenters from the universities; the lack of
burial rights in parish churchyards. They secured a general registration
and the right to be married in their own chapels in 1836, but they
failed in the other three. The Whig government's proposal to abolish
Church Rates and replace them with a grant from direct taxation was
fiercely criticised (33) and then dropped. Although several petitions
for change at Oxford and Cambridge were presented to
Parliament (including one circulated by Thomas Arnold (32)), a bill
to change the situation was defeated in the House of Lords. Nothing
was done about burials.[10]

The Methodists tended to remain aloof from these battles. All
the Methodist denominations had a 'no politics' rule (e.g. 34b, 36)
by which chapels could not be let for political meetings and ministers
were not supposed to speak at such meetings. The Wesleyans did
not share many of the 'Dissenting grievances' because they did not
object to being married in the Church of England, etc. But although
this was the majority view, there were some who disagreed. The
Rev. J. R. Stephens was expelled from the Connexion in 1834 for
disobeying a district meeting's order to give up his involvement in
the Ashton-under-Lyne Church Separation Society, which favoured
the separation of Church and State.[11] In this case, as in that of Dr
Warren the following year, it was widely felt that, although the
reason for expulsion had been ostensibly one of internal discipline,
behind this there lay differences of outlook in secular as well as
ecclesiastical politics. It was a Wesleyan who remarked that 'the
neutrality between the Established Church and political Dissent had
proved to be a one-sided neutrality', because Jabez Bunting, the
effective leader of Wesleyanism at this time, had publicly stated his
belief in Church Rates.[12]

But it is too easy to call some denominations conservative and others liberal. As has been pointed out, the 'no politics' rule applied to all Methodist denominations, but it is only the Wesleyans who have been called Tory because of it. The London Congregational ministers were regarded as conservative by their provincial brethren (37). The father of Newman Hall, the Congregational minister, was a Nonconformist 'but in politics he was an old-fashioned Tory and was opposed to the separation of Church and State'.[13] Most denominations in the 1830s contained both Whigs and Tories. It is thus a mistake to see Dissent as being wholly committed to social and political change (25).[14]

But a movement was beginning, particularly in provincial Dissent. The Municipal Corporations Act of 1835 brought Nonconformists to political power in many provincial towns, and many local political divisions polarised around the Anglican/Dissenter line, particularly over Church Rates. It was from this context that Edward Miall, a former Congregational minister in Leicester and much involved in Church Rate battles there, founded the *Nonconformist* in 1841. Miall attacked the piecemeal approach to redress Dissenting grievances (42) and argued that only the separation of Church and State would solve the problem. Miall and his supporters were usually political Radicals, who were disillusioned with the Whig government and wanted more political reform as well. At the same time Richard Cobden was seeking to harness the moral feeling that Nonconformists had shown over the slave trade behind his campaign to repeal the Corn Laws. A conference of Dissenting ministers in Manchester in 1841 backed the Anti-Corn Law League. But whilst there is no doubt that many Nonconformists felt strongly on the Corn Laws, it is clear that this conference was stage-managed (43) and the strength of the new radical movement should not be exaggerated.[15]

The controversies over education after 1839 were probably more important in uniting the Nonconformist denominations against the government. In 1839 the Whigs proposed to extend the possibility of receiving school grants to Dissenting and Roman Catholic schools that did not belong to either the National (Anglican) Society or the British and Foreign (Dissenting) Society, to have all grant-aided schools inspected by government inspectors, and to build a government teacher-training college in which 'general' rather than denominational religious instruction would be given. The Church of England opposed the proposals because of the recognition given to Dissent and the government interference proposed in their own schools. Some Nonconformists, including the Wesleyans, opposed them because of the recognition given to Roman Catholics.[16] The government withdrew the plan for a training college, but kept inspection. But their troubles were mild compared with those that broke over the heads of the Tory government in 1843, when it was proposed in the Factories Bill to include provisions for factory schools run by a committee of trustees with the vicar in the chair. Despite modifications the clauses were bitterly opposed, and eventually withdrawn (44).

The address of the Wesleyan Conference to its societies in 1843 is particularly interesting on this point, because it sums up the trends which were now taking even the Wesleyans steadily in a liberal direction (45). The Wesleyans joined in the agitation against the education clauses, and even Bunting opposed them. The Disruption of the Church of Scotland in 1843, when some 500 ministers left the established Church of Scotland, not because they disbelieved in establishment but because they thought the State was trying to usurp the rights of the Church, made many Wesleyans aware of the defects in establishment: and they saw in the education clauses an example of these defects. Their suspicion was also increased by the news coming from Oxford about the 'Romanising tendencies' of the Puseyites. The Church of England which Wesley knew and his followers admired was changing too, and not in directions they liked; and as it did, the case of the Dissenters against it became more plausible. In 1843 Bunting told the Wesleyan Conference, '*No doubt we are Dissenters. We are not Churchmen....* In a *sense* we are *Dissenters*; yet there is a sense in which we are not, but only *Nonconformists.*'[17] The Disruption of the Church of Scotland first made the term 'Free Church' known south of the border. United action by Nonconformists or 'Free Churchmen' became a more popular rallying point than united action by 'Dissent'.

Curiously enough the Oxford Movement shared with the Nonconformists this movement of thought in favour of the Church's autonomy, and the belief of men like Thomas Arnold that the doctrine of the king's supremacy was a providential discovery of the Reformation (40) became less widely shared. Belief in 'comprehension' (of Anglicans and Dissenters in a national Church) became more difficult as the basis of that belief (that Church and State were co-extensive) was challenged. Thus the Arnold who championed the cause of Dissenters in 1834 was for the same reasons their critic six years later.

20   A Methodist view of Catholic emancipation, 1829

An extract from *Memoir of the Rev. Joseph Entwisle* (by his son) (1848), pp. 436–7.

Joseph Entwisle was one of the most respected Wesleyan preachers of his day, and his very cautious attitude to collective political involvement, even when he was sympathetic to the cause, is typical.

Mar. 14.—Received a letter from Mr. Mason, as Secretary of the Committee of Privileges. They have met, and come to the following resolution:—'That with respect to the Bill for the Relief of His Majesty's Roman Catholic subjects, now before the House of Commons, the Committee of Privileges do not think it their duty to take any proceedings in their collective capacity; but every member of the Methodist Society will of course pursue such steps in his individual capacity on this occasion, as he may think right.' *A wise conclusion*, in my opinion; for, *as a religious body, I trust the Methodists will never move collectively on any civil or political question.*

Thurs. 26.—Received a letter from the Secretary of the Brunswick Club in Dublin, requesting the Methodists everywhere to petition against Popery. I doubt the propriety of this. I have signed petitions, in common with the citizens and inhabitants of Bristol, to the Lords and Commons, and to the King; but I doubt the propriety of the Methodists, *as such*, embarking in political matters. It would create much contention too in our own societies, as there exists a great difference of opinion on the Catholic question.

21 Resolutions of the Wesleyan Conference on slavery, 1830

Minutes of the Wesleyan Conference, 1830, collected edition, vi, pp. 613–15.

Feeling against slavery was common to all evangelicals from Anglicans to Quakers. The resolutions of the Wesleyan Conference are interesting, partly because they are typical of the attitude of evangelical Nonconformists, partly because they refer to the missionary situation where Nonconformists were involved, and also because they advocate use of the vote in the cause, a significant step for Wesleyans.

1 That, as a body of Christian Ministers, they feel themselves called upon again to record their solemn judgment, that the holding of human beings in a state of slavery is in direct opposition to all the principles of natural right, and to the benign spirit of the religion of Christ.
2 That the system of bondage existing in our West India colonies is marked with characters of peculiar severity and injustice; inasmuch as a great majority of the slaves are doomed to labours inhumanly wasting to health and life; and are exposed to arbitrary, excessive, and degrading punishments, without any effectual protection from adequate and impartially administered laws.
3 That the Conference, having long been engaged in endeavouring the instruction and evangelization of the Pagan Negroes of our West India colonies by numerous and expensive Missions, supported by the pious liberality of the friends of religion at home, have had painful experience of the unfavourable influence of a state of slavery upon the moral improvement of a class of men most entitled to the sympathy and help of all true Christians; that the patient and devoted men who have laboured in the work of Negro conversion, have too often been made the objects of obloquy and persecution, from that very contempt or

fear of the Negroes which a system of slavery inspires; that the violent prejudices of caste, founded upon the colour of the skin, and nurtured by a state of slavery, and inseparable from it, have opposed the most formidable obstacles to the employment of coloured teachers and Missionaries, who would otherwise have been called into useful employment, in considerable numbers, as qualified instructers of their fellows; that the general discouragement of slave marriages, and the frequent violent separation of those husbands and wives who have been united in matrimony by Missionaries, have served greatly to encourage and perpetuate a grossness of manners which might otherwise have been corrected; that the nearly absolute control of vicious masters, or their agents, over those under their power, is, to a lamentable extent, used for the corrupting of the young, and the polluting of the most hallowed relations of life; that the refusal of the Lord's day to the slave, as a day of rest and religious worship, besides fostering the habit of entire irreligion, limits, and in many cases renders nugatory, every attempt at efficient religious instruction;—all which circumstances, more or less felt in each of the colonies, demonstrate the incompatibility of slavery with a general diffusion of the influence of morals and religion, and its necessary association with general ignorance, vice, and wretchedness.

4   That the Preachers assembled in Conference feel themselves the more bound to exhort the members of the Methodist Societies and congregations at home, to unite with their fellow-subjects in presenting their petitions to the next Parliament to take this important subject into its earliest consideration, because of the interesting relation which exists between them and the numerous Methodist Societies in the West Indies, in which are no fewer than 24,000 slaves, who, with their families, have been brought under the influence of Christianity, and who in so many instances have fully rewarded the charitable toil of those who have applied themselves to promote their spiritual benefit, and whose right to exemption from a state of slavery, is, if possible, strengthened by their being partakers with us of 'like precious faith', and from their standing in the special relation of '*brethren*' to all who themselves profess to be Christians.

5   That the Conference fully concur in those strong moral views of the evil and injustice of slavery which are taken by their fellow-Christians of different denominations, and in the purpose which is so generally entertained of presenting petitions to Parliament from their respective congregations for its speedy and universal abolition; and earnestly recommend it to all the congregations of the Wesleyan Methodists

throughout Great Britain and Ireland, to express in this manner—that is, by petitions to both Houses of Parliament from each congregation, to be signed at its own chapel, and presented, as early as possible, after the assembling of the next Parliament—their sympathy with an injured portion of their race, and their abhorrence of all those principles on which it is attempted to defend the subjection of human beings to hopeless and interminable slavery.

6 That the Conference still further recommend, in the strongest manner, to such of the members of the Methodist Societies as enjoy the elective franchise, that, in this great crisis, when the question is, whether justice and humanity shall triumph over oppression and cruelty, or nearly a million of our fellow-men, many of whom are also our fellow-Christians, shall remain excluded from the rights of humanity, and the privileges of that constitution under which they are born; they use that solemn trust to promote the rescue of our country from the guilt and dishonour which have been brought upon it by a criminal connivance at the oppressions which have so long existed in its colonies, and that, in the elections now on the eve of taking place, they will give their influence and votes only to those candidates who pledge themselves to support, in Parliament, the most effectual measures for the entire abolition of slavery throughout the colonies of the British empire.

22   Primitive Methodist regulations for camp meetings, 1830

Various Regulations made at and by the Primitive Methodist Conference begun at Hull, 1830, pp. 5–6.

Camp meetings became a regular part of Primitive Methodist life, but they were governed by detailed regulations as this extract shows.

CAMP MEETINGS

16   Q. What is the order for these?

A. The Conference Camp Meeting at Hull was arranged as follows:

1   Each preaching service in the general course, to be three quarters of an hour, and each praying service half an hour. That two preachers should preach in each preaching service; and be allowed to speak twenty minutes each and not to exceed, unless sinners were actually falling down under the word. And that each one keep to a form of sound things. To avoid all apologies as being *frivolous*, as well as all attempts to tell over again what has been said, with such phraseology as, 'You have heard so and so,' or 'Our brethren have told you so and so,' or any such sort of *chaffy* discourse. Also not to use such expressions as 'My time's short'—'I must give over before it's long,' or any such sort of *trash*; or any *cant* expressions about 'doing justice to my subject'. But keep to a form of sound words that cannot be reproved, and make an honourable and useful conclusion.

2   That the Conductor give each preacher a signal, by pressing the point of an umbrella or something else, against his foot, five minutes before his time is expired; and during that five minutes, if not before, he is advised to press a present faith,

and a present salvation; and conclude with leaving such impression as full and as strong as possible on the minds of the people.

3 That the Conductor repeat the signal if need be, when the time expires, and that then the preacher at once break off.

4 That there be one sermon or more, preached to Children.

5 The praying services to be lengthened or varied in case of the work breaking out.

6 That this order be made general throughout the Connexion.

N.B. If on any occasion there be not a full supply of preachers, the order may be varied to suit; as also if there be not a sufficient supply of pious praying labourers. Also a reading service may on any occasion, be put in place of a sermon. And towards a close, a short service may be held, or the services varied to fill up the time, or produce an effect.

[In 1831 the time limit was altered to one minute's notice, with a shilling fine for exceeding it: *Minutes 1831*, p. 2, q. 4.]

23 Nonconformity in 'Cowfold', c. 1830

An extract from Mark Rutherford, *The Revolution in Tanner's Lane* (1887), chapters 16 and 17.

Mark Rutherford was the pseudonym of W. Hale White (1831–1913),[18] who was brought up an Independent and went to Cheshunt College and then New College, London, to train for the ministry. He was later expelled for unsound views on the Biblical canon. He wrote a number of novels against the Nonconformist background, of which *The Revolution in Tanner's Lane* is probably the best known. The description of Cowfold given here is based on Bedford in the 1830s. It may be compared with documents 28 and 38.

The rest of Cowfold was Dissenting or 'went nowhere'. There were three chapels; one *the* chapel, orthodox, Independent, holding about

seven hundred persons, and more particularly to be described presently;
the second Wesleyan, new, stuccoed, with grained doors and cast-
iron railing; the third, strict Baptist, ultra-Calvinistic, Antinomian
according to the other sects, dark, down an alley, mean, surrounded
by a small long-grassed graveyard, and named ZOAR in large letters
over the long window in front. The 'went nowhere' class was apparently not very considerable. On Sunday morning at twelve o'clock
Cowfold looked as if it had been swept clean. It was only by comparison between the total number of church-goers and chapel-goers
and the total population that it could be believed that there was anybody absent from the means of grace; but if a view could have been
taken of the back premises an explanation would have been discovered.
Men and women 'did up their gardens', or found, for a variety of
reasons, that they were forced to stay at home. In the evening they
grew bolder, and strolled through the meadows. It is, however, only
fair to respectable Cowfold to say that it knew nothing of these
creatures, except by employing them on week-days.

With regard to the Wesleyan Chapel, nothing much need be said.
Its creed was imported, and it had no roots in the town. The Church
disliked it because it was Dissenting, and the Dissenters disliked it
because it was half-Church, and, above all, Tory. It was supported
mainly by the brewer, who was drawn thither for many reasons, one
of which was political. Another was, that he was not in trade, and
although he objected to be confounded with his neighbours who stood
behind counters, the church did not altogether suit him, because there
Mr. and Mrs. Muston and the seminary stood in his way. Lastly, as he
owned beer-shops, supplied liquor which was a proverb throughout
the county, and did a somewhat doubtful business according to the
more pious of the Cowfold Christians, he preferred to be accredited
as a religious person by Methodism than by any other sect, the stamp
of Methodism standing out in somewhat higher relief.

As for Zoar, it was a place apart. Its minister was a big, large-jawed,
heavy-eyed man, who lived in a little cottage hard by. His wife was
a very plain-looking person, who wore even on Sundays a cotton
gown without any ornament, and who took her husband's arm as they
walked down the lane to the chapel. The Independent minister, the
Wesleyan minister, and, of course, the rector had nothing to do with
the minister of Zoar. This was not because of any heresy or difference
of doctrine, but because he was a poor man and poor persons sat under
him. Nevertheless he was not in any way a characteristic Calvinist.
The Calvinistic creed was stuck in him as in a lump of fat, and had

no organising influence upon him whatever. He had no weight in Cowfold, took part in none of its affairs, and his ministrations were confined to about fifty sullen, half stupid, wholly ignorant people who found in the Zoar services something sleepier and requiring less mental exertion than they needed elsewhere; although it must be said that the demands made upon the intellect in none of the places of worship were very extensive. There was a small endowment attached to Zoar, and on this, with the garden and house rent free, the minister lived. Once now and then—perhaps once in every three or four years— there was a baptism in Zoar, and at such times it was crowded. The children of the congregation, as a rule, fell away from it as they grew up; but occasionally a girl remained faithful and was formally admitted to its communion. In front of the pulpit was an open space usually covered; but the boards could be taken up, and then a large kind of tank was disclosed, which was filled with water when the ceremony was performed. After hymns had been sung the minister went down into the water, and the candidate appeared dressed in a long white robe very much like a night-gown. The dear sister, during a short address, stood on the brink of the tank for a few moments, and then descended into it beside the minister, who, taking her by the neck and round the waist, ducked her fairly and completely. She emerged, and walked dripping into the vestry, where it was always said that hot brandy and water was ready. . . .

The Reverend John Broad was minister of Tanner's Lane Chapel, or, more properly, Meeting-house, a three gabled building, with the date 1688 upon it, which stood in a short street leading out of North Street. . . . There were about seven hundred and fifty sittings in it, and on Sundays it was tolerably full, for it was attended by large numbers of people from the surrounding villages, who came in gigs and carts, and brought their dinners with them, which they ate in the vestry. It was, in fact, the centre of the Dissenting activity for a whole district. It had small affiliated meeting-houses in places like Sheepgate, Hackston Green, and Bull's Cross, in which service was held on Sunday evening by the deacons of Tanner's Lane, or by some of the young men whom Mr. Broad prepared to be missionaries. For a great many years the congregation had apparently undergone no change in character; but the uniformity was only apparent. The fervid piety of Cowper's time and of the Evangelical revival was a thing almost of the past. The Reverend John Broad was certainly not of the Revival type. He was a big, gross-feeding, heavy person with heavy ox-face and large mouth, who might have been bad enough for anything if

75

nature had ordained that he should have been born in a hovel at
Sheepgate or in the Black Country. As it happened, his father was a
woollen draper, and John was brought up to the trade as a youth; got
tired of it, thought he might do something more respectable; went to a
Dissenting College; took charge of a little chapel in Buckinghamshire;
married early; was removed to Tanner's Lane, and became a preacher
of the Gospel. He was moderate in all of what he called his 'views';
neither ultra-Calvinist nor Arminian; not rigid upon Baptism, and
certainly much unlike his lean and fervid predecessor, the Reverend
James Harden, M.A., who was educated at Cambridge; threw up all
his chances there when he became convinced of sin; cast in his lot
with the Independents, and wrestled even unto blood with the world
the flesh, and the devil in Cowfold for thirty years, till he was gathered
to his rest. . . .

24 A Nonconformist Sunday in the 1830s

An extract from *The Autobiography of Mark Rutherford* (1881),
chapter 1.

Mark Rutherford's *Autobiography* is based on the life of W. Hale
White. In this extract he gives a vivid picture of the atmosphere of
the Old Dissent and its Sunday worship. This way of spending
Sunday would have been typical of the majority of Nonconformist
homes, with very little modification before the end of the century.

. . . On the Sundays, however, the compensation came. It was a season
of unmixed gloom. My father and mother were rigid Calvinistic
Independents, and on that day no newspaper nor any book more
secular than the Evangelical Magazine was tolerated. Every preparation for the Sabbath had been made on the Saturday, to avoid as much
as possible any work. The meat was cooked beforehand, so that we
never had a hot dinner even in the coldest weather; the only thing hot
which was permitted was a boiled suet pudding, which cooked itself
while we were at chapel, and some potatoes which were prepared after

we came home. Not a letter was opened unless it was clearly evident that it was not on business, and for opening these an apology was always offered that it was possible they might contain some announcement of sickness. If on cursory inspection they appeared to be ordinary letters, although they might be from relations or friends, they were put away. After family prayer and breakfast the business of the day began with the Sunday-school at nine o'clock. We were taught our Catechism and Bible there till a quarter past ten. We were then marched across the road into the chapel, a large old-fashioned building dating from the time of Charles II. The floor was covered with high pews. The roof was supported by three or four tall wooden pillars which ran from the ground to the ceiling, and the galleries by shorter pillars. There was a large oak pulpit on one side against the wall, and down below, immediately under the minister, was the 'singing pew', where the singers ꞏnd musicians sat, the musicians being performers on the clarionet, flute, violin, and violoncello. Right in front was a long enclosure, called the communion pew, which was usually occupied by a number of the poorer members of the congregation. There were three services every Sunday, besides intermitting prayer-meetings, but these I did not as yet attend. Each service consisted of a hymn, reading the Bible, another hymn, a prayer, the sermon, a third hymn, and a short final prayer. The reading of the Bible was unaccompanied with any observations or explanations, and I do not remember that I ever once heard a mistranslation corrected. The first, or long prayer, as it was called, was a horrible hypocrisy, and it was a sore tax on the preacher to get through it. Anything more totally unlike the model recommended to us in the New Testament cannot well be imagined. It generally began with a confession that we were all sinners, but no individual sins were ever confessed, and then ensued a kind of dialogue with God, very much resembling the speeches which in later years I have heard in the House of Commons from the movers and seconders of addresses to the Crown at the opening of Parliament. . . . Nobody ever listened to this performance. I was a good child on the whole, but I am sure I did not; and if the chapel were now in existence, there might be traced on the flap of the pew in which we sat, many curious designs due to these dreary performances. The sermon was not much better. It generally consisted of a text, which was a mere peg for a discourse, that was pretty much the same from January to December. The minister invariably began with the fall of man; propounded the scheme of redemption, and ended by depicting in the morning the blessedness of the saints, and in the evening the doom of the lost. There was a tradition that in the morning there should be 'experience', that is to say, comfort for the elect, and that the evening should be appropriate to their less fortunate brethren. . . .

25   A Congregational Sunday school in the 1830s

An extract from G. J. Holyoake, *Sixty Years of an Agitator's Life* (1893), i, p. 33.

G. J. Holyoake, the Secularist organiser and lecturer, here describes his disillusionment with the political attitudes of the Congregationalists—which in this respect were not untypical. Birmingham was, of course, the centre of Thomas Attwood's Political Union prior to the Reform Bill; the Rev. John Angell James, minister of Carr's Lane chapel, was one of the leading Congregational ministers of the period. Most Nonconformist Sunday schools did not give any other secular instruction than reading and writing, and concentrated on Bible teaching.

For five years I was a scholar in the Carr's Lane Sunday Schools, yet save Watts's hymns and reading in the Bible, I had learned nothing. There was a sand class for seven or eight boys, in which lessons in rudimentary writing were given. But beyond this, secular instruction in these schools did not go. Once the Rev. John Angell James, the pastor, delivered a week-night public address, in which he counselled young men to be content in the station and with the lot which Providence had assigned them. Dissent was no better than the Church as regarded secular progress. When I heard Mr. James's counsel, I believed it. It was logical Christian doctrine I knew, and I could see that if acted upon, the Political Union was an organized sin—as its object was to alter and raise the condition of the people. Had Mr. James himself acted upon his own principle, he would not have been a preacher.

26   Aims of the Congregational Union, 1831

Report in the *Congregational Magazine*, 1831, pp. 372-3.

Both the Congregational Union and the Baptist Union were formed in their present form in 1832, following earlier ventures which had only been partially successful (see document 10). The resolutions containing the principles of the Congregational Union and the reasons for its formation were discussed at meetings of ministers and church officers on 10, 13 and 20 May 1831. The words in italics were added to resolution 1 by the Provisional Committee, and the words in brackets replaced the original phrase 'the broadest'.

I   That it is highly desirable and important to establish a Union of the Congregational Churches *and Ministers* throughout England and Wales, founded on (a full) recognition of their own distinctive principle, namely, the scriptural right of every separate church to maintain perfect independence in the government and administration of its own particular affairs; *and therefore that the Union shall not in any case assume legislative authority, or become a court of appeal.*

II   That such Union consist of County and District Associations.

III   That the following be the objects contemplated in its formation:—

  1 To promote Evangelical Religion in connection with the Congregational denomination.

  2 To cultivate brotherly affection and sincere co-operation in every thing relating to the interests of the associated Churches.

  3 To establish fraternal correspondence with Congregational Churches, and other bodies of Christians, throughout the world.

  4 To address an Annual Letter to the associated Churches, accompanied with such information as may be deemed necessary.

  5 To obtain accurate statistical information relative to the Congregational Churches, throughout the kingdom and the world at large.

  6 To enquire into the present methods of collecting funds for the

erection of places of worship, and to consider the practicability of introducing any improved plan.

7 To assist in maintaining and enlarging the civil rights of Protestant Dissenters.

IV To promote the accomplishment of these objects and the general interests of the Union, That an Annual Meeting shall be held consisting, if practicable, of an equal number of ministers and laymen, and that each Association may appoint such a number of representatives as it may deem necessary; and that the Annual Meeting be held in London, or such other town or city, as may from time to time be appointed; that at the Annual Meetings of Delegates, every minister and officer connected with any Association, united in the general body, shall be eligible to attend and vote.

27 Primitive Methodist minute on temperance, 1832

Minutes of the Primitive Methodist Conference, 1832, p. 3.

At the Primitive Methodist Conference of 1831 in Leicester, Hugh Bourne introduced a discussion on temperance, as a result of which a number of local societies were set up. The minute of 1832 recorded here gave official approval to the new movement, and Primitive Methodists were one of the first denominations to do so. Bourne had been a teetotaller for several years, and by 1841 the General Committee in a circular to all stations said, 'It is well known that our Connexion approves of Teetotalism, and recommends the prudent advocacy of it'.[19] It should be remembered that in the early years temperance did not necessarily mean teetotalism.

10 Q. What is the opinion of Conference in regard of Temperance societies?

A. We highly approve of them, and recommend them to the attention of our people in general.

28 Dissent, the Industrial Revolution and reform, c. 1832

An extract from G. Eliot, *Felix Holt* (1866), chapter 3.

George Eliot (Mary Ann Evans) was born and brought up in the Midlands, and this is the scene for her novel *Felix Holt*. Her description of Dissent in Treby Magna shows a real awareness of the changes wrought in Dissent by the Industrial Revolution and the new mood in the years before the Reform Act of 1832. Compare her picture with the static society of Mark Rutherford (document 23).

In this way it happened that Treby Magna gradually passed from being simply a respectable market-town—the heart of a great rural district, where the trade was only such as had close relations with the local landed interest—and took on the more complex life brought by mines and manufactures, which belong more directly to the great circulating system of the nation than to the local system to which they have been superadded; and in this way it was that Trebian Dissent gradually altered its character. Formerly it had been of a quiescent, well-to-do kind, represented architecturally by a small, venerable, dark-pewed chapel, built by Presbyterians, but long occupied by a sparse congregation of Independents, who were as little moved by doctrinal zeal as their church-going neighbours, and did not feel themselves deficient in religious liberty, inasmuch as they were not hindered from occasionally slumbering in their pews, and were not obliged to go regularly to the weekly prayer-meeting. But when stone-pits and coal-pits made new hamlets that threatened to spread up to the very town, when the tape-weavers came with their news-reading inspectors and book-keepers, the Independent chapel began to be filled with eager men and women, to whom the exceptional possession of religious truth was the condition which reconciled them to a meagre existence, and made them feel in secure alliance with the unseen but supreme rule of a

world in which their own visible part was small. There were Dissenters
in Treby now who could not be regarded by the Church people in the
light of old neighbours to whom the habit of going to chapel was an
innocent, unenviable inheritance along with a particular house and
garden, a tan-yard, or a grocery business—Dissenters who, in their
turn, without meaning to be in the least abusive, spoke of the high-
bred Rector as a blind leader of the blind. And Dissent was not the
only thing that the times had altered; prices had fallen, poor-rates had
risen, rent and tithe were not elastic enough, and the farmer's fat sorrow
had become lean; he began to speculate on causes, and to trace things
back to that causeless mystery, the cessation of one-pound notes. Thus,
when political agitation swept in a great current through the country,
Treby Magna was prepared to vibrate. The Catholic Emancipation
Bill opened the eyes of neighbours, and made them aware how very
injurious they were to each other and to the welfare of mankind
generally. Mr Tiliot, the Church spirit-merchant, knew now that
Mr Nuttwood, the obliging grocer, was one of those Dissenters,
Deists, Socinians, Papists, and Radicals, who were in league to destroy
the Constitution. A retired old London tradesman, who was believed
to understand politics, said that thinking people must wish George
the Third alive again in all his early vigour of mind; and even the
farmers became less materialistic in their view of causes, and referred
much to the agency of the devil and the Irish Romans. The Rector,
the Rev. Augustus Debarry, really a fine specimen of the old-fashioned
aristocratic clergyman, preaching short sermons, understanding business, and acting liberally about his tithe, had never before found himself in collision with Dissenters; but now he began to feel that these
people were a nuisance in the parish, that his brother Sir Maximus
must take care lest they should get land to build more chapels, and
that it might not have been a bad thing if the law had furnished him
as a magistrate with a power of putting a stop to the political sermons
of the Independent preacher, which, in their way, were as pernicious
sources of intoxication as the beer-houses. The Dissenters, on their side,
were not disposed to sacrifice the cause of truth and freedom to a
temporising mildness of language; but they defended themselves from
the charge of religious indifference, and solemnly disclaimed any lax
expectations that Catholics were likely to be saved—urging, on the
contrary, that they were not too hopeful about Protestants who
adhered to a bloated and worldly Prelacy. Thus Treby Magna, which
had lived quietly through the great earthquakes of the French Revolution and the Napoleonic wars, which had remained unmoved by the

'Rights of Man', and saw little in Mr Cobbett's 'Weekly Register' except that he held eccentric views about potatoes, began at last to know the higher pains of a dim political consciousness; and the development had been greatly helped by the recent agitation about the Reform Bill. . . .

29 The political influence of Dissent, 1833

An extract from a letter of 6 March 1833 from the Duke of Wellington to John Croker in L. J. Jennings, *The Correspondence and Diaries of John Wilson Croker* (1885), ii, pp. 205–6.

Among the newly enfranchised voters of 1832 were many Dissenters. In this letter Wellington is writing about Berkshire, but he also says the same is true of Northamptonshire, Gloucestershire and especially Scotland and Ireland. It is not clear how Dissenters in the strict sense could have increased substantially in influence in Scotland or Ireland, and it is certain that Wellington was exaggerating the degree to which power had been transferred: rather it now had to be shared. But the division between Dissent and the Church of England did give a new edge to politics in the 1830s.

I will endeavour to obtain for you the details which you require regarding the state of the representation in the House of Commons. I know none, excepting regarding this county. I have compared notes with others, and I think that all agree in the same story. The revolution is made, that is to say, that power is transferred from one class of society, the gentlemen of England, professing the faith of the Church of England, to another class of society, the shopkeepers, being dissenters from the Church, many of them Socinians, others atheists.

I don't think that the influence of property in this country is in the abstract diminished. That is to say, that the gentry have as many followers and influence as many voters at elections as ever they did.

But a new democratic influence has been introduced into elections, the copy-holders and free-holders and lease-holders residing in towns which do not themselves return members to Parliament. These are all dissenters from the Church, and are everywhere a formidably active party against the aristocratic influence of the Landed Gentry. But this is not all. There are dissenters in every village in the country; they are the blacksmith, the carpenter, the mason, &c. &c. The new influence established in the towns has drawn these to their party; and it is curious to see to what a degree it is a dissenting interest. I have known instances of a dissenting clerk in the office of the agent in a county of an aristocratical candidate, making himself active in the canvass of these dissenters, to support the party in the town at the election.

30   Ordinary chapel folk, c. 1833

An extract from *The Life of Joseph Barker written by himself* (1880), pp. 149–50.

The ordinary folk in the pew were the backbone of Nonconformity. They were often of quite humble origins, though, as this extract shows, they often prospered. Joseph Barker here describes a couple belonging to the Methodist New Connexion at the time he was in the Sunderland circuit.

At Easington Lane, I used to stay at Joseph Love's. Joseph Love was the son of a collier at Whitby, near Shields; and he himself, while a youth, had worked in the pit. By some means or other he contrived to save a little money, and began shop-keeping. He prospered in his new business, and now had a large shop at Easington Lane, and was doing a good deal of business in other places besides. He had, in fact, become rather a rich man. He had had no education beyond being taught to read and write a little, and even his ability to read and write, I fancy, was not very considerable till after he became a man. He was a free, kind person, and his wife was as free and friendly as himself, and both together did what they could to make the preachers comfortable during the time which they spent in their house. They were very kind to me. Both took delight in spreading for the preacher a good table, in pouring out for him a good glass of ale or whiskey grog, and in supplying him with pipes and tobacco. They took care to give him a good, warm, comfortable bed; and laboured to make his stay with them agreeable by their kind and cheerful conversation, and they did what they could to secure, for such preachers as they thought good for anything, a large congregation.

31 The Lady Hewley case, 1833

An extract from *Lady Hewley's Charities: A Full Report of the Hearing in the House of Lords . . . to which are prefixed the Judgment of the Vice-Chancellor . . . 1833, the Judgment of Lord Lyndhurst . . . 1836, the Case of the Appellants, the Case of the Respondents* (1839), pp. i–iii, vi–vii.

The Lady Hewley case concerned the right of Unitarians to enjoy the benefits of a Trust Fund, where no doctrinal limitation was stated but which was dated before Unitarianism was either common or legal. The judgment of the Vice-Chancellor, Sir Lancelot Shadwell, on 23 December, given here, was upheld on appeal by Lord Lyndhurst in 1836 and by the House of Lords in 1842. The case, which went against the Unitarians, threatened all property held by them on trust deeds dated before 1813, until the law was changed by the Dissenters' Chapels Act in 1844.

Before stating my opinion upon the trust, I must first of all say, that I should be extremely sorry if any person entertained an opinion that I thought harshly of the Unitarians as a body; because it has happened to me to have had intercourse with various persons, from the earliest part of my life, and whom I have known for many years, who are of that persuasion, and with whom I have lived with great cordiality and friendship; but it does not appear to me that the question in this case to be determined is, whether they were properly called Christians or not; but whether it was consistent with what appeared on the trust-deeds of Lady Hewley, having regard to such evidence as had been produced of what her sentiments were, that the Unitarians could be allowed to participate in the benefit of her charity; she having stated, that the first trust was for 'poor and godly preachers, for the time being, of Christ's holy Gospel'; and then repeating phrases which evidently showed that she alluded to the same sort of persons who might happen to be widows of persons, or exhibitioners, and so on, as would fall under the first denomination. . . .

Now the first donation in Lady Hewley's trust was to 'poor and godly preachers of Christ's holy Gospel'. I cannot but suppose, as she was not a Conformist, that she did mean those persons, not being members of the Church of England, who did entertain, among others, the firmest belief in the divinity of our Redeemer's person, in the necessity of the sacrifice he made, because of the universality of sin, commonly called original sin; and that she would, as Sir Edward Sugden has stated with great propriety, have shaken with horror at the notion of her charity being given to the sustenance of persons, who not only disbelieved these two doctrines, but who actually preached against them. It has also been argued (and I must say I do not remember a case which has been argued with more ingenuity and ability by all the members of the bar concerned in it), that the principal object of this lady was to support poor ministers, widows of poor ministers, and the other persons included in her trust-deed, who would themselves be the supporters of what was called the great doctrine of the Presbyterians—that sort of unrestrained method of disseminating the faith which would not submit to be bound by any test or creed, or by anything except the words of Scripture.

Now, the book mentioned in the Catalogue of Books at the end of the Sixth Report of the Unitarian Society, which was called an Improved Version of the New Testament, afforded a strong inference that persons who would assist the publication of it cannot come under the description of 'poor and godly preachers of Christ's holy Gospel', even according to the view which had been taken of those words by the defendants' counsel. . . .

In the progress of improvement, it may be discovered, that no parts of Scripture are genuine and authentic, except the first verse of Genesis and the last of Revelation; and, according to the argument for the defendants, the preachers upon those two verses only might still be considered, as godly preachers for the time being of Christ's holy Gospel, within the intent and meaning of Lady Hewley's trust-deeds. I find, by the evidence, that Mr Wellbeloved and Mr Kenrick, and some third trustee, were subscribers to the institution called the Unitarian Society, which enumerated amongst the books it circulated this improved version of the Scriptures, as it was called; and my opinion is, that the question being, not who should participate, but what given individuals should be excluded, it is satisfactorily made out that no person who believes as Mr Wellbeloved has stated in his sermon he believes, or who acts as Mr Wellbeloved has acted with regard to supporting that Unitarian Society which had published such a book as the Improved Version, could be considered as entitled to share in the charity of Lady Hewley.

Therefore I think it clear, that no stipend ought to be continued to Mr Wellbeloved, or to any person preaching the doctrines he does; and it is also clear, that the charity itself cannot be administered according to the intention of Lady Hewley, at least there is no reasonable security that it can be administered according to her intention, if it is allowed to remain in the hands of persons who thought as he did, and who had acted as he had. I have no evidence whatever to induce me to believe that he had anything to do with the Improved Version, more than in assisting by his subscription the publication of it; nor have I ever heard, nor have I the slightest conception, who were the fabricators of the book; but I am quite certain Lady Hewley never would have thought this book did contain Christ's holy Gospel, or that the persons who disseminated this book were to be considered disseminators of Christ's holy Gospel.

Therefore, my decree must, in substance, declare, that NO PERSONS WHO DENY THE DIVINITY OF OUR SAVIOUR'S PERSON, AND WHO DENY THE DOCTRINE OF ORIGINAL SIN, AS IT IS GENERALLY UNDERSTOOD, ARE ENTITLED TO PARTICIPATE IN LADY HEWLEY'S CHARITY; AND THAT THE FIRST SET OF TRUSTEES MUST BE REMOVED.

It is sufficiently manifest that this lady never intended that there should be trustees of one sort to administer the dealing out of the funds amongst the persons who were named in the first deed, and trustees of a second sort to superintend the hospital which contained the poor almswomen.

I therefore think, that ALL THE TRUSTEES WHO ARE DISSENTERS AND DENY THE DOCTRINE OF OUR SAVIOUR'S DIVINE PERSON, AND THE DOC-TRINE OF ORIGINAL SIN, MUST BE REMOVED; AND THOUGH THERE IS NO OBJECTION PERSONALLY TO MR. PALMES, YET AS IT APPEARS THAT HE IS A MEMBER OF THE CHURCH OF ENGLAND, HE OUGHT NOT TO BE CON-TINUED A TRUSTEE.

32   Declaration on the admission of Dissenters to Oxford and Cambridge, 1834

Quoted in A. P. Stanley, *The Life and Correspondence of Dr Arnold* (12th ed., 1881), i, pp. 330–1.

A number of senior members of both Oxford and Cambridge petitioned that Dissenters should be admitted to the universities in the early 1830s. This particular declaration was circulated by Thomas Arnold, headmaster of Rugby. Although the matter was debated in the House of Commons, in both universities those who favoured the move were in a minority and the attempts were unsuccessful.

The undersigned members of the Universities of Oxford and Cambridge, many of them being engaged in education, entertaining a strong sense of the peculiar benefits to be derived from studying at the Universities, cannot but consider it as a national evil that these benefits should be inaccessible to a large proportion of their countrymen.

While they feel most strongly that the foundations of all education must be laid in the great truths of Christianity, and would on no account consent to omit these, or to teach them imperfectly, yet they cannot but acknowledge, that these truths are believed and valued by the great majority of Dissenters, no less than by the Church of England; and that every essential point of Christian instruction may be communicated without touching on these particular questions on which the Church and the mass of Dissenters are at issue.

And, while they are not prepared to admit such Dissenters as differ from the Church of England on the most essential points of Christian truth, such as the modern Unitarians of Great Britain, they are of opinion, that all other Dissenters may be admitted into the Universities, and allowed to take degrees there with great benefit to the country, and to the probable advancement of Christian truth and Christian charity amongst members of all persuasions.

33 Debates in the House of Commons on Church Rates, 1834

Extracts from *Parliamentary Debates* (third series), xxii, cols. 382–6, 389–90, 1013–15, 1025–6, 1031–3.

The first two extracts come from the debate on Divett's motion on 18 March 1834, and the remainder from the discussion of Lord Althorp's proposals on 21 April.

Church Rates was the first of the Dissenting grievances to be raised in the reformed House of Commons, when Mr Divett moved, 'That in the opinion of this House, it is just and expedient that effectual measures should be taken for the abolition of the compulsory payments of Church Rates in England and Wales.' Divett (Member of Parliament for Exeter) was an Anglican, but his analysis (a) was that of a moderate Churchman. Lord Althorp's reply (b) showed awareness of the Dissenters' grievances, but his proposals a month later to abolish the rates and make an annual grant for the maintenance of parish churches from general taxation (c) failed to satisfy either side. Tories like Sir Robert Inglis regarded the rate as falling on property not persons (d), whilst Nonconformists like Wilks, secretary of the Protestant Society, opposed the principle of State support for parish churches, not the method (e). As a result nothing was done.

---

a.

Mr. *Divett*: . . . Every hon. Member must be aware that, in the course of the last few months, there had been an increasing disposition on the part of the people to avoid the payment of Church-rates,—a feeling which had been growing up for many years. It had arisen in consequence of the increase of the impost, but still more in consequence of the continual and great increase of Dissenters. To what cause it was to be attributed, he would not stop to inquire, though it was, no doubt, greatly owing to the measures which took place as far back as 1819. In that year, an Act passed granting 1,000,000*l.* for the building of churches and chapels. That million coming from the general revenue of the country, was paid equally by Dissenters and Churchmen. But, besides this, in many districts, there was a great increase of parochial taxes to keep up the churches. He need hardly say, that was strong ground for complaint on the part of the Dissenters. Perhaps it was right that he should state to the House the amount of the Church-rates. In the return of the local taxation of the country, for the year ending the 27th of March, 1827, the Church-rates were stated to amount to 564,000*l.* . . . His own opinion was, that no man could be justly charged for the support of a religion to which he dissented; and, there-fore, the principle upon which money should be raised for the necessary expenses of the Church was exclusively that of voluntary contribution. But it would be said, that it was impossible to maintain the Church by such means. To disprove that assumption, he would refer to the case of the Dissenters, who had 8,000 places of worship; and for their maintenance they did not raise in any year less than a million. Surely, if the Dissenters could effect this, the members of the Church of England might be called upon to do something also for the support of their religion. The Dissenters not only contributed the sum which he had mentioned for the support of their places of worship, but their subscriptions, for missionary and other purposes connected with religious and moral improvement, exceeded those of the Established Church. . . . He was aware, that some persons conceived that to attack the principle of Church-rates was to attack also the principle of tithes; but that such a construction could justly be put upon the proposition which he brought forward, he must beg leave to deny; and, if it could, he must assert, that he would not be instrumental in promoting a measure of that nature. . . . In looking at certain accounts, he was astonished to observe the progress which dissent had made of late years. In many towns, the Dissenters outnumbered the members of the Church of England. In the principality of Wales, there were more dissenting places of worship built than there were churches belonging to the Establishment. . . . He wished to call the attention of the House to the oppressive character of the Church-rates, as they affected Dis-senters, and to impress upon the minds of members of the Church of England, that, by showing a conciliatory spirit to their dissenting fellow-subjects, they would best promote the interests of that Church to which they were attached, and contribute to its stability hereafter. In almost all parishes, particularly in large towns, there was at present a bitter feeling of hostility entertained by the Dissenters towards the Church of England. He believed it was yet possible to do away with the acrimony which existed. . . . There had never been a time when the Church was apparently stronger in the support of a great portion of the people of England than at present; but there had never been a time when there were greater apprehensions that inroads might be made upon it. . . .

b.

Lord *Althorp*: . . . The subject which the hon. Gentleman who had last spoken most properly placed first amongst the general grievances under which the Dissenters laboured, was the payment of Church-rates; then came the subject of marriage; and thirdly that of a general registration; and although this matter concerned every class of the community, yet he was ready to admit, that the want of a general registration pressed more heavily upon the Dissenters than upon the members of the Established Church. The fourth point, of which they complained was that which related to their exclusion from the Universities. These were the main points which were urged on behalf of the Dissenters. There was, also, as he was reminded by an hon. friend near him, a complaint with regard to burial in Church-yards without the ceremonies of the Church. . . .

c.

Lord *Althorp*: . . . Another proposition . . . was, to continue Church-rates as at present, but to exempt Dissenters from the payment of them. As far as the Dissenters were concerned, this would, of course, satisfy them; but it would be detrimental in the highest degree to the interests of the Established Church. If any person could exempt himself from the payment of Church-rates by saying he was a Dissenter, he apprehended that the number of Dissenters would be greatly and rapidly increased. . . . While the Dissenters had a right to call upon the Legislature not to require them to pay money for a Church which was contrary to their principles, the members of the Establishment had a right also to say, that their interests should receive all due attention, and that their principles should be respected. One of those principles certainly was—one of the consequences of having an Established Church was—that means should be provided by the Legislature for the support of the fabric of the Church. . . . The plan he had to propose was, that Church-rates should be entirely abolished, and that in lieu of them the sum of 250,000*l*. should be annually charged upon the

Land-tax. . . . The mode in which he suggested, that the sum should be expended was not that it should be applied to all purposes to which Church-rates were now applicable, but merely to the maintenance and support of the parish churches and chapels. . . .

d.

Sir *Robert Inglis*: . . . He would ask the hon. Member to tell him, whether any Dissenters had ever purchased or taken a lease of a house, without the charge of Church-rate having been taken as an element in the calculation of its value, as much as the Land-tax, or Poor-rate, or Water-rate, or any other charge whatever? And, he would then ask him, if that were so, whether that person paid the Church-rate as a Dissenter, or as the owner or occupier of number 10 or 12 in such or such a square? It was precisely and strictly as an element of charge upon his property, as he had bought it, that a Dissenter, as well as every other man, was called upon to pay his proportion of Church-rates. . . .

e.

Mr *Wilks*: . . . It was not the amount of the tax, but the principle of taxation, which lost England her American colonies. It was not the amount of ship-money, but the principle of extortion, which Hampden resisted. On similar grounds, he should say, that whether the sum were 560,000*l*., or 250,000*l*., the Dissenters were equally called upon to resist the payment. As conscientious men, the Dissenters were called upon to refuse contributions to a Church from which they were in their religious capacity as much separated as it was possible. In no point of view could this question of Church-rates be presented, in which it did not appear as a grievous and distressing impost—as an infringement of religious liberty—for the restraint was the same whether it presented itself in the form of a pecuniary payment, or of personal imprisonment. The principle for which the Dissenters contended was, 'that every man has a right to worship his God according to his own conscience, and that he cannot be required, consistently with justice, to contribute a doit to the support of a form of worship which his conscience condemns'. . . . It was said that to assent to the principle of voluntary payments for the support of religion, would be the destruction of all religion; and that there would be no pious homage to our Creator, if extorted contributions should cease. The best practical reply to that was the fact, that upwards of 3,000,000*l*., within the last century, had been contributed by Protestant Dissenters, to rear their own places of worship, and maintain their own ministry. Though they might be as destitute of wealth as the hon. Baronet had assumed, and he admitted that they had no sinecures, nor cathedrals, nor palaces; but still they had been able to provide for the worship of their Maker. Nor was the present race, increasing in numbers, less attentive to this. The Dissenters were at this time paying annually from 300,000*l.* to 400,000*l.* to support their chapels, to maintain their ministers, to educate the poor, to circulate the Scriptures, and to diffuse Christianity on earth. . . . The present proposition must rather increase than lessen their complaints. Now they had power in vestries to interfere and could often prevent the charge; but of that right, by the proposed boon of the Government, they would be deprived. They objected to an alliance of the Church and the State, which this boon would render firm, and rivet for ever. . . . Tithes were bad enough; but Church-rates were far more indefensible and harsh. They were imposed in a manner that opened the door to every abuse. No purchasers of property could calculate the amount that, by waste or extortion, they might be bound to provide. They were levied too by an annual vote of Church-men, and were peculiarly irritating, because the persons taxed derived no benefit from the burthen. . . .

34   The expulsion of the Rev. J. R. Stephens from the Wesleyan Conference, 1834

Minutes of the Wesleyan Conference, 1834: collected edition, vii, pp. 417–20.

Joseph Rayner Stephens was suspended by the Manchester District for his involvement in the Ashton-under-Lyne Church Separation Society. He appealed to the Conference on the ground that the district meeting had no business to pronounce on the matter. His appeal was rejected after a long discussion on Church and State which reiterated the Wesleyan desire to hold a midway position between the Church of England and Dissent. Stephens was expelled, and subsequently became a Chartist leader. The first extract contains part of the resolutions of the district meeting affirmed by the Conference; the second is a general comment made by the Conference following the case making clear the ban on the use of chapels for political meetings.

a.

1   That in these proceedings Brother Stephens has flagrantly violated the peaceable and anti-sectarian spirit of Wesleyan Methodism so strongly enjoined in the writings of our Founder, enforced by repeated acts of the Conference since his decease, and required as a necessary qualification of every Methodist Preacher. . . .

2   That the above-mentioned speeches of Brother Stephens are directly at variance with the general sentiments of Mr Wesley and the Conference, and are distinguished by a spirit highly unbecoming a Wesleyan Minister, and inconsistent with those sentiments of respect and affection towards the Church of England which our Connexion has, from the beginning, openly professed and honourably maintained.

3   That, as far as his influence extends, Brother Stephens has committed the character of the Connexion on a question involving its public credit as well as its internal tranquillity. . . .

4   That he has endangered the peace, and acted prejudicially to the spirituality, of the Connexion, by giving occasion to the introduction, amongst our people, of unprofitable disputations on Ecclesiastical Politics, thus violating the directions of the last Conference in its 'Pastoral Address' to the Societies. . . .

5   That Brother Stephens, in accepting the office of Corresponding Secretary to the Ashton Church-Separation Society, has acted contrary to his peculiar calling and solemn engagements as a Methodist Preacher.

6   That the culpability of these proceedings is aggravated by the fact, that they were pursued by Brother Stephens without consultation with his Superintendent, and contrary to his example and expressed opinion.

7   That Brother Stephens be authoritatively required to resign his office as Secretary to the Church-Separation Society, and to abstain, until the next Conference, from taking any part in the proceedings of that Society, or of any other Society or Meeting having a kindred object: and that, in the event of a violation of this injunction, he be forthwith suspended until the Conference. . . .

The above Resolutions having been read to Brother Stephens, he declared that, on the finding of the second and third, he *could not acknowledge the authority of the Meeting, and that he would not resign his office* of Corresponding Secretary to the Church-Separation Society of Ashton-under-Line.

He is, therefore, now suspended from the exercise of his ministry until the next Conference. . . .

b.

The Conference takes this opportunity of declaring its grateful satisfaction with the peaceable spirit and conduct of the very great majority of our Preachers and people, in reference to certain questions of national polity, which have been agitated during the past year; and earnestly exhorts our Societies to a steadfast perseverance in the same course, as being most conducive to their own spiritual prosperity, and to the tranquillity, reputation, and general usefulness of our Connexion.

The Conference, however, has learned with surprise and deep regret, that, in two or three cases, our Chapels have been used for the purpose of public Meetings having more or less of a political object and character; and expresses its strongest disapprobation of any such appropriation of our places of worship.

35   Revivalism in Sheffield, c. 1835

An extract from *The Life of Joseph Barker, written by himself* (1880), pp. 185–91.

Some Nonconformist ministers were not satisfied with spontaneous revivals, and sought to achieve the same result by organisation. Other ministers disapproved strongly of these techniques. Joseph Barker's description is obviously hostile, but there is no reason to doubt its accuracy. He is certainly right to stress how quickly the converts made in this kind of situation fell away.

Preparations were therefore made for getting up a revival. Meetings were appointed, and parties were fixed upon to take part in them. I was myself urged to take part in those meetings; but hesitated and objected. I was afraid that harm would be done by them, and stated my fears. . . .

No matter; they had formed their plan, and they were determined to carry it out. They accordingly commenced their revival meetings, the preachers began to preach revival sermons; and their labours appeared to be attended with very great success. The body of Scotland Street chapel was crowded at the prayer-meetings, and scores in a night professed to be converted. . . . Burrows prayed and shouted with all his might, and Lynn, with his bulky frame, almost as tough as iron, and with lungs like leather, shouted and sang, and ranted with all his powers. Their manner of proceeding was truly dreadful. They jumped over the forms, climbed over the pews, kneeled down and prayed beside such as they supposed to be penitents, whispered in their ears, urged them to believe, talked in sterner ways to such as they supposed to be unawakened, thundered in their ears the horrors of damnation and eternal wrath, scores of them joining together to raise the wild excitement to its highest pitch. The screams, the shouts, the jarring songs, the disorders and indecencies were at times quite horrible. On many occasions, three, four, or five, and at times even ten or twenty would be praying and shouting together. While some were praying, others would be singing; while some were moaning and groaning, crying or shrieking, others would be shouting with all their might, 'Glory, Glory!' 'He is coming, He is coming, He is coming!' 'He is here, He is here!' while others would be exclaiming, 'I believe it, I believe it, I believe it!' 'I feel Him, I feel Him!' 'He is knocking at my heart!' 'He will save! He is saving!' 'Glory, Glory!' 'He has pardoned my sins!' 'I am saved!' 'My soul is at liberty!' No sooner would the last expression gain the ears of any of the preachers or leaders in the meeting, than they would call out at the highest pitch of their voices 'Another soul is saved! Another soul is pardoned! Let us praise God!' and at once they would strike off the Old Hundred:

'Praise God from Whom all blessings flow,' etc.

And while some scores were singing this verse, some scores or hundreds more would be still groaning, shouting, whispering, screaming, leaping over the forms, falling down on the floor, climbing over the pews, whispering in people's ears, or lifting up the loud voice of warning to some apparent triflers who had come to gaze upon the awful scene. At times two or three lots would be singing together, while six or eight groups more would be praying or talking in other parts of the chapel, all at the same moment. Occasionally Burrows would retire into the vestry to recruit himself with a glass of wine or a little brandy and water, and then return to his labours again in the chapel. And thus would things go on for two or three hours, till the leaders of the revival were utterly exhausted and their voices gone; and then, after a while, they would dismiss the meeting. These meetings were held almost every night for several weeks, and in the course of a month or two it was stated that some hundreds had found peace, or got into liberty at these meetings. . . .

At the following quarter-day, the number of the members in the Circuit was considerably greater than it had previously been, but not so much greater as the reported number of converts had led some to expect. Out of the three or four hundred converts, not more than a hundred or a hundred and fifty could be found. Many of the converts had already fallen away. Some that were converted at night, were converted back again before the morning. Others were found to have been converted and counted several times over. Some of the converts were drunk at the time of their conversion; and when the influence of the drink and the excitement had passed away, they were as far from God, and as far from meeting in class, as they had been before they attended the revival meetings. Others, again turned out to be persons who had begun to meet in class before the revival commenced, and who had given every sign of a determination to learn and do God's will. They had not, however, experienced a sudden and miraculous conversion. They could not tell the time and the place where their souls were set at liberty. Hence they were called to the penitent bench at the revival meetings with the rest, and some of them were wrought into the necessary state of excitement, and made to believe that they were converted. But as these had been numbered before they added nothing to the increase of the Society.

I may also observe, that after the revival had subsided, the societies began to diminish in numbers. Instead of being gratified by the continuance of that regular increase which I had witnessed previous to the revival, I was doomed, now that the revival was over, to behold a perpetual falling away, a continued diminution of numbers. The revival had caused no increase of religious feeling; it had only occasioned a sudden and a premature explosion of that feeling. It had not improved the character of the congregations; it had only hurried some to a premature step, and ruined others by driving them, first into wild excitement, and secondly into hypocritical professions. The revival, as it was called, had, in fact, done infinite mischief. It had suspended all rational operations for the spread of truth and the promotion of righteousness. It had interrupted all rational and deliberate thought, and involved the religious feelings and rational principles of many in disorder, if not in ruin. It had, besides, interrupted the meetings for business and discipline. Its disorders and indecencies had disgusted many of the congregations, and driven them further from connexion with us. It had strengthened false notions about religion and conversion in many, and increased their inability to understand the truth. It had thrown some good people into needless alarm about their spiritual state, by making them fear or fancy that they had not been rightly converted. It did harm in many ways; incalculable harm! And it is a fact, that from that period to the present, the societies in Sheffield have never recovered from the bad effects of that revival. They have gradually, and, I believe, continually gone down. Before the revival commenced, there were in the Sheffield societies, and in the country places, somewhere about sixteen hundred members. That number had dwindled down to six or seven hundred some years ago; and I question whether it has not continued to dwindle to the present time.

36 The 'no politics' rule in Methodism, 1835-6

Extracts from the *Minutes of the Primitive Methodist Conference, 1835,* pp. 9–10; *1836*, p. 9.

The 'no politics' rule was not unique to the Wesleyan Methodists but common to all the Methodist denominations. These extracts constitute the ruling of the Primitive Methodist Conference on the subject. The rule has sometimes been regarded as prima facie evidence of Toryism, but it should rather be seen as evidence of the desire to separate religious from political concerns and avoid divisions.

a.

14 What is the order of the Conference relative to public speechifying on politics?

A. That none of our travelling preachers be allowed to make speeches at political meetings, nor at parliamentary elections. And it is strongly recommended to our local preachers to avoid such things.

15 How shall the cause of piety be further guarded from injury?

A. That none of our chapels or preaching rooms be lent on any account, for either political or religious controversy.

b.

8 The conference of 1835, in order more fully to guard the course of piety, made a Minute that none of our chapels or preaching rooms be lent on any account, for either political or religious agitation; has this been duly attended to?

A. It has, with the exception of two or three instances, in which we are sorry to say, piety has suffered; but our brethren regret it, and we hope there will be more firmness in future.

37   The London Congregational ministers in the 1830s

An extract from J. G. Rogers, *An Autobiography* (1903), pp. 158–9.

The conservatism of Dissent in the 1830s was attributed by the ministers of the Midlands and north, led by Edward Miall, to the influence and prestige of the southern ministers, who were not interested in further changes. The Rev. J. Guinness Rogers, a leading Congregationalist of the second half of the century, describes the London ministers as he saw them from Manchester in his early years.

Most of these men came from a somewhat higher stratum in society than the majority of their brethren, and they all succeeded in preserving a grace of manner and a singularly refined and gentlemanly bearing. Some of them were positively Tory in politics, and all had a distinctly Conservative tendency both in mind and temperament, greatly disliking everything that savoured of Democratic Radicalism, proud of their moderation and using that word in a very emphatic sense. . . .

The influence exerted by some of these men in circles generally inaccessible to Dissenting ministers was one of the features of the time. The Duke of Sussex was said to be a frequent visitor at the Peckham Congregational Church and reckoned Dr. Collyer amongst his personal friends. Dr. Vaughan, during his ministry at Kensington, attracted even more attention from an aristocratic circle, of whom the Duchess of Sutherland was the most remarkable member. His successor, Dr. Stoughton, who had been well known and respected at Windsor, preserved, to some extent, the traditions of his predecessor. They were a class very faithful to the spiritual principles of Congregationalism, and earnest in their service of the churches. . . . They had come into the full enjoyment of a liberty which their fathers hardly anticipated, and they were very much disposed to the 'rest and be thankful' policy of Lord John Russell, who represented the extreme form of Liberalism which any of them approved. They were so satisfied with mere toleration that they hardly dreamt of religious equality.

38   Church life in Prescot, 1837-8

An extract from J. G. Rogers, *An Autobiography* (1903) pp. 19–21.

The Rev. J. G. Rogers was brought up in Prescot, near Liverpool, where his father had moved in 1829. Prescot contained more denominations than 'Cowfold' or 'Treby Magna' (documents 23 and 28), but is strikingly similar to those fictional places. The Congregational church where Rogers's father was minister is not mentioned in this extract.

It is astonishing how many of the varieties of church life were represented in this little town of five thousand people, and how keenly each maintained its own isolation. What Roman Catholics there were in the place were an Irish element occupying a little corner of their own, and not represented by either chapel or priest. I remember still the Unitarian Chapel—an old, gloomy-looking building, shadowed by trees—which had formerly belonged to the English Presbyterians. Its congregation was not large, but their influence in the town was greater than their number, for the few it included were men of high character, public spirit, and considerable intelligence, on whom it was possible to rely for sympathy in all works of philanthropy or reform. The Methodists were a very strong element in the religious life of Prescot; but their ministers and their leading lay members were very far from being in sympathy with other Dissenters. . . . To-day it is very hard to realise that there was a high wall of separation between these different classes of Nonconformists, each of which was regarded, by the members of the Established Church, as an unauthorised intruder into its own special domain. . . .

Perhaps it was all the more so because there was another Methodist body, consisting of members of the Association (the Warrenite section) which had drawn off most of the progressive and liberal spirits of the older Society. The leading Wesleyan layman was a man of high social standing in the town, employing a large number of workpeople, but maintaining an aloofness from other Dissenters, and giving an impression of High Toryism which may, possibly, have been exaggerated by those who knew him only from the outside. At all events, between the two bodies of Nonconformists there was comparatively little intercourse and still less of vital sympathy. Jews had no dealings with the Samaritans. We used to visit each other's chapels on the occasion of an anniversary or the visit of some well-known preacher, and such visits were amongst the pleasures of my own early days. . . .

Interchanges of occasional visits, however, like these, did not mean any active co-operation in public work. In the education controversies of that early period, one of which I remember, we could never count upon the absolute sympathy and perfect co-operation of the Methodists. The truth is, they did not like our Calvinism upon the one hand, or our strong Liberalism upon the other. Since those days we have abated in the first, and they have relaxed their dread of the other.

But, as I have said, the dominating influence in such a town was the Established Church, which moved quietly on its own solitary path and took no notice of the unhappy things who failed to appreciate the beauties of the old National Church. . . .

39   A Dissenting academy, 1837-41

An extract from N. Hall, *An Autobiography* (1898), pp. 38-9.

By the nineteenth century the old Dissenting academies were for the most part theological colleges. In this extract Newman Hall, another leading Congregational minister of the second half of the century, describes his training at Highbury College, where he was one of the first to benefit from the opportunity of taking degrees of the University of London. The description may be compared with that in the *Autobiography of Mark Rutherford*, chapter 2.

At Highbury College, besides tuition, board and lodging were free. I had £20 yearly of my own, and resolved to make this suffice for personal expenses. Some students engaged a servitor to light their fire, black their boots, and sweep their room. I thought it no degradation to perform these offices for myself rather than be dependent on others. So I rose a few minutes earlier, and at 6 a.m. was generally ready for devotion and study.

The number of students, all training for the Congregational ministry, was forty, for four years, ten leaving and as many entering every year. Some of these had scarcely any other qualification than piety and a natural fitness for preaching. All of the same year were placed together in a class, and thus I found myself sitting with men who were beginning the Greek grammar, and stumbling over the *pons asinorum*. . . .

Dr Halley was Principal, and, after two years, Professor Godwin succeeded. His class on the Greek Testament I thought invaluable—so much so that on my coming to reside near 'New College', in London, I partially renewed my student-life by regularly attending his weekly Greek Testament class. Dr Henderson, the learned Hebraist, held the Theological Chair.

Though I needed little time to prepare for lectures, ten hours a day were spent in diligent study. I am not sure I was wise in my selection of subjects. I read poetry, a little fiction, Gibbon, Rollin, and Hume, writing long abstracts. I was enamoured of mental philosophy, reading Brown, Stewart, Reid and Locke. I also enjoyed books on natural science. I have several thick quarto manuscript volumes full of condensed epitomes. I have scarcely ever read a line of any of them. No doubt, writing them did me good; but they have been dry bones— very, very dry—ever since.

At the end of three years the charter of the London University was extended to Highbury and other colleges, and to meet the case of students who were in their last year the matriculation or 'Little-Go' examination was dispensed with. I wished to secure this opportunity of taking my degree. So did the occupant of the adjoining study. He was worthy of his imposing name, Bernard Bolingbroke Woodward, a relative of the eminent scientist. He was a good German scholar, and seemed to have a vocation rather for the literary path of usefulness than the pastoral. We agreed to 'coach' each other, and so, after reading during the week the same subject, we spent Saturday evenings in a mutual written examination, each supplying to the other a list of questions, omitting none we thought might possibly be asked. At the close of the anxious days at Somerset House, we were rewarded by finding our names in the First Class of the B.A. candidates. . . .

40   Thomas Arnold on Dissenters, 1840

An extract from A. P. Stanley, *The Life and Correspondence of Dr Arnold,* (12th ed., 1881), ii, pp. 161–2.

In this letter from Arnold to James Marshall, dated 23 January 1840, his attitude to the Church and Dissent is succinctly set out. His belief in the 'Broad' Church was an inevitable consequence of his idea of the unity of Church and State. There are some points in common with his son Matthew's criticism of Dissent too (see document 71).

I look to the full development of the Christian Church in its perfect form, as the Kingdom of God, for the most effective removal of all evil, and promotion of all good; and I can understand no perfect Church, or perfect State, without their blending into one in this ultimate form. I believe, farther, that our fathers at the Reformation stumbled accidentally, or rather were unconsciously led by God's Providence, to the declaration of the great principle of his system, the doctrine of the King's Supremacy;—which is, in fact, no other than an assertion of the supremacy of the Church or Christian society over the clergy, and a denial of that which I hold to be one of the most mischievous falsehoods ever broached—that the government of the Christian Church is vested by divine right in the clergy, and that the close corporation of bishops and presbyters,—whether one or more, makes no difference,—is and ever ought to be the representative of the Christian Church. Holding this doctrine as the very corner stone of all my political belief, I am equally opposed to Popery, High Churchism, and the claims of the Scotch Presbyteries, on the one hand; and to all the Independents, and advocates of the separation, as they call it, of Church and State, on the other; the first, setting up a Priesthood in the place of the Church, and the other lowering necessarily the objects of Law and Government, and reducing them to a mere system of police, while they profess to wish to make the Church purer. And my fondness for Greek and German literature has made me very keenly alive to the mental defects of the Dissenters as a body; the characteristic faults of the English mind,—narrowness of view, and a want of learning and a sound critical spirit,—being exhibited to my mind in the Dissenters almost in caricature. It is nothing but painful to me to feel this; because no man appreciates more than I do the many great services which the Dissenters have rendered, both to the general cause of Christianity, and especially to the cause of justice and good government in our own country; and my sense of the far less excusable errors, and almost uniformly mischievous conduct of the High Church party, is as strong as it can be of any one thing in the world.

41 The Wesleyan Conference on teetotalism, 1841

An extract from B. Gregory, *Side Lights on the Conflicts of Methodism 1827–52* (1898), p. 318.

Although teetotalism is widely associated with Nonconformity, it had difficulty in winning approval at first. The Wesleyans were suspicious of the excitability of the teetotal campaigners, and treated them as they did political movements. This extract describes discussions at the Conference of 1841.

Dr Bunting spoke of 'the annoyance arising from teetotalism. There are two points on which we must insist: (1) The use of *bona fide* wine in the Lord's Supper; (2) the not allowing teetotal meetings in our chapels. I question whether we have any legal power to do this. I have spoken of mutual forbearance on this question at former Conferences.'

Dr Beaumont: 'I agree with Dr Bunting that we ought not to allow anything but wine to be drunk at the Lord's Supper. It requires great knowledge to determine whether any beverage is the pure blood of the grape and yet altogether free from *alcohol*.'

Mr Marsden quoted specimens of the intemperate and excited and exciting talk of teetotal advocates. Cornish Methodism was described as in a state of 'fermentation' on the subject, and the Rev. W. Burt said: 'If a teetotaler be not appointed to Penzance, I fear there will be a division.'

Dr Bunting's points were passed in the form of resolutions, but Dr Beaumont objected to the closing of our chapels against teetotal meetings, and said that he believed there had been but one case in which any liquid had been substituted for wine in the Lord's Supper.

42   Edward Miall on the 'grievance' error, 1841

An extract from E. Miall, *The Nonconformist's Sketch Book* (1842), pp. 3–6.

In 1841, Edward Miall, a Congregational Minister, resigned his pastorate in Leicester, and founded *The Nonconformist*, pledged to work for the separation of Church and State. *The Nonconformist's Sketch Book* contained four essays from the paper, each urging that the reason for the failure of Nonconformists to make progress in securing their just demands was their failure to see the necessity of campaigning against the establishment as such. In the first essay, from which this extract is taken, he criticises the policy of rectifying only Dissenting grievances.

How does it happen that in looking over the records of our legislature, we find every reference now made to dissenters by men of all parties, marked by a tone so different from that which formerly prevailed? Whence comes the seemingly mysterious change that has passed upon them since the great campaigns which terminated in the repeal of the Test and Corporation Acts, and the emancipation of our Roman-catholic fellow-countrymen? Ten years since their voice commanded a respectful attention; their movements were bold, vigorous, and successful. Now, although they have gained in numbers, are possessed of equal wealth, and superior intelligence, they are despised, and, what is worse, despised with impunity.

A Registration Act and a Marriage Bill have been ceded to them, it is true, by a reformed parliament. But setting these aside, to what quarter can they look for self-gratulation. The continuation of church-rates, ecclesiastical imprisonments, workhouse chaplains, colonial bishoprics, and demands for church extension, prove that they are no longer formidable. Their own movements are not what they once were, well planned and skilfully conducted enterprises. They are more like insurrections,—fitful, sudden, partial in extent, easily suppressed, productive of no beneficial result. Dissenters are without union; they have lost heart, the *prestige* of their power is gone.

When, however, they are taunted by whigs, tories, and radicals, with their mutual disagreements, and sectarian jealousies, whilst there may be some truth in the reproach, it does nothing to lay open the true cause of their present weakness. Differences of opinion, strong and even bigoted attachment to theological creeds are not things of yesterday's growth. . . .

The secret of the present humiliating position of dissenters is, that their proceedings have, of late, been based on no intelligible principle at all. They put forward the redress of 'practical grievances' as their bond of union. . . . Their mistake was, perhaps, natural, but it was fatal. From the moment this system of tactics was adopted, energy began to decline, zeal to grow cold, and disunion to appear. The timidity, the selfishness, the petty character of the proposed enterprise, quickly produced their baneful results. One unsuccessful contest decided the matter. Then came languor, indifference, mutual recriminations and disastrous defeat. Dissenters are now like a disbanded army. The materials of strength exist among them in abundance, but without the discipline which once combined them and rendered their strength available, against the foes of religious freedom. Why should dissenters conceal from themselves what is known to all the world? They are no longer respected—they are feared by none.

In tracing their present weakness to its right source, we indicate the only efficient remedy. They must begin again the struggle with intolerance. Let them begin wisely. Ultimate success will require union, patience, persevering energy, and considerable self-sacrifice. Their aim must therefore be a worthy one. It must involve a noble principle. It must be honest, direct, and final. THE ENTIRE SEPARATION OF CHURCH AND STATE is really their object. It becomes dissenters fairly to avow it, soberly to set about it, and in all earnestness to gird and discipline themselves for a final grapple with ecclesiastical tyranny.

43   The Anti-Corn Law Convention, 1841

An extract from J. Waddington, *Congregational History: continuation to 1850* (1878), pp. 563–4.

The Anti-Corn Law League organised a conference of Dissenting ministers in Manchester in August 1841, in order to win the support of Dissent for the League. The more conservative ministers were very suspicious, and in this letter from the Rev. Robert Halley, a leading Congregationalist, to a friend dated 21 August it becomes clear that the conference had been organised as a demonstration rather than as an opportunity for the spontaneous expression of views.

. . . Of the late meeting, I should say it cannot be viewed as the expression of opinion of our denomination. The persons present represent themselves as, at most, their own congregations, and, in each denomination, constituted but a small part. Yet, still, it was a very important meeting, and has excited amazing interest throughout the manufacturing districts. I felt rather jealous for the *honour of our own body, and did not quite like the multitude of sects with which they were mingled, and the persons of all sorts who called themselves preachers.*

Of the meeting I must say it was managed with amazing tact, skill, energy, and power. . . . This arose partly from the boundless liberality of the Anti-Corn-Law League, who furnished clerks, messengers, door-keepers, assistants of all kinds, printing, feeding, etc., at the will of the secretaries; partly from the power, and energy, and untiring perseverance of the secretaries and committees. What a wonderful man this Massie is! He has worked night and day—writing, talking, debating, contriving, watching, soliciting, refusing, urging—I know not what, and never tired. . . . Then there were many of the Manchester ministers, who devoted themselves to preparing measures, and several others who were scarcely ever in the Hall, but sitting in the committee rooms from seven in the morning until ten in the evening. Moreover, the thing never came to a *Conference* at all, but only a convocation.

There was no discussion. The Committee took care to provide resolutions which were moved and seconded, and then to receive information. The room being crowded with spectators checked discussion, which was, I think, fortunate. Besides, the feeling was so general in favour of the extreme view—no 'protection', no 'fixed duty'—that no person on the other side would have any chance. As an effort of generalship, nothing could have been more complete.

44   Debates on the education clauses of the Factories Bill, 1843

Extracts from *Parliamentary Debates* (third series), lxvii, cols. 87–90; lxviii, cols. 1104–5, 1117; lxix, cols. 537–8; lxx, cols. 94, 95–6.

As a result of the outcry from Nonconformists, the education clauses of Sir James Graham's Factories Bill of 1843 were dropped. The sections to which objection was later taken are described in Graham's speech introducing the Bill (a) on 28 February 1843. Graham recognised the hostility felt towards the Bill, and introduced new amendments on 1 May, at the same time warning the Commons about the danger of the educational system foundering on controversy (b). Radicals, such as Roebuck who introduced a motion against State religious instruction on 18 May (c), were as hostile to the Dissenters as to the Church of England. After the clauses had been dropped, the Bill received its third reading on 19 June. Lord Shaftesbury suggested that Dissent must bear the blame (d) and said that the real losers were the children, but this was indignantly repudiated by Gibson, Liberal Member of Parliament for Manchester, (e), who pointed out the very limited application of the whole scheme.

a.
Sir *James Graham*: . . . Then comes the question, 'How are these district schools to be managed?' I propose that they shall be managed by

trusts; and the composition of these trusts I will now state to the House. I propose that the trust shall contain seven individuals, and that any officiating clergyman of the district shall be one; if the district contains only one officiating clergyman, then such clergyman shall be a trustee *ex officio*. If the district contain more than one clergyman, or where the school shall be intended for two or more, or parts of two or more ecclesiastical, districts, I then propose to give the bishop of the diocese the power of selecting a clergyman to be such trustee. I propose that two of the churchwardens for the year shall be chosen by the clerical trustee, and added as trustees. I then propose a property qualification for all who are not thus *ex officio* trustees, and that the remaining four shall be appointed by the magistrates in a special session assembled for that purpose out of persons assessed to the poor-rate at a certain rate; and I further propose that two out of the four chosen trustees shall be mill-owners. . . . The general management of the schools will be under the control of the trustees; they will have the power of appointing the master, subject to the approval of the bishop of the diocese as to his competency to give religious instruction to members of the Established Church. The Holy Scriptures are to be taught daily, but no child will be required to receive instruction in the Catechism of the Church of England or to attend the Established Church whose parents object on religious grounds. The children of parents belonging to the Church of England are to be instructed in the Catechism and Liturgy of the Church of England separate from the other children, and that daily. The schools are to be inspected by the clerical trustees. . . .

Then, as to the children of Dissenters, if the parents desire it, they need not be present at the periods at which the Church catechism or any portion of the Liturgy is taught. . . .

The House will perceive that I provide only, that in all schools the authorised version of the Scriptures shall be read; no special religious instruction will be given to the children of Dissenters if their parents object. The constitution of the trust, in itself, is a sufficient security that no undue influence in religious matters will be resorted to, but, beyond that, the trustees will be subject to the control of the inspectors of the committee of the Privy Council. I have dealt specially with the case of Roman Catholic children. . . . As regards Dissenters I have followed the general outline of Lord Brougham's bill, introduced in 1820, and in some instances I have almost adopted his words, and I have reason to believe, that on the whole, Dissenters will be satisfied when they see that we have provided their children with instruction by the best masters, who will be subject to constant inspection—that they are only required to read the authorised version of the Scriptures, and that all attempts at proselytism are prevented by the strongest guards....

b.

Sir *James Graham*: ... I cannot dissemble for myself that although that spirit of calm forbearance prevails within these walls which is worthy of a deliberative assembly, much heat and excitement have arisen out of doors upon this very subject. The petitions which have been presented against those clauses of the Factories Bill to which I am about to advert have been numerous almost without a parallel. I might, if I thought it worth while, make some observations respecting the manner in which, in particular places, some of these petitions have been got up; I might point out the very gross misrepresentations which have been made out of doors, with respect to the scope, the objects, and the intentions of this measure; I might remark upon the means, that have been used to excite and stimulate opposition to it; but I shall abstain from all this. It is enough for me to know that these petitions are numerous, and have received the signatures of so many parties, that they are entitled to the utmost respect and attention from this House. I am at once ready to admit, that amongst the great Dissenting bodies of this country there does prevail at the present moment a very unanimous feeling against the educational clauses in this bill....

... I feel that I am justified in saying that these alterations have been framed with the respect which is due from her Majesty's Government to the Church established in this country, and, at the same time, with the respect which is due to that perfect liberty of conscience and those tolerant principles which are no less established by law. I have stated to the House, not more warmly and deeply than I feel it, that the necessity of some such measure as this is urgent. It is my belief that imminent danger would result from its postponement. I may be wrong, but I feel intimately persuaded that if this measure, modified as it now is—a measure treated with signal forbearance by the political opponents of the Government, and with respect to which an earnest desire has been manifested to arrive, if possible, at a conciliatory adjustment—if a measure so proposed, so supported, and so treated in Parliament, shall fail to effect the great object of a combined system of education, from this time all further attempts to attain that end will be hopeless, and henceforth we must expect nothing but a system of education conducted on adverse principles, and in an antagonist spirit, which, I say it with deference, instead of producing a feeling of unity and good will amongst all classes of her Majesty's subjects, will but aggravate the bitter spirit which now exists; and I venture to predict that the most fatal consequences will ensue.

c.

Mr *Roebuck*: . . . Had the Churchmen on the one hand abstained from grasping at power? And had the great Dissenting body shown themselves ready to participate in the benefits which they might have been instrumental in carrying out? He thought he had shown that the Church was desirous to grasp at power—(*No.*) You cry no; and when I come to the Dissenters I shall be told no, by hon. Gentlemen on this side. And yet I say with regard to the Dissenters, that I do see on the other hand an unwillingness to enter into any accommodation expressed by the Dissenting body, a cry of no surrender. . . . There were two distinct things which showed a want of judgment in the framing of this measure. It was founded on the narrow basis that education should depend upon the accidental circumstance, or test of employment. When there was no employment there was to be no instruction. It was a partial measure—it was not for the extension of education, but for a system of education dependent on the merest chance in the world— namely, that of employment. . . . In the next place, the working of the machinery was thrown into the hands of Churchmen. First, from the Secretary of State to the very teachers, they must be members of the Church of England. The Secretary of State was a portion of the machinery—Privy Councillors in the same way—and then came the teachers —(*Hear*). What, must they not also be of the Church of England by the bill? Was not the instruction to be given by teachers of the Church of England? Was not the appointment of the teachers dependent on the bishops of the Church of England? . . . The grand faults of the bill were, that it went first on a narrow basis, and next on a sectarian basis; and when he saw this narrow, grasping disposition manifested on one side, and on the other a feeling so averse to conciliation that conciliation would not be listened to, he had no hopes of the measure.

d.

Lord *Ashley* said, although he deeply regretted the loss of the educational clauses, he, for the sake of the rest of the bill, approved of the resolution the Government had come to. Even had it been possible for the Government to have carried the measure in that House, he did not think it would have met with that cordial sympathy and co-operation from the different classes affected by it, without which it could not have been effectually carried out. It should be borne in mind, that the Church, with a view to conciliation, were ready to make the very largest concessions, larger certainly than it had ever made before, but concessions made in the hope of conciliation and peace. But when the Church found that the terms which it proposed, so far from leading to conciliation and peace, only led to greater disunion and almost to effectual war, it had no alternative but to stop, at all events, at the point to which it had already advanced. Somewhere or other, however, a very great and deep responsibility did lie; it was not for him to point out who were the parties really responsible for the position at which they had now arrived. He certainly must say that the Government had shown their readiness to act. He saw the Church prepared to make concessions for the sake of conciliation and peace, and on the other hand he saw the great body of Dissenters rejoicing that they had been successful in their efforts to defeat the measure. Wherever the fault lay one thing was quite clear—that the really suffering parties were the vast body of neglected children, who, as present appearances went, were now consigned to an eternity of ignorance. . . .

e.

Mr *M. Gibson* could not understand how it was that the noble Lord used the word 'concession', as regarded the conduct of the Church with respect to the education clauses of the Factory Bill. . . . He could tell the noble Lord that it was because the framers of that measure had proceeded on the doctrine that there was some recognised superiority in Churchmen—some sort of divine right in them to trample on the religious liberty of the Dissenters, and to take the money of the Dissenters to teach the tenets of the Church of England; —it was because they persisted in recognising this sort of superiority that they had failed in accomplishing the object of a general system of education. Proceed on the real principle of religious freedom; let men be treated not with reference to their theological opinions, but simply as citizens of a free country, having the right to worship their God in their own way, freely according to their own conscience—adopt this as the principle of legislation and it would not fail. . . . If the Ministerial plan had been carried, it must be admitted that it was a very partial and pitiful proposal, considering the great amount of destitution with regard to religious education that prevailed in the manufacturing districts. It was admitted by all parties that the measure now abandoned would not have led to the education of a single child in the large city of Glasgow, and of not many more in the manufacturing districts in

England, than were educated now, for it was only intended to apply to cotton, flax, silk, and woollen factories; and it left the children in mines and collieries, and in many other employments, wholly unprovided with education. The small amount of education that would have been afforded by the measure was one reason for not so much regretting its rejection. It was a plan that could not have effected much good, but which was certain to have done much harm.

45   Address of the Wesleyan Conference to the societies, 1843

Minutes of the Wesleyan Conference, 1843: collected edition, ix, pp. 555–8.

This important address marks the beginning of the movement of the Wesleyan Methodists away from their uncritical support of the establishment principle. The Disruption of the Church of Scotland raised doubts about the possibility of an acceptable establishment; the education clauses of the Factories Bill had brought Wesleyans into alliance with Dissenters to defeat them; and the increasing influence of the Oxford Movement alarmed Wesleyans about the Protestantism of the Church of England. The address was not approved without a lengthy debate, but it is significant that it was written by Dr Osborn, described by Benjamin Gregory as 'the stoutest defender of the Establishment in the Conference'.[20]

We allude further to the calamitous events which, during the last year, have issued in the secession of nearly five hundred Ministers from the Established Church of Scotland, and the formation of the Free Protesting Church in that country. . . . We do not feel ourselves called upon to express to you, in this official form, our individual opinions on some of the legal and historical details which have been connected with this question in the various stages of its progress. But we do unhesitatingly declare our adherence to what we consider to be by much the most important principle involved in the recent discussions;—the one great principle, namely, That it is the right of every Christian church to claim, in matters which are plainly, and in their very nature, spiritual and ecclesiatical, and especially in reference to the Sacred Functions belonging to the Admission, Appointment, Ordination, Suspension, or Deposition of Ministers, an unfettered freedom of acting according to those deliberate convictions which it may have been led to form, and to embody in its standing Rules and Discipline, as to what is required from it, in such cases, by the Laws of Christ contained in the Holy Scriptures.

If the Civil Courts may regulate the terms of Christian communion, may interpose their authority to compel the ordination of candidates for the ministry, may allow or forbid the exercise of its sacred functions, then the word of God is become of none effect, and we must judge of right and wrong in church-matters by another standard than that which is set up in Zion. To such a conclusion, we are persuaded that you are altogether opposed; and we confidently trust, that, as you have opportunity, you will rejoice to show your sympathy with men who have nobly suffered the loss of all things, for maintaining the supremacy of Christ as the King of his people, and the paramount authority of his word as the law of the church. We have heard with much satisfaction that some of our people, in a few Circuits, have already given practical proof of their high regard for these excellent Ministers and their flocks, by affording their pecuniary aid to the Free Church of Scotland, either in concurrence with the general efforts made in their several localities, by Christians of other communities, or by a Public Collection in our own chapels; and we shall rejoice to learn that similar aid has been afforded in other Circuits, at such time and in such manner as may be deemed most convenient in each particular Circuit to which any application may be made.

There remains yet another subject to which we deem it right to refer. In the commencement of the present session of Parliament, a measure was introduced to promote the better education of the poor in the manufacturing districts, and, as it was generally supposed, with the intention of ultimately extending its application, substantially, to the entire kingdom. On a careful examination of this measure by the United Committees of Privileges and of Education, it was found to be based on unjust principles; to be defective in its provisions; and calculated to produce serious injury to many excellent schools now in existence, to sow the seeds of discord in every place in which it might come into operation, and to inflame, almost beyond the possibility of healing, those unhappy dissensions which at present exist in our land. They therefore recommended that our congregations and schools should petition Parliament against it; a recommendation which was very cheerfully and extensively complied with. The strong and general feeling of disapprobation which this measure excited, in various influential quarters, has led its proposers to withdraw it for the present; and we heartily congratulate you on this result. But we must not disguise or overlook the fact, that our recent proceedings, in reference to public education, have involved us in a most serious responsibility. The case stands thus: A large number of the youth of our country are found to be greatly in need of education. It is proposed to give them a certain amount of education upon certain terms; but we, in common with other bodies, object to the terms proposed, and are understood thus to prevent them from receiving the education offered. Unless, therefore, the education offered was itself an evil as great or greater than absolute ignorance, or unless the terms proposed were such as to neutralize the benefit of education altogether, it is manifest that we must either exert ourselves to the utmost of our power for the instruction of the people on a better system, or we must incur the guilt of depriving them of instruction altogether; neither giving it ourselves, nor allowing it to be given by others. We would have you, dear brethren, deeply impressed with this conviction; and zealous to extend to the children of the poor in your several neighbourhoods the blessing of a truly Christian education. We do not suppose, indeed, that any private or denominational efforts can effect an amount of good equal to that which would result from a well-devised and equitable measure of national education; but we are sure that patient zeal and self-denying liberality may find ample scope, and secure an ample reward, in almost any Circuit in our Connexion. The establishment and maintenance of efficient *Week-Day and Infant Schools* in large towns; and the further improvement of our valuable Sunday-schools everywhere, are objects which we once more earnestly commend to your kind and most careful attention.

It has been publicly stated, that *one* ground of our strenuous opposition to the lately-projected measure of public education was, its obvious tendency to give to the Clergy of the Established Church, an unfair and undue control over the religious teaching in the schools which it would have established. We think it right to confirm this statement, not out of any hostile feeling towards the Established Church as such, for this has never been the feeling of our Body, but with a view to bear our distinct and solemn testimony against those grievous errors which are now tolerated within her pale. We have been hitherto accustomed to regard her as one of the main bulwarks of the Protestant faith; but her title to be so regarded has of late been grievously shaken. Opinions concerning the insufficiency of Scripture, as the sole authoritative and universal rule of faith and practice, the exclusive validity of Episcopal Ordination, and the necessarily saving efficacy of the Sacraments, which can only be distinguished from Popery by an acute and practised observer, and which in their necessary consequences lead directly to Popery, have been revived when they were almost extinct, have spread with fearful rapidity, and are now held by a large number of the Established Clergy. As a natural result of such a state of opinion, an exclusive and persecuting spirit has appeared in many parts of the land. The influence of rank and station is arrayed in various forms of annoyance and intolerance against liberty of conscience; the common offices of good neighbourhood are often denied to all but strict Conformists; and every approach to Christian intercourse and co-operation for religious purposes with those beyond the pale of Episcopal jurisdiction, is repudiated almost with indignation. A preference for Papists over their brethren of the Reformation is in some cases openly avowed; and feelings of tenderness, and even veneration, for the Church of Rome are carefully cultivated by this party. The simple worship hitherto practised in this country, is depreciated by them in comparison with the gorgeous ritual of Rome; and the appliances of art are in constant and increasing requisition for the purpose of bringing Englishmen nearer to that standard of supposed perfection. Amidst all this zeal about externals, the vital and essential doctrine of *Justification by Faith only* is awfully obscured or denied. We deeply condemn and deplore this alarming departure from the truth of the Gospel in doctrine, and from its godly simplicity in divine worship and ecclesiastical observance. Yet we are aware that there is a numerous and powerful body of holy and faithful men to be found in the ranks of the National Church; and we cherish the hope that they, and the authorities of that Church, may soon feel it to be a duty which they owe to Christ and to the souls of men, to stand forth, and, by a more vigorous, explicit, and united assertion of the doctrine of the Reformation, purify their branch of the Christian community from the evils which at present threaten its destruction.

Notes

1 J. G. Rogers, *An Autobiography* (London, 1903), p. 8.
2 G. S. R. Kitson Clark, *The Making of Victorian England* (London, 1962), p. 148.
   For another description see E. Gosse, *Father and Son* (London, 1907), pp. 273–5.

3 J. G. Rogers, *An Autobiography*, pp. 12–13; *Minutes of the Wesleyan Conference, 1855*, collected edition, xiii (1859), p. 125.

4 See the discussion at the Wesleyan Conference of 1837 described in B. Gregory, *Side Lights on the Conflicts of Methodism, 1827–52* (London, 1898), pp. 246–7.

5 H. Carter, *The English Temperance Movement* (London, 1933), i. pp. 21–63; E. R. Taylor, *Methodism and Politics, 1791–1851* (Cambridge, 1935), pp. 140–1.

6 J. Waddington, *Congregational History: continuation to 1850* (London, 1878), pp. 359–62; A. Peel, *These Hundred Years* (London, 1931), pp. 58–74.

7 E. A. Payne, *The Baptist Union* (London, 1959), pp. 60–3.

8 B. L. Manning, *The Protestant Dissenting Deputies* (Cambridge, 1952), pp. 53–93; W. O. Chadwick, *The Victorian Church* (2 vols, London, 1966 and 1970), i, pp. 392–4.

9 J. B. Braithwaite, *Memoirs of Joseph John Gurney* (2 vols, Norwich, 1854), i, p. 184.

10 W. O. Chadwick, *The Victorian Church*, i, pp. 79–95, 147–8.

11 Stephens subsequently became a Chartist leader.

12 B. Gregory, *Side Lights on the Conflicts of Methodism*, p. 252; E. R. Taylor, *Methodism and Politics*, pp. 155–8; J. Kent, *The Age of Disunity* (London, 1966), pp. 92–3, 127–45.

13 N. Hall, *An Autobiography* (London, 1898), p. 24.

14 In this respect R. G. Cowherd, *The Politics of English Dissent* (London, 1959), is apt to be misleading.

15 J. Waddington, *Congregational History: continuation to 1850*, pp. 557–64; G. S. R. Kitson Clark, *The English Inheritance* (London, 1950), pp. 126–7.

16 *Minutes of the Wesleyan Conference, 1839*, collected edition, viii (1841), pp. 514–15.

17 B. Gregory, *Side Lights on the Conflicts of Methodism*, p. 512.

18 See C. M. Maclean, *Mark Rutherford* (London, 1955).

19 Quoted in H. B. Kendall, *Origin and History of the Primitive Methodist Church* (2 vols, London, n.d.), i, p. 472.

20 B. Gregory, *Side Lights on the Conflicts of Methodism*, pp. 348–53.

Three   Starts and Stops

From the formation of the Anti-State Church Association to the bicentenary of the Great Ejectment, 1844-62.

The period sees the emergence of the disestablishment movement from the position of a suspected minority to one of increasing strength. The Disruption of the Church of Scotland and the Dissenters' victory over factory education encouraged the extremists to press for disestablishment right away. In December 1843 a conference of delegates from various parts of the country met in Leicester and decided that the time was ripe to launch a wider movement. It should be remembered also that this was a time when the rights of the Church of England in Canada and Australia were also being warmly debated. The Anti-State Church Association was formed in April 1844 (46) as a result of this movement.[1] It met a mixed reaction (47), again showing that not all Nonconformists, even among the Old Dissent, were behind it. In fact, it was rather overshadowed by the activities of the Anti-Corn Law League (on which in many respects it was modelled) and the Chartists, and the early years of its history are quiet. It was born just as the divisions between Trinitarian and Unitarian dissenters were at their worst over the Dissenters' Chapels Bill,[2] and although it was stimulated by the agitation over Peel's decision to make a government grant to the Roman Catholic seminary at Maynooth (where again Wesleyans felt strongly (50)), that was soon forgotten in the political turmoil over the repeal of the Corn Laws. In 1854 the A.S.C.A. changed its name to the Society for the Liberation of the Church from State Patronage and Control, or the Liberation Society. But its fortunes were not thereby substantially changed. The Church Rates battle died down after the House of Lords' decision in the Braintree case in 1852 (58), and this had been the issue at local level which had most mobilised opinion in favour of disestablishment.[3] Nevertheless, there is some evidence that the movement fed the growth of a new popular Liberalism in the constituencies.[4]

The 1840s do, however, demonstrate the extent to which Wesleyans, Congregationalists and Baptists have moved into the centre of the Nonconformist stage. The Unitarian troubles were cleared up by the Dissenters' Chapels Act, but it left a sour taste in the mouth. From 1845 the Unitarians were engaged in a valuable new enterprise in the industrial towns—the Domestic Missions, which concentrated on house to house visitation in slum areas (103). But they were a declining denomination in numerical terms. So were the Quakers, who had not been particularly concerned in the movements to redress Dissenting grievances because they had secured exemption from them f r themselves in the previous century. To a large extent their decline was the result of their own policy (63). They remained influential in particular ways, through their philanthropy, through the Peace Society, and in education, for example, but they had little share in the general movement of Nonconformity.[5] Their views on peace could, however, expose them to attack at times of national bellicosity, such as the Crimean War (59).

The Wesleyans' internal troubles entered a new phase with the *Fly Sheets* controversy, and this virtually paralysed the denomination for a decade in the later 'forties and early 'fifties. The *Fly Sheets* were anonymous pamphlets circulated to all Wesleyan ministers and some laymen between 1844 and 1849. They attacked what they considered to be abuses in Wesleyanism, in particular the central administration in London and the powers exercised by a few leading ministers over the life of the whole Connexion. In brief, they attacked Jabez Bunting. The Wesleyan leaders responded by circulating a declaration, which all ministers were invited to sign, saying that they were not the authors of the *Fly Sheets*, and knew nothing about the authors. A majority of ministers signed, but a number of 'liberal' ministers refused to do so on principle. In 1849 the man most suspected of being the author, James Everett, was expelled from the Connexion for refusing to answer the question whether he was the author (52). With him were expelled two other ministers, Samuel Dunn and William Griffiths, for their association with 'opposition' Wesleyan newspapers, the *Wesley Banner* and the *Wesleyan Times*, which had also been critical of the leadership. The expelled ministers were supported by other Nonconformists, and even by *The Times*. Mass expulsions of ordinary members in the circuits followed if there was any hint of support for the expelled ministers, and the Wesleyans lost 100,000 members in the next five years. In many places they never recovered their former position relative to population.[6]

The Primitive Methodists were entering a period of consolidation.

In 1842 both Hugh Bourne and William Clowes were super-
annuated: the effective leadership was passing from the pioneers
to a new generation; and increasingly the denomination was
'coming inside'. The 1840s and 1850s began a great age of chapel-
building. In 1847 the number of rented rooms outnumbered the
chapels by two to one: by 1868 the chapels outnumbered the
rented rooms.[7] The picture one gets of Primitive Methodist life
is of steady advance (48).

The Primitive Methodists, of course, were strong among the
working classes. Another denomination with great strength there
was the New Connexion of General Baptists, in which John
Clifford was brought up (49). Both denominations were affected
by the economic difficulties of the time. They seem to be in a
completely different world from the more prosperous
Nonconformists (66), though all met with social discrimination.
The appeal of Nonconformity to the middling ranks of society
was beginning to be widely noticed (61, 57) and Anglican clergymen
were probably right to attribute this to the failure of the Church
of England to offer responsibility to these classes. The closed social
world of many Nonconformist chapels may have been partly
responsible for the rather trivial internal disputes that periodically
arose (69).

The census of religious worship of 1851 provides a useful
picture of the state of Nonconformity at mid-century (57). This
count of the numbers attending worship at each service on 30 March
1851, the day of the decennial census, is uniquely complete.
Subsequent proposals for a government census foundered because
the Church of England, horrified by the numbers of Nonconformists
the census revealed, would only accept a census of religious
profession, whilst the Nonconformists, realising that this would give
a very different view, insisted on a census of attendance. The
report contains an analysis of the reasons for non-attendance as well
as an account of the statistics. The census figures showed that the
strength of the various denominations varied regionally, with
Wesleyans stronger in the north than the south, and Baptists and
Congregationalists stronger in Wales, the Midlands and East Anglia
than either north or south. It also seemed that the rate of increase
was dropping after 1841, quite apart from the Wesleyan troubles.
All the main denominations were stronger in the countryside
than the towns. The census confirmed that the largest Nonconformist
denomination was the Wesleyans, followed by the Congregationalists,

Baptists and Primitive Methodists: the significance of this, however, is off-set by the fact that locally the balance could be very different. Even Nonconformists were surprised by their strength as revealed by the census, but the Liberation Society claimed that they were even stronger. There followed a number of attempts to make the census show things it was incapable of showing, the main effect of which was to cast doubt on the figures altogether.

The 1840s and 1850s were a period of new movements within and new problems for Nonconformity. One of the new denominations which the census revealed was the Mormons. They spread quite rapidly in the late 'forties, and the main reason for their decline seems to have been the effect of polygamy and the stress placed on the trip to Salt Lake City. Eleven thousand Mormons emigrated between 1848 and 1854. The atmosphere of Mormon worship seems to have been very like that of the more orthodox revival movements (55), and their appeal may have been very similar to that of the Primitive Methodists (56). At a different level the 1850s saw the appearance in London of C. H. Spurgeon, a young Baptist preacher who consistently had to hire larger halls to accommodate the crowds who flocked to hear him. The climax came at a meeting in 1856 in the Surrey Gardens music hall which held 10,000 people: someone screamed 'Fire!' and in the panic seven people were killed and twenty-eight injured (60). The story provoked considerable public controversy about Spurgeon's methods, but he continued to attract congregations of 4,000 to 5,000 people by his evangelical preaching. Spurgeon was brought up in a small country chapel, and this was the milieu of the other new movement of the period. The 1850s saw the strengthening of a number of smaller groups which attempted to return to a primitive, New Testament Christianity. The Brethren are the largest and best known; another was the Churches of Christ; other congregations were not formally attached to any denomination and had a purely local existence. All had in common a deep attachment to the Bible, which they studied closely. Nor is it without interest that all the new movements just described practised believer's baptism (64), though Spurgeon believed in open communion (i.e., that unbaptised people could share in communion) somewhat surprisingly for one who was Calvinist in other respects.

Nonconformists were also becoming more self-critical. Edward Miall's book, *The British Churches in Relation to the British People*, showed that he recognised that establishment was not the only problem for the Church. It was published in 1849 and he criticised Nonconformists as well as the Church of England. Miall was one of the first to analyse the extent to which class divisions existed in the churches (54), a subject which occupied the Congregational Union's Assembly for a whole session in 1848.[8] He also attacked what he called the 'trade spirit', one of the few criticisms of prevailing economic morality and its assimilation into Christianity in the first half of the century. Again Miall was one of the few people inside the churches to criticise Sabbatarianism (53), a movement which was if anything gaining ground in the 1850s with opposition being expressed to Sunday rail travel, Sunday opening of museums and public places, and, of course, Sunday opening of public houses.[9] Although not seen as such at the time, this attempt to restrict the pursuit of pleasure on the Lord's Day, in which Nonconformists were very prominent, was helping to deepen the cultural gap between the churches and many ordinary people.

Finally it is in the 1850s that the suburban problem begins to appear. The continuing growth of cities was beginning to produce social segregation, as Engels noted in Manchester in the 1840s.[10] Nonconformist churches were particularly exposed in areas where the richer people moved away, because they depended on them for their contributions. One consequence was that Nonconformist churches often followed their congregation to the suburbs, by rebuilding in a 'more desirable location' (62). The Wesleyan Conference of 1855 bewailed the tendency to move house and the social separation it produced.[11]

The 1850s seem to have been a time of stagnation or even decline for Nonconformity as a whole: certainly there is a pause before the advance is resumed. The reasons are unclear: emigration may have had something to do with it; high prices in the early 'fifties were alleged to have caused hardship; the Wesleyan troubles certainly affected Wesleyanism, a significant proportion of Nonconformity in itself, but it is difficult to understand why this should have affected other denominations. Local reasons may also be important.[12] By the end of the decade new initiatives in church extension were being tried: from 1860 the Congregationalists adopted a system of country evangelists to supplement the regular ministry and begin new causes; Baptists supported colporteurs and Spurgeon ran a colportage society supplying tracts for distribution.

The bicentenary movement—to celebrate the ejectment of Nonconformist ministers in 1662—was intended by its initiator,

Joshua Wilson, energetic secretary of the Congregational Home
Missionary Society, to be a movement for church extension (67).
Significantly he saw that the real initiative must come in the towns.
But the bicentenary movement was also seen as an opportunity once
again to make the case for disestablishment, even though it had to
be recognised that this was not what the ejected ministers had stood
for (68). The effect of this movement was to arouse the hostility
of many Anglicans, even though this had not been intended.[13]
It also prepared the way for a fresh attempt by the Liberation
Society to influence political action. In 1863, disillusioned with
Lord Palmerston, the Liberation Society decided to support the
Liberals only in so far as they showed themselves willing to support
Nonconformist principles, and they planned to push this policy
in the more radical local party associations.[14] This time their
policy was destined to yield rather more fruit.

46   Constitution of the Anti-State Church Association, 1844

Extracts from a report in the *Eclectic Review*, 1844, pp. 736–8.

It was decided to launch a movement for the separation of Church
and State at a meeting in Leicester on 4 December 1843, and a
conference met in London for three days, beginning on 30 April
1844, at which the constitution for the Anti-State Church Association
was approved. The organisation was typical of the pressure groups
of the time, and the list of 'modes of action contemplated by the
Society' in clause 15 is particularly interesting. The details of the
composition and duties of committees, etc., have been omitted.

I   That a society be now formed, to be intituled 'The British Anti-
state-church Association'.
II   That this Society be based upon the following principle: 'That
in matters of religion man is responsible to God alone; that all legisla-

tion by secular governments in affairs of religion is an encroachment upon the rights of man, and an invasion of the prerogatives of God; and that the application by law of the resources of the state to the maintenance of any form or forms of religious worship and instruction is contrary to reason, hostile to human liberty, and directly opposed to the word of God.'

III   That the object of this Society be, the liberation of religion from all government or legislative interference.

IV   That this object be sought by lawful and peaceful means, and by such means only.

V   That every individual subscribing to the principle upon which this Society is based, and contributing not less than one shilling annually to its general fund, be admissible as a member.

VI   That the officers of this Society consist of a treasurer, three secretaries, three auditors, a council of five hundred, and an executive committee of fifty members; that the place of meeting of the executive committee be in London; and that the members of the council be entitled, when in London, to sit at the committee board, and to take part in their deliberations. . . .

XV   That the following be among the modes of action contemplated by this Society.

1 The collection and digest, from authentic public documents, of all such information as may throw light upon the nature and tendency of state churches.

2 The securing original essays on the question of state churches, for popular use, and fitted to supply to the public, and especially to dissenters, needful and useful information on the subject.

3 The employment of lecturers, gratuitous or otherwise, under the sanction and direction of the executive committee, to explain and enforce the fundamental principle of this society; to expose the evils which have resulted and are inseparable from any form of alliance between church and state; and to rouse the public, and especially professed nonconformists, to an earnest consideration of their duty in this matter.

4 The giving of advice to individuals wishing to form similar associations, for the purpose of diffusing correct information, and of bringing public opinion to bear, as prudence may dictate, upon the composition of the House of Commons, and upon the decisions of the imperial parliament.

5 The promotion of the return to parliament, wherever practicable, of men of known integrity and ability, conversant with the

principles of this Society, and disposed to avail themselves of all suitable occasions for exciting discussion thereupon, and ready to promote its object; and the furnishing of such members, when returned, with all the special information the Society can command.

6 The support of such members whenever the council shall deem it advisable to agitate the question of state churches in the legislature, by means of petitions to the houses of parliament, and memorials to the throne, and in other appropriate and constitutional ways.

7 The removal of the question of national religious establishments as much as possible from under the influence of party feeling; the placing it upon the ground of what is due to pure and undefiled religion, and to the best interests temporal and spiritual, of the people; and the enlistment of the sincerely religious of all classes of the community by energetic appeals to conscience.

8 The adoption of preparatory measures for obtaining the repeal of all existing laws directly or indirectly involving the union of the church with the state; and the enactment of laws adapted to carry out, to their legitimate extent, the principles of religious liberty.

9 The employment of whatsoever lawful and peaceful means may be adapted to promote the one great object of 'the British Anti-state-church Association'.

47   Two reactions to the Anti-State Church Conference, 1844

Extracts from (a) the *Congregational Magazine*, 1844, pp. 393–4, and (b) the *Eclectic Review*, 1844, p. 738.

Two different reactions to the Anti-State Church Conference are illustrated in these extracts from contemporary comment in the religious journals. The editor of the *Congregational Magazine* (a) rejected the political involvement which the Association implied, whilst Dr Price in the *Eclectic Review* (b) commented on the lack of political discussions. Both magazines circulated mainly among Congregationalists.

a.   *(Congregational Magazine)*
We object to this Conference as a means for the promotion of religious ends, the right government of the Church of Christ, because, according to its constitution, it is to consist of Christians, Socinians, and men of no religion. . . . The Conference must, we think, to be consistent, act on the low views and principles which are the only common ground on which its members can meet. Thus our religious influence, wherein our real strength lies, is necessarily diminished. . . .

   Again, we object to this Conference as a means for the promotion of political ends—for the redress of civil grievances—because we think that in such an object Christian ministers have no special concern, and Christian Churches and congregations, as such, no proper concern at all. We think that our ministers have nobler and better objects to pursue— that few are qualified for successful political agitation, and that all may be more usefully employed. Our Christian societies are formed for mutual improvement in piety, and for the extension of Christian truth and privileges to all. If they are ever made political associations, so far their Christian character must be obscured, and their Christian usefulness lessened. . . .

In conclusion, we cannot but regard the Anti-State Church Conference as liable to the same objections as the State Church itself. Its design is to employ worldly influence for the advancement of Christian objects, and to use Christian Churches for the promotion of political objects. We think that Christian societies should be used only for Christian ends, and that these will only be attained when sought by Christian means.

b.   (*Eclectic Review*)

We notice as a striking feature of these meetings, the entire absence of all political discussions. Not a petition to parliament, nor a memorial to the queen, nor even a resolution expressive of a political sentiment was adopted. This was the more remarkable, as a great part of the men assembled were known to entertain very decided political views, and to be thoroughly earnest in their maintenance. . . . A proposition to send a petition from the Conference to parliament, was submitted by a minister of deserved repute, but was withdrawn on a general expression of opinion unfavourable to its adoption. We need not say how many predictions this fact falsified, but we do trust that the utterers of such predictions will deem it befitting,—an act of common integrity due alike to themselves and to their brethren,—to acknowledge their error, and repudiate the spirit under which they wrote. Never was any public meeting of dissenters held, so absolutely free from the charge alleged against this conference of being 'a means for the promotion of political ends—for the redress of civil grievances'.

48 A Primitive Methodist quarterly meeting, 1845

An extract from the *Primitive Methodist Quarterly Meeting Minute Book, Earl Shilton Circuit*, pp. 7–10 (Leicestershire County Records Office, N/M/142/57).

The normal business of a Methodist circuit was discharged at the quarterly meeting. Among Primitive Methodists this was divided into two parts: the first was attended only by the preachers and dealt with preaching appointments, discipline of the preachers and preaching places; the second (the full board) was attended by representatives from each society and dealt with more general business. The extract gives a good picture of the variety of business handled. Note the references to a woman preacher, to camp meetings and to the appointment of a new minister.

Minutes of a Quarter Day Meeting Nuneaton Mar^h 16th 1845. Resolved 1st That Sister Corbett have but one appointment this next Quarter, and that be at Peckleton.

2nd That Bro Dingley's name stand over to the full Board.

3rd That Brother Everitt's name come of the Plan for non-attendance to Class.

4th That Brother Gisbourn's name come of the Plan on account of sickness.

5th That Bro Colton's name come of the Plan, he having left the Circuit.

6th That Bro Lucas come on the Plan on Trial.

7th That Bro W. King and Bro Newcom come on the Plan with a Star.

8th That Shilton stand at the top of the Plan.

9th That Bro Bayliss's request be granted with respect to appointments.

10th That Attleborough come on the Plan at five O'Clock.
11th That Coaton Heath End come on the Plan at two O'Clock.
12th That Whittleford come on the Plan at six O'Clock.
13th That Coaters come on the week night Plan.

S. Gee   President
B. Blackburn   Secrey

Full Board
Resolved 1st   That the account of members be satisfactory.
2nd   That the Book Steward's account is correct.
3rd   That the Book Steward be allowed the whole of the Book proffits during the time he as to pay in advance to the Book Room.
4th   That Barlestons School Sermons be according to their request.
5th   That Atherstone Sermons be on the 27 of April.
6th   That Atherstone Camp meeting be on Whitsunday.
7th   That Bro Blackburn preach Nuneaton School Sermons.
8th   That Burbage and Hinckley have a union Camp meeting.
9th   That Hunts Lane Camp Meeting be the Second Sunday July.
10th   That Bro Blackburn preach Barwell Sermons Second Sunday in the new plan.
11th   That Desford School Sermons be in June.
12th   That Bro Corbett be Circuit Steward.
13th   That the former Committee be realected with the addition of Bro Wood and Bro Winderage to meet once at Barwell Barlestone and Atherstone in the Quarter.
14th   That Bro Gee write a letter in answer to the District Committee Letter with regard to Shilton Chapel.
15   Nuneaton Trustees pay of Mr Bassets bill as far as possible.
16   That the next Quarterly Meeting be at Shilton this day thirteen weeks.
17   That Bro Simpson be delegate to the District Meeting.
18th   That Bro Corbett be vice delegate.
19th   That the Circuit report and historical account of the preachers be filled up in the ushual way.
20th   That Bro Blackburn be Superintendant untill June Q^r day.
21st   That Bro W. Martin of Bedford be written too imediaetly to come into this Circuit.
22   That boath the Preachers live in Shilton Chapel house.
23   That Mrs Plant have a quarters notice that the Preachers are removing to Shilton.
24   That Bro Blackburn be treasurer for Nuneaton.

25 That Bro Blackburn be subtreasuerer and Bro Martin be subSec^ty and that the Circuit Committee be the subCommittee of the Missionary regulations.

26 That Mr Gee have a credential given him signed by this board.

Thos Simpson President
Thos Corbett Secratary

49 Working-class Nonconformity in the 1840s

An extract from Sir J. Marchant, *Dr John Clifford, C.H.* (1924), p. 1.

These are the opening words of John Clifford's scraps of autobiography, written towards the end of his life, and they give a vivid picture of the atmosphere of working-class Nonconformity in the 1840s. Clifford was a Baptist minister who took a leading part in the agitation against the 1902 Education Act. He was born in 1836 and was brought up in the General Baptist (New Connexion) church at Sawley near Derby.

I began life in a factory and I have never forgotten the cruel impressions I received there of men and work. Ebenezer Elliott's prayer was on our lips daily—'When wilt Thou save the people?' Chartists were alive and eloquent. Feargus O'Connor, Thomas Cooper, Henry Vincent, William Lovett were fighting. Holyoake later was going to prison; Fox, the Quaker, was having his goods sold in Nottingham Market Place because he would not pay the Church dues. Edward Miall and J. P. Mursell were preaching for individual freedom. So I came to have sympathy with the working classes, of which I was one, who are said to form eighty per cent or more of the population of these Isles, and I have it still and I have never lost it after eighty years, and I feel it stronger to-day than ever.

50   Resolutions of the Wesleyan Conference on the Maynooth grant, 1845

Minutes of the Wesleyan Conference, 1845: collected edition, x, pp. 243–4.

The government grant to the Roman Catholic seminary at Maynooth in 1845 united a variety of Dissenters—some because of the recognition given thereby to Roman Catholicism, others because of opposition to State endowment on principle. The Wesleyans objected more on the first ground than the second, and their resolutions sum up the kind of objections felt under this heading. As in the case of slavery (document 21) there is a recommendation to use the vote to change the policy.

1.   Resolved, That the recent Measure for the permanent National Endowment of the Roman Catholic College of Maynooth, together with the purpose expressed by many leading Statesmen of all parties, to promote a legal endowment of the Priesthood of the Church of Rome in Ireland,—a measure which we believe would inevitably extend the power and influence of that Church, not only in Ireland, but in the United Kingdom generally, and elsewhere,—constitutes, in the judgement of the Conference, a just ground of apprehension and alarm for the stability of our Protestant institutions, both civil and religious.
2.   That the Conference deems it seasonable to express its deep conviction that this country is indebted, under Divine Providence, to the Reformation from Popery, together with the subsequent establishment of the Protestant Faith, for the high measure of religious prosperity which, at different periods, has been vouchsafed to it; that the rights of conscience and freedom of worship, so fully enjoyed by the several Christian denominations, have been secured by the same arrangement; and that the equitable laws, and remarkable strength and glory of this great nation have rested on its recognition of Protestant truth. . . .
3.   That the Conference, in common with other Protestant bodies,

is penetrated with the conviction that the Romish system embraces and propagates fatal error, and is, in its distinctive peculiarities, essentially antagonist to the vital truths of the Gospel, and to the free use of the holy Scriptures by the people; they believe that its worship is defiled with superstition and idolatry, and that its ecclesiastical government is despotic and oppressive.

4. That therefore the Conference cannot but consider the national and legislative establishment of a system so obviously anti-Christian, as being directly sinful, and calculated to expose the country to the displeasure of Almighty God, and to draw down upon it the judgements which he has denounced against those nations who practically renounce his authority, and adopt a course opposed to the teachings of his holy word.

5. That in the prospect of these threatening dangers, the Conference deems it an imperative duty, while maintaining perfect loyalty to the throne of Her Most Gracious Majesty, our beloved Queen, and unwavering attachment to the laws and institutions of the country, to declare it to be their fixed resolution, by all constitutional and Christian means, to oppose the further national endowment of the Romish Church in any part of the United kingdom.

6. That, in conformity with this resolution, the Conference pledges itself, as a body of Ministers, to employ all its fair and Christian influence in promoting a general, united and persevering resistance to any further national endowment of the Church of Rome; and earnestly recommends the Methodist Societies and Congregations to employ all the constitutional resources and legitimate means at their command, in order to avert this imminent evil.

7. More particularly, the Conference recommends and entreats those members of our Societies and Congregations who possess the elective franchise, to exercise it irrespectively of merely political partialities, and of local and temporary considerations, in favour of candidates of approved Protestant principles. In the maintenance of these principles there are involved the freedom of the British churches, the interests of pure religion, and the continuance of the divine favour; while the abandonment of them would have the effect of compelling the vast majority of the people of this country to support a system of religion which they solemnly believe to be, in its spirit, doctrine, and polity, directly opposed to the Gospel of Christ.

51   The 'Fly Sheets', no. 4, 1848

An extract from *All the Numbers of the 'Fly Sheets'* (1849), pp. 83-5.

The *Fly Sheets* were circulated anonymously to all Wesleyan
ministers from 1844. They consisted of a systematic, bitter and clever
attack on the leading figures in the Connexion, especially (but
not only) Jabez Bunting and on the way the Connexion was run.
No. 1 appeared in 1844, no. 2 in 1846, no. 3 in 1847, no. 4 in 1848
and no. 5 in 1849. The search for their author (suspected to be James
Everett) precipitated the split which led to the Wesleyan Reform
movement. This extract from no. 4 summarises the main arguments.

It is a fact, to which we refer with great satisfaction, that amid the
heavy censures which have fallen on us, no one has dared to say that
our *facts* are *fictions*, and that our *reasonings* are *sophisms*. Their truth in
the one case, their force in the other, is their power. No refutation
has been attempted—for the most weighty of reasons—*no refutation
was possible.*

Most sincerely do we wish that there had been no personalities
in our Fly Sheets. But this was impossible. We must have abandoned
our object altogether, had we resolved to give no pain to any one
individual. The men were implicated in the measures;—the abettors
were the very life and soul of the system. No weapon could reach *it*
without piercing *them*. This was our *misfortune*, but their *fault*.

We proceed with our work. And here let us remind our readers of
what we have already done.

1   We have infixed in the minds of the preacher generally, this
point:– *there shall henceforth be no re-election of the President of the
Conference.* Till the publication of No. 2 of the Fly-Sheets, this matter
had scarcely been discussed anywhere or by any one. It seemed to
occur, as a matter of course, that the Presidental Chair should be
reserved for a very elect few; who, for life, as often as the constitution

of the body would allow, should engross this honour to themselves. No. 2 was a bomb-shell, thrown into this coterie of Presidents elect.

2 We have exposed the evils inherent in the modern system of *location*, *centralization*, and *secularization* in Methodism.

Of *location*, we have shewn—and who in Conference or out of Conference has been venturous enough to dispute our position?—that it is opposed to the spirit and practice of our venerable founder; prevents a fair distribution of ministerial talent; excuses ministers of Christ, moved of God to preach the gospel to perishing sinners, from delivering more than one sermon in seven days throughout the year, these ministers being the very men who have most to do with ordaining young men to the ministry, and with urging on them the solemn and tremendous obligations of the ministerial office.

Of *centralization*, we have shewn it to be a vortex engulphing every interest of Methodism, as the Maelstroom sucks in every vessel afloat in its vicinity.

Of *secularization*, its evils we summed up in one sentence, '*This endangers their souls.*' Being located, and constituting a centre, towards which money is constantly flowing, and where matters of finance constitute the grand staple of their business and conversation, scarcely any thing, save that which is wordly, is permitted to come over their spirits.

3 We have proved that *there exists a settled purpose of centralising everything in London*. Nothing can be done for Methodism but in London. The utmost jealousy is shewn by the clique, if it be attempted to draw away from London to the provinces.

4 We have shewn that *when a man has wriggled himself into office, he somehow continues to stick there much longer than he is useful to the body, creditable to himself, or acceptable to many of his brethren;* probably to a majority of them, if their votes were so taken that their individual decision was not known.

5 We have shewn that *the various Connexional Committees have been formed on the most manifest partiality and exclusiveness.* The same names occur everlastingly on the numerous committees. It would seem as though there was an awful paucity of men of ability, and character in the connexion. The prospects of the connexion are awful, if these men may not live, if not for ever, for ages!

6 We have shewn that *those who are for ever lauding Mr Wesley's plans and proceedings, are as constantly and effectually perverting them* by squatting themselves down on one spot for life, carefully avoiding the proper work (in Mr Wesley's opinion) of a Methodist Preacher, and making

their official seats, on one respect, like the Lord Chancellor's, easy as a wool-sack. Methodist Preachers resident in one town for 15, 20, and even 30 years!! And these are itinerant! These the admirers and eulogists of Wesley!

7   We have shewn that *the cost of the Mission House is excessive, averaging for each Secretary £500 per annum.* We have asked why four Secretaries, and one lay-agent, besides clerks, are necessary in the Wesleyan Mission House, when two Secretaries can transact the business of the London Missionary Society?

8   We have shewn,—and once again we challenge the clique, aided by Osborn and Co., to a refutation, to a denial, or to a vindication, of the charge, that *the grossest partiality has been shewn by the dominant party in cases of discipline, when the delinquent has been from their own rank.* Witness the case of Mr Cubitt, as contrasted with Overton:—the latter a fifty pence debtor, with many extenuating circumstances; but in his case the law must take its course; no shield of power is thrown before him. The former is screened, is aided, is elevated into the rank of Editor; but, then, he belongs to the party in power;—he is subservient.

9   We have shewn that *in the distribution of office the same shameless partizan partiality exists.* It does not ooze out. It does not sneakingly peep out. It is unblushing. It is open.

10   We have shewn that the *stationing committee deserves the appellation we have given it,*—'THE SLAUGHTER-HOUSE OF MINISTERIAL CHARACTER:' Where character is assassinated, and years elapse before the man knows that the bowie knife has been plunged into it.

11   We have shewn that *the Nomination Committee is a mere instrument in the hands of the Dictator and his tools for carrying their principles out in every department of Methodism.* By its means 'the station-master' has his men everywhere.

12   We have shewn that *the preservation of the liberties of the preachers makes the use of the Ballot indispensible* in all decisions in which the unbiassed votes of the Conference are of moment.

52 The expulsion of the Rev. James Everett from the Wesleyan Conference, 1849

An extract from R. Chew, *James Everett: A Biography* (1875), pp. 381-4.

James Everett was suspected of being the author of the *Fly Sheets*, partly because he was known to have written the anonymous *Wesleyan Takings* (1840), and partly because he refused to sign the declaration against the *Fly Sheets* circulated by the Rev. G. Osborn. He was expelled in 1849 for refusing to answer the question whether he was the author. This extract comes from his Journal, and may be compared with that in Benjamin Gregory's *Side Lights*, pp. 445-60.

July 30th, Monday. Proceeded to Conference at Manchester, in company with my friend, the Rev. John Burdsall, both being summoned by the President, the Rev. Thomas Jackson, on the motion of the Rev. W. M. Bunting, to appear before the Conference, without assigning any reason or preferring any charge against either of us. We entered the Conference in Oldham Street chapel on Tuesday morning, and took our seats in the large square pew in the corner next the wall, on the right of the pulpit. There we sat during the various sittings till Friday evening, when it turned out that we were to be subjected to 'question under penalty', as in the Star-chamber and High Commission court.

The question related to certain missiles called 'Fly-Sheets', which were circulated privately among the preachers, and which exposed the proceedings of the executive of the Connexion, the malappropriation of moneys, etc., giving facts, figures, and published documents as evidence of the truth of the charges alleged. On Friday evening I was selected by the holy inquisitors to lead the way, and Dr Hannah, secretary of the Conference, was appointed to propose the question. I was ordered to appear at the bar of the Conference, and there I stood! Why?

1st. The President's summons gave no notice of a charge, which according to rule ought to have been specified in writing, two or three days before, with the names of the accusers. This not being done, I was left to guess out the cause or reason of this strange procedure. 2nd. The York district minutes, which had been handed to the Conference, were free from any charge against me, having in their entries, 'Are there any objections against James Everett?' Answer, 'None'. 3rd During a period of forty-three years the same question had been annually asked, and the same answer given! No charge! 4th. The Conference avowed that it had no charge to prefer! But to evade all rule and order, and to accomplish a despotic purpose, which could not with any show of decency be effected in any other way, the question was put in the shape of a 'friendly inquiry'.

Dr Hannah, with a paper in his hand, containing a string of questions, commenced with, 'Are you the author of the "Fly-Sheets"?' Being pretty firm and recollected, and indignant at the mode of proceeding adopted, regarding it as an un-scriptural, un-English, and cruel attempt to get a man to criminate himself, when the basest villain in civil society is cautioned not to say anything to criminate himself, I demanded to know, first, by what law of the body I was summoned to appeal at the bar of the Conference, without any notice of a charge. Secondly, Why the secretary had reversed the order of calling over the districts, having passed over several districts to reach that of York? There were brethren in those districts who had not signed George Osborn's 'declaration', and were therefore open to the same inter-rogatory mode of procedure. And thirdly, Why I, on the York district, should be selected for interrogation before my venerable friend Mr Burdsall? He was my senior both in years and office, and stood precisely in the same position as myself, having been summoned to Conference by the same authority, by the same post, and apparently for the same object, owing, it was presumed, to his not having signed the said 'declaration'.

Dr Hannah, good man, who had a curious look with his eyes, seemed at a loss for an answer. This caused him to assume a still more singular expression, partly simpering and partly blank, as he turned right and left, to the President on the one hand and to Dr Bunting on the other. After a short pause he replied, 'You are called first because you are the most suspected'. To this I promptly returned, 'If I am the most suspected, you, of course, have the most evidence against me.' 'Oh', he subjoined, 'there is no charge; it is only a "friendly inquiry," ' styled afterwards a 'brotherly' inquiry. 'Then if you have no charge,' I said, 'I have no answer to give'; adding, 'Prefer your charge in writing, according to rule, if you have one, and I pledge myself to meet it at any time and in any place; but I will not be the man, even at the risk of expulsion from the body, to convert a Methodist Conference into a Romish inquisition.'

What a buzz! What a clamour from all parts of the house! I made short work of it, withdrew from the front of the platform, and resumed my seat. My noble friend Mr Burdsall was next called. He took the ground which I had taken, answering the question in the same brief way, only varying a little in expression, and accompanied with a remark condemnatory of the novel and unlawful mode of procedure. He was not entrapped by the insidious 'brotherly inquiry'.

The dominant party, who sought by clamour and intimidation to stifle the charges preferred against them in the 'Fly-Sheets', were evidently met in a way not anticipated. We were ordered to withdraw from the Conference, when we returned to our lodgings.

We had not been long in the house before a deputation from the Conference waited upon us. The deputation consisted of the Revs. William Vevers and Joseph Cusworth. They requested us to attend the Conference at nine o'clock next morning. Our reply was brief, stating that we would answer no question, but were ready at any hour and in any place to meet any charge, regularly preferred, agreeably to the rules of the body. The good men reasoned, entreated, coaxed; but in vain. A committee was appointed to deliberate and decide on our case, consisting of the President, secretary, ex-president, four chairmen of the large districts, viz. George Taylor, William Burt, Henry Davies, and Robert Young, together with George Osborn, Jonathan Crowther, and William Naylor, the latter of whom, all good men and true on the dominant side, were on the minor district committee which condemned Daniel Walton without evidence of guilt, for the disreputable conduct of his accuser could not be twisted into proof of authorship of the 'Fly-Sheets'.

We were never called before the committee which had to consider our case; and in the Conference we were permitted to give no answer, except 'Yes' or 'No', an answer which, in fact, belonged to the proposers, not to us, as they wished to put it into our mouths, and then for us to give it as our own, without being allowed to assign a single reason for any answer we might feel disposed to give. This committee (both of us, I repeat being unheard) recommended my expulsion; and Mr Burdsall, who stood in precisely the same position as myself, was to be reprimanded! The one condemned to ecclesiastical death, and the other left in full possession of all his funded and other privileges!

Left Manchester Sunday, August 5, disgusted with the Conference
and their ultimate designs; and not less so with the unprincipled
conduct of many of the preachers, who, while they could inveigh in
my hearing against the dominants, were still found supporting them
in their measures.

53   Edward Miall criticises Sabbatarianism, 1849

An extract from E. Miall, *The British Churches in Relation to the British People* (1849), pp. 167–8.

Although a rigid attitude to Sunday observance characterised many
Nonconformists (see document 24), it was not without its critics,
even among Nonconformists. This extract comes from Edward
Miall, founder of the *Nonconformist*, and an ex-Congregational
minister.

The British Churches, but particularly those of Scotland, evince a
strong, and I fear it must be added, a growing disposition, to attack
irreligion in its external manifestations, and that with weapons which
do not so much as touch, and therefore cannot destroy, the internal
causes of it. I submit as the most vivid, but not by any means the only,
illustration of it, what is commonly called 'the Sabbath question'.
Means, it appears, must be taken by religious society to prevent the
desecration of the day by men indifferent or hostile to the claims of the
gospel—as if such men could possibly present other homage to the
sanctity of the day than one which their hearts refuse, and as if this
were better than no homage at all. Suppose the object aimed at could
be compassed. Suppose all the means and opportunities of openly
violating the Sabbath were cut off—every tavern and tea-garden shut—
every vehicle prohibited—every avenue to pleasure barred—and every
act expressive of contempt for the institution rendered impossible.
What then? There would not be more religion—if by religion it

meant sympathy with God, in the gospel of Jesus Christ—in consequence of the arrangement, than there was before—not one single additional element of the social state upon which, the eye of the Supreme could rest with approval. There would be nothing more than an imposing show without any corresponding reality—towards God a mockery—to the Churches a blind, concealing from them the actual spiritual condition of the world—and operating upon the ungodly themselves as a delusion and a snare. Strange that Christianity should be so completely misunderstood! Stranger still that the misunderstanding should be exhibited in connexion with the most general and strenuous advocacy of the doctrine of justification by faith!

54 Religion and class, 1849

An extract from E. Miall, *The British Churches in Relation to the British People* (1849), pp. 210–13, 222–3.

Sensitivity to class distinction in the churches was growing in the 1840s. These two passages from Edward Miall's survey of British Christianity in 1849 form one of the more perceptive analyses of the problem.

But I am bound to say, that in watching the operations of our religious institutions, whenever I have endeavoured to put myself in the position of the humbler classes, and have asked myself, 'What is there here to interest such?' I have been at a loss for a reply. I do not arraign architectural magnificence—we cannot, indeed, boast much of it outside of the Establishment—for in continental countries I am not aware that it discourages the humblest worshipper. But here, in Great Britain, we carry our class distinctions into the house of God, whether the edifice be a splendid monument of art, or whether it be nothing superior to a barn. The poor man is made to feel that he is a poor man, the rich is reminded that he is rich, in the great majority of our churches and chapels. The square pew, carpeted, perhaps and curtained, the graduated scale of other pews, the free-sittings, if there are any, keep up the separation between class and class; and even where the meanly-clad are not conscious of intrusion, as is sometimes painfully the case, the arrangements are generally such as to preclude in their bosoms any momentary feeling of essential equality. We have no negro pews, for we have no prejudice against colour—but we have distinct places for the pennyless, for we have a morbid horror of poverty. Into a temple of worship thus mapped out for varying grades of worshippers, in which the lowly and the unfortunate are forbidden to lose sight of their worldly circumstances, some such, spite of all discouragements, find their way. In the singing, it may be, they can join, and mingle their voices and their sympathies with those around them—unless, indeed, the more respectable tenants of the pews, deeming it ill-bred to let themselves be heard, leave the psalmody to the Sunday-school children, and the vulgar. Possibly, their emotions may be elicited by prayer—seldom, we should think, by the discourse. It may be excellent, persuasive, pungent—but, in multitudes of cases, it will also be cast in a mould which none but the educated can appreciate. Let it not be said that this is owing exclusively to their ignorance. 'The common people heard' our Lord 'gladly'—the early reformers won their way to the inmost hearts of the lowliest of men—and even those who in our day are judged to be too uncultured to profit by the ministry of God's word from the pulpit, are sufficiently intelligent to derive interest from a public political meeting, to appreciate the points of a speech from the hustings, and to feel the force of an argument when put to them in private. . . . It is the entire absence of coloquialism from the discourse—an absence imposed upon the speaker by that sense of propriety which the aristocratic sentiment engenders. The etiquette of preaching prescribes an exclusively didactic style—and an address, the aim of which is to save souls, is supposed to approximate towards perfection, in proportion as it is free from conversational blemishes and inaccuracies, satisfies a fastidious and classical taste, and flows on in one unbroken stream from its commence-ment to its close. The consequence is, that whilst some few are pleased, and perhaps, profited, the mass remain utterly untouched. Oh! for some revolution to break down for ever, and scatter to the four winds of heaven, our pulpit formulas and proprieties, and leave men at liberty to discourse on the sublime verities of the Christian faith, with the same freedom, variety, and naturalness, with which they would treat other subjects in other places! The service concludes, and the worshippers retire. Communion with God has not disposed them to communion with each other, beyond the well-defined boundaries of class. The banker or the merchant pays no more attention to the sm tradesman, or the tradesman to the labourer, in the sanctuary than out of it. All is artificial and conventional there as elsewhere. The distinctions which obtain in the world, and which do little to improve it, obtain likewise in the Church, and are preserved with the same unyielding tenacity. And every arrangement appears to have been conceived upon a principle precisely identical with that denounced with such severity by the Apostle James. . . .

There are few, I should imagine, who will controvert the statement, that religious profession, and respect for the public means of grace, are far more common amongst, and characteristic of, the middle, than the labouring classes, in Great Britain. The bulk of our manufacturing population stand aloof from our Christian institutions. An immense majority of those who in childhood attend our Sabbath schools, neglect, throughout the period of manhood, all our ordinary appliances of spiritual instruction and culture. When disease creeps upon them, or death looks them in the face, early association may have power enough over many to induce them to send for a minister of the gospel, and request his conversation and his prayers. But evidence is abundant and conclusive that they generally pass through the prime of life, and too frequently reach its appointed term, without being even momentarily attracted, and without being in the slightest degree interested, by what the Churches of Christ are doing in their respective neighbourhoods. The operatives of these realms, taken as a body, and the still more numerous class whose employment is less regular, and whose temporal prospects are still more discouraging and precarious, must be described as living beyond even occasional contact with the institutions of Christian faith and worship. They feel no sympathy with them— they evince no respect for them. Their views, their tastes, their habits, their pursuits, if influenced at all by Divine revelation, are influenced only by its extremely indirect and reflex power.

55 Mormonism in England, 1849

An extract from Mrs T. B. H. Stenhouse, *An Englishwoman in Utah* (1880), pp. 11–13.

Descriptions of Mormonism in England during its early flourishing period from the early 1840s to the mid-1850s are rare. Mrs Stenhouse's account is therefore particularly interesting, even though it is written from the point of view of one who renounced Mormonism eventually because of polygamy. This extract describes the atmosphere of Mormon worship, which was probably similar to that in many working-class religious groups.

I shall never forget the trial it was to my pride to enter the dirty, mean looking room where the Saints assembled at that time. No one would rent a respectable hall to them, and they were glad to obtain the use of any place which was large enough for their meetings. On the present occasion there was a very fair gathering of people, who had come together influenced by the most varied motives. The Presiding Elder . . . called the meeting to order, and read the following hymn:

> The morning breaks, the shadows flee;
> Lo! Zion's standard is unfurl'd!
> The dawning of a brighter day
> Majestic rises on the world.

> The clouds of error disappear
> Before the rays of truth divine;
> The glory bursting from afar,
> Wide o'er the nations soon will shine!

> The Gentile fulness now comes in,
> And Israel's blessings are at hand;
> Lo! Judah's remnant, cleansed from sin,
> Shall in the promised Caanan stand.

> Angels from heaven and truth from earth
> Have met, and both have record borne;
> Thus Zion's light is bursting forth
> To bring her ransom'd children home.

Every word of this hymn had a meaning peculiar to itself, relating to the distinctive doctrines of the Saints. The congregation sang with an energy and enthusiasm which made the room shake again. Self and the outer world were alike forgotten, and an ecstasy of rapture seemed to possess the souls of all present. Then all kneeled down, and prayer was offered for the Prophet, the apostles, high-priests, 'seventies', elders, priests, teachers, and deacons; blessings were invoked upon the Saints, and power to convert the Gentiles; and as the earnest words of supplication left the speaker's lips, the congregation shouted a loud 'Amen'.

There was no prepared sermon. There never is at a Mormon meeting. The people are taught that the Holy Ghost is 'mouth, matter, and wisdom'. Whatever the preaching Elder may say is supposed to come directly by inspiration from heaven, and the Saints listening, as they believe, not to his utterances but to the words of God Himself, have nothing to do but to hear and obey.

The first speaker on this occasion was a young gentleman of respectable family, who had been recently baptized and ordained. . . . He spoke of the joy which he had experienced in being baptized into the Mormon Church and realizing that he had received the 'gift of the Holy Ghost'. The simplicity with which he spoke, his evident honesty, and the sacrifices he had made in leaving the respectable Baptists and joining the despised Mormons, were, I thought, so many evidences of his sincerity. . . .

56   Mormonism and Methodism, 1849

An extract from Mrs T. B. H. Stenhouse, *An Englishwoman in Utah* (1880), pp. 20–1.

The secret of the success of the Mormons was probably nothing more than that in their revival methods they were indistinguishable from other Nonconformist denominations. Mrs Stenhouse's description may be compared with Joseph Barker's description of revivalism in Sheffield in the Methodist New Connexion (document 35). In 1852 the Mormons claimed to have fifty conferences, 700 organised branches and 6,000 men ordained to the priesthood.[15]

At the time of which I speak, the Primitive Methodists in England were doing a great work in the way of converting sinners. Their missionaries were zealous and devoted men, though generally poor and uneducated. They resembled very closely the Mormon elders in their labours; and, in fact, a very large number of the leading Mormons had been Methodist local-preachers and exhorters; and the greater number of the new-born Saints had come from that denomination with their former teachers, or else had followed them soon after.

The change from Methodist to Mormon, was, in course of time, very strongly marked; but for a considerable period the same, or what seemed the same, influences were at work among the people. Remarkable scenes of excitement were often witnessed at the 'love feasts'; and from the 'anxious seats', as they were called, might be heard, the entreaties of self-accusing souls, frightened by a multitude of sins, crying earnestly, nay, wildly, for grace, mercy, and the Holy Ghost; while many of the supplicants would fall upon the ground, completely overcome by nervous excitement. Then they would have visions, and beheld great and unutterable things; received the forgiveness of their sins; and, coming back to consciousness, believed themselves now to be the children of God, and new creatures; doubting not that they would ever after be happy in the Lord. . . .

The Mormon Missionary often came upon whole communities in the rural districts of England, where this 'good time', was in full operation; and being a man of texts he would follow up the revival, preaching that the spirit of the the prophet was subject to the prophet, and not the prophet subject to the spirit. Controversy would arise, and his appeal to Scripture, literally interpreted, was almost invariably triumphant.

57 Report of the Census of Religious Worship, 1851

Extracts from the *Report of the Census of Religious Worship, 1851*: H.C. 1852–53, lxxxix, pp. cxliii–cxlvi, cxlviii, clvi–clviii, clxiv–clxv.

The report on the census of religious worship was prepared by Horace Mann, a young barrister in the Registrar-General's office. It is the only comprehensive source of religious statistics for all denominations in England and Wales in the nineteenth century, and was based on a count of all those attending worship on 30 March 1851, together with averages for the preceding six months. The extracts here refer to the regional distribution of the Nonconformist denominations, their progress in the first half of the century, the estimated total numbers of attendants (figures which are disputable in detail but useful in giving orders of magnitude) and the attempts of Nonconformists to reach the working classes.

The most numerous religious bodies, next to the Established Church, are the Wesleyan Methodists, the Independents or Congregationalists, and the Baptists. The first and the last of these denominations are respectively dispersed into several sections; but the Independents form a compact and undivided body. If we consider the Wesleyans and the Baptists in their aggregate combined capacity, the three denominations

F

will contribute each as follows towards the general religious accommodation of the country:

	Places of Worship	Sittings
Wesleyan Methodists	11,007	2,194,298
Independents	3,244	1,067,760
Baptists	2,789	752,343

Many of these places of worship are, however, merely *parts* of buildings, rooms in houses used as mission stations in poor neighbourhoods unable to support a regular chapel. The number mentioned in the return as 'not separate buildings' is,—Wesleyan Methodists, 2,155; Independents, 284; and Baptists, 304; but there seems to be some reasons for conjecturing that these are under-statements, that the number of 'separate and entire' religious edifices has been somewhat exaggerated, and the number of rooms, etc. correspondingly reduced. The WESLEYAN METHODISTS are found in greatest force in *Cornwall, Yorkshire, Lincolnshire, Derbyshire, Durham*, and *Nottinghamshire*; their fewest numbers are in *Middlesex, Surrey, Sussex, Essex, Warwickshire* and *Hertfordshire*. The INDEPENDENTS flourish most in *South Wales, North Wales, Essex, Dorsetshire, Monmouthshire*, and *Suffolk*; least in *Northumberland, Durham, Herefordshire*, and *Worcestershire*. The BAPTISTS are strongest in *Monmouthshire, South Wales, Huntingdonshire, Bedfordshire, Northamptonshire, Leicestershire*, and *Buckinghamshire*; weakest in *Cumberland, Northumberland, Westmorland, Cornwall, Staffordshire*, and *Lancashire*.

The following statement, derived from the column of *dates*, will show, as far as can be gathered from that source, the rate at which each body has progressed in the present century. But great reliance cannot safely be reposed in inferences from dates in the case of dissenting places of worship, since a certain number (merely rooms) have undoubtedly, though only occupied in *recent* years for religious purposes, been returned with the date of their erection—not that of their first appropriation to such uses. . . . Subject to whatever reservation may be thought essential, Table 17, will display the progress of these three bodies since 1801.

From this it appears that neither of these bodies is advancing at a rate so rapid as formerly. But then it must also be remembered, that neither is there *room* for such a rapid increase, since the aggregate rate of increase during the half century has been so much more rapid than the increase of the population that whereas, in 1801, the number of

TABLE 17

RATE of INCREASE, in Decennial Periods, of the WESLEYAN METHODISTS, INDEPENDENTS, and BAPTISTS respectively, in the whole of ENGLAND and WALES

PERIODS	WESLEYAN METHODISTS (All branches)			INDEPENDENTS			BAPTISTS (All branches)		
	Number of Places of Worship and Sittings at each Period		Rate of Increase per cent at each Period	Number of Places of Worship and Sittings at each Period		Rate of Increase per cent at each Period	Number of Places of Worship and Sittings at each Period		Rate of Increase per cent at each Period
	Places of Worship	Sittings		Places of Worship	Sittings		Places of Worship	Sittings	
1801	825	165,000	—	914	299,792	—	652	176,692	—
1811	1,485	296,000	80·0	1,140	373,920	24·7	858	232,518	31·6
1821	2,748	549,600	85·0	1,478	484,784	29·2	1,170	317,070	36·4
1831	4,622	924,400	68·2	1,999	655,672	35·2	1,613	437,123	37·9
1841	7,819	1,563,800	69·2	2,606	854,768	30·4	2,174	589,154	34·7
1851	11,007	2,194,298	40·3	3,244	1,067,760	24·9	2,789	723,343	27·7

sittings provided for every 1,000 persons was—by Wesleyans 18, by Independents 34 and by Baptists 20; in 1851, the provision was—by Wesleyans 123, by Independents 59, and by Baptists 42.

We have seen how far the Christian churches generally and the Church of England in particular provide for the religious teaching of the masses in large towns. A similar view of the achievement of the three important bodies named above is presented in Table (18). . . . Next to these three denominations of Dissenters come, in the order of magnitude, the *Calvinistic Methodists*, divided into two classes, the Welsh and the English—the latter being known as the *Countess of Huntingdon's Connexion*. Together they supply 250,678 sittings, mostly in Wales. The remaining Protestant sects thus range themselves:

	Places of Worship	Sittings
Society of Friends	371	91,559
Scottish Presbyterians	160	86,692
Unitarians	229	68,554
Brethren	132	18,529
New Church	50	12,107
Moravians	32	9,305
Sandemanians	6	956
Reformed Irish Presbyterians	1	120

And then a great crowd of what are called, for want of a better term, 'Isolated Congregations,' refusing to acknowledge connexion with any particular sect, make up together as many as 539 places of worship with 104,481 sittings.

In the aggregate, the Protestant Dissenting churches of England provide accommodation for 4,657,422 persons, or for 26 per cent of the population and 45·6 per cent of the aggregate provision of the country. The proportion of this accommodation which is *available* at each period of the day is—*morning*, 3,428,665 sittings; *afternoon*, 2,367,379 sittings; *evening*, 3,855,394 sittings; making a total, at all three portions of the day, of 9,651,438 sittings; . . .

The only other prominent sect which appears to possess a noticeable degree of influence, is the 'Church of the Latter Day Saints,' known better by the name of *Mormons*. Within the short period since the introduction of this singular creed, as many as 222 chapels or stations have been established, with accommodation for 30,783 worshippers or hearers. The activity of the disciples of this faith is evidenced by the frequency with which they occupy these meeting places; out of the

TABLE 18

COMPARATIVE VIEW of the ACCOMMODATION in Rural and Large Town Districts, provided by the WESLEYAN METHODISTS, INDEPENDENTS, and BAPTISTS respectively

	WESLEYAN METHODISTS			INDEPENDENTS			BAPTISTS		
	Number of Places of Worship and Sittings		Proportion per cent of Sittings to Population	Number of Places of Worship and Sittings		Proportion per cent of Sittings to Population	Number of Places of Worship and Sittings		Proportion per cent of Sittings to Population
	Places of Worship	Sittings		Places of Worship	Sittings		Places of Worship	Sittings	
Large Town Districts	3,050	896,372	9·7	936	454,729	4·9	839	318,013	3·5
Country Districts	7,957	1,297,926	14·9	2,308	613,031	7·1	1,950	434,330	5·0
England and Wales	11,007	2,194,298	12·2	3,244	1,067,760	6·0	2,789	752,343	4·2

TABLE 23

Estimated Total Number of Attendants

	Estimated Total Number of Attendants	Proportion per 1000 Of the Population	Proportion per 1000 Of the Number of Attendants of all Denominations
PROTESTANT CHURCHES			
Church of England	3,773,474	210	520
Scottish Presbyterians:			
Church of Scotland	8,712	1	1
United Presbyterian Church	23,207	1	3
Presbyterian Church in England	28,212	2	4
Independents	793,142	44	109
Baptists:			
General	12,323	1	2
Particular	471,283	26	65
Seventh Day	52	—	—
Scotch	1,246	—	—
New Connexion General	40,027	2	5
Undefined	63,047	4	9

	Estimated Total Number of Attendants	Proportion per 1000 Of the Population	Proportion per 1000 Of the Number of Attendants of all Denominations
PROTESTANT CHURCHES (continued)			
Sandemanians	587	—	—
New Church	7,082	—	1
Brethren	10,414	1	1
Isolated Congregations	63,572	4	9
Lutherans	1,284	—	—
French Protestants	291	—	—
Reformed Church of the Netherlands	70	—	—
German Protestant Reformers	140	—	—

	Attendants		
Society of Friends	18,172	1	3
Unitarians	37,156	2	5
Moravians	7,364	1	1
Wesleyan Methodists:			
Original Connexion	907,313	51	125
New Connexions	61,319	3	8
Primitive	266,555	15	37
Bible Christian	38,612	2	5
Wesleyan Association	56,430	3	8
Independent Methodists	1,659	—	—
Wesleyan Reformers	53,494	3	7
Calvinistic Methodists:			
Welsh Calvinistic Methodists	151,046	8	21
Lady Huntingdon's Connexion	29,679	2	4
OTHER CHRISTIAN CHURCHES			
Roman Catholics	305,393	17	42
Greek Church	240	—	—
German Catholics	567	—	—
Italian Reformers	20	—	—
Catholic and Apostolic Church	4,908	—	1
Latter Day Saints	18,800	1	3
Jews	4,150	—	1
Estimated Total Number of Attendants:	7,261,032	405	1000

total number of 222, as many as 147 (or 66 per cent) were open in the morning, 187 (or 84 per cent) were open in the afternoon, and 193 (or 87 per cent) were open in the evening. Comparison with similar statistics of the other churches will show that this is much above the average frequency of services. . . .

Of the total existing number of 10,212,563 sittings, the Church of England contributes 5,317,915, and the other churches, together 4,894,648. . . . [For estimated numbers of attendants, see Table 23.]

With reference to the particular periods of the day preferred by different bodies . . . the members of the Church of England choose the earlier, while the members of the principal dissenting churches choose the later portion of the Sunday for attendance at religious worship. Thus, while the number of sittings out of every 100 occupied by the former is 48 in the morning, 36 in the afternoon, and only 16 in the evening; the number, out of every 100, occupied by the other Protestant Churches in the aggregate, is 40 in the morning, 26 in the afternoon, and 45 in the evening. This fact exhibits strikingly the different social habits of the members of these bodies; and, even if we did not know as much already, would suffice to prove their difference of social station.

It must not be overlooked, when considering the amount of *afternoon* attendance, that, amongst Dissenters more especially, that period is occupied to very great extent by *Sunday-school instruction*. Of the number of children thus instructed at this portion of the day we have no account, but as the total number of Sunday Scholars in attendance every Sunday is as many as 1,800,000, the number present every Sunday afternoon must be considerable. The religious knowledge thus administered to children is by no means ineffective; probably, indeed, this mode of spiritual teaching is far better suited to a child's capacity than is the more elaborate service of the church or chapel. . . .

By the various Protestant Dissenting churches too, the question of the readiest way to reach the working classes has of late had much attention. Lectures, specially addressed to them, and services conducted in the public halls or rooms with which they are familiar and to which they will resort without objection though deterred from church or chapel, are (as we have seen) amongst the means adopted to attract them to religious habits. In these various operations lay exertion is of course encouraged, but—excepting by the Methodists, with whom it has been long adopted to the utmost—not to that extent which, from the views which most Dissenting bodies entertain upon the subject of the ministerial office, might have been expected. The Independents and the

Baptists have each a 'Home Missionary Society'; and the members of these bodies aid in supporting such undenominational societies as the 'London City Mission'. But the amount of lay exertion proceeding from individual churches (congregations), though considerable, is much less, especially in large towns, than might, from their professed opinions on the nature of the Christian ministry have been anticipated. . . .

At present, the grand employers of lay agency, amongst Dissenters, are the Methodists, who, in the aggregate, possess perhaps as many as 20,000 preachers and class leaders not belonging to the ministerial order. Nothing, probably, has more contributed than this to their success amongst the working population. The community whose operations penetrate most deeply through the lower sections of the people is the body called the *Primitive Methodists*; whose trespasses against what may be thought a proper order will most likely be forgiven when it is remembered that perhaps their rough, unformal energy is best adapted to the class to which it is addressed, and that, at all events, for every convert added to their ranks, society retains one criminal, one drunkard, one improvident the less.

58   The Braintree Church Rates case, 1852

An extract from the evidence of Stephen Lushington, D.C.L., to the House of Lords' Select Committee on Church Rates: *H.C. 1859, Sess. 2,* v, pp. 175–6.

The Braintree case (1837–52) was the most famous case in the Church Rates battle and arose out of a disputed rate at Braintree, Essex. The churchwardens, frustrated by their inability to gain the vestry's support for a rate, had levied one on their own authority. The case went through a number of courts and eventually to the House of Lords where in 1852 the original decision of Judge Lushington in the Consistory Court, that a majority of the vestry had to approve any rate, was upheld. This decision effectively ended Church Rates in all parishes where there was a large number of Dissenters. Lushington here gives an account of the case to a House of Lords committee in July 1859.

1442   ... In the Braintree case the majority refused the rate, and the churchwardens made a rate of their own authority. I believe that there were some parishioners who joined them, but they were a minority. The churchwardens made a rate of their own authority, and that was the contest that came originally before me, sitting as Judge of the Consistory Court.

1443   Upon what authority did the churchwardens conceive themselves entitled to make a rate in opposition to the vestry?
     I believe, it was upon the advice of some gentleman at the bar. I do not know upon whose.

1444   How did you decide that case when it came before you?
     When it first came before me—it has gone through a great many stages—upon the strength of the case of Gordon v. Selby, I allowed what we call the admission of the libel pleading the rate. I held it *prima facie* to be valid; but I did it upon the authority of Gordon v. Selby,

which was a case in the Arches, and the Arches being a superior Court, governed my judgement; but I doubted exceedingly the law at the time. The case afterwards went to the Court of Queen's Bench and the Court of Queen's Bench unanimously pronounced against the rate so made. Then they brought the matter back again in another shape, and then I followed the doctrine of the Court of Queen's Bench, upon which it went to Sir Herbert Jenner, who went the other way. Then it went to the Court of Queen's Bench again, and they changed their opinion. It then went to the Court of Exchequer Chamber, and eventually to the House of Lords.

1445 The decision of the House of Lords, I believe, coincided with your judgement in the first instance?
Yes.

1446 What is the effect of that judgement in the present state of the law?
The effect of that judgement would be, that it would be impossible to enforce any rate made by the churchwardens, such rate having been refused by the parish.

59 A hostile view of Quakers, 1855

An extract from A. Tennyson, *Maud* (1855), lines 366–81.

Several of Tennyson's poems in the early 1850s attack the 'peace at any price' school associated with Richard Cobden and John Bright. The *Westminster Review* said that this stanza in *Maud* was an attack on Bright, but Tennyson said that he did not realise Bright was a Quaker.[16] Bright's campaign against the Crimean War was not popular.

> Last week came one to the county town,
> To preach our poor little army down,
> And play the game of the despot kings,

Though the state has done it and thrice as well:
This broad-brimmed hawker of holy things,
Whose ear is crammed with his cotton, and rings
Even in dreams to the chink of his pence,
This huckster put down war! can he tell
Whether war be a cause or a consequence?
Put down the passions that make earth Hell!
Down with ambition, avarice, pride,
Jealousy, down! cut off from the mind
The bitter springs of anger and fear;
Down too, down at your own fireside,
With the evil tongue and the evil ear,
For each is at war with mankind.

60   Spurgeon at the Surrey Gardens, 1856

Two extracts from *C. H. Spurgeon's Autobiography by His Wife and His Private Secretary* (1897–8), ii, pp. 204–6.

Charles Spurgeon arrived in London as an unknown Baptist preacher in 1853. While his chapel was being enlarged he preached at Exeter Hall, and when this proved too small he hired the largest public amusement hall in London, the Surrey Gardens music hall. During the first meeting there was a panic rush for the doors in which seven people were killed and twenty-eight injured. From this point onwards Spurgeon was a controversial public figure. The first extract is from a description by Dr Alexander Fletcher, and the second is the sermon, as far as Spurgeon preached it.

a.

As early as five o'clock, thousands of persons were filling up the approaches to the Surrey Gardens. By five minutes after six, the hall was filled to overflow; it is supposed that not fewer than 12,000 persons were present, and many thousands were on the outside, and still as many more were unable to gain admittance even to the Gardens. While the service was being conducted in Mr. Spurgeon's usual way, during the second prayer, all of a sudden there were cries simultaneously, doubtless preconcerted, from all parts of the building, of 'Fire!' 'The galleries are giving way!' 'The place is falling!' the effect of which on the audience it is impossible to describe. Many hundreds of persons rushed towards the place of exit, at the risk of their own lives, and sacrificing those of their fellow-creatures. In vain did Mr. Spurgeon, with his stentorian voice and self-possession, assure the alarmed multitude that it was a *ruse* on the part of thieves and pickpockets; the people in the galleries rushed down, precipitating themselves almost headlong over, or breaking down the balustrade of the stairs, killing some and fearfully wounding others. Those who fell through force, or fainting, were trampled under foot, and several lives were lost in the *mêlée*. To make 'confusion worse confounded', it is also said that, as fast as one portion of the multitude made their exit, others from without entered. Mr Spurgeon, who was ignorant of any of these fatal consequences, after a temporary lull, was persuaded to make an effort to preach; but, after one or two attempts, he found it impossible to proceed, owing to the noises which the swell-mobsmen continued to make. Wishing to get the people gradually out of the hall, he gave out a hymn, requesting the congregation to withdraw while it was being sung. He then pronounced the Benediction, and, at length, overcome by emotion, which he had long striven to repress, he was led from the platform in a state of apparent insensibility. The results of this dreadful panic are most calamitous and distressing. Seven lives have been sacrificed, and serious bodily injury inflicted upon a great number of persons.

b.

My friends, you bid me preach, but what shall I preach about? I am ready to do all I can, but, in the midst of all this confusion, what shall be my subject? May God's Holy Spirit give me a theme suited to this solemn occasion! My friends, there is a terrible day coming, when the terror and alarm of this evening shall be as nothing. That will be a time when the thunder and lightning and blackest darkness shall have their fullest power, when the earth shall reel to and fro beneath us, and when the arches of the solid heavens shall totter to their centre. The day is coming, when the clouds shall reveal their wonders and portents, and Christ shall sit upon those clouds in glory, and shall call you to judgment. Many have gone away to-night, in the midst of this terrible confusion, and so shall it be on that great day. I can, however, believe that the results of that time of testing will show that there will be many—not a less proportion than those who now remain to those who have left—who will stand the ordeal even of that day. The alarm which has just arisen has been produced, in some measure, by that instinct which teaches us to seek self-preservation, but in the more numerous of the cases, it is not so much the dread of death which has influenced them, as 'the dread of something after death—the undiscovered country, from whose bourn no traveller returns'. 'Tis conscience that has made cowards of them. Many were afraid to stop here, because they thought, if they stayed, they might die, and then they would be damned. They were aware—and many of you are aware—that, if you were hurried before your Maker to-night, you would be brought there unshriven, unpardoned, and condemned. But what are your fears now to what they will be on that terrible day of reckoning of the Almighty, when the heavens shall shrink above you, and hell shall open her mouth beneath you? But know you not, my friends, that grace, sovereign grace, can yet save you? Have you never heard the welcome news that Jesus came into the world to save sinners? Even if you are the chief of sinners, believe that Christ died for you, and you shall be saved. Do you not know that you are lost and ruined, and that none but Jesus can do helpless sinners good? You are sick and diseased, but Jesus can heal you; and He will if you only trust Him. I thought of preaching to-night from the third chapter of Proverbs, at the 33rd verse: 'The curse of the Lord is in the house of the wicked: but He blesseth the habitation of the just.' I feel that, after what has happened, I cannot preach as I could have wished to do; I fear that you will have another alarm, and I would rather that some of you would seek to retire gradually, in order that no harm may be done to anyone.

61   The attraction of Dissent, 1858

An extract from the evidence of the Rev. T. F. Stooks, secretary of the London Church Building Society, to the House of Lords Select Committee on 'The Deficiency of Means of Spiritual Instruction . . .': *H.C. 1857–8*, ix, p. 95.

The Nonconformist denominations offered more scope for ordinary people to take part in the life of the Church than the Church of England. This point is made here by an Anglican minister as one of the reasons for the attraction of Dissent to such people.

837 Do you happen to know whether in dissenting chapels the charges for the seats are much higher than for the Church of England sittings?
—I believe they are as high.

838 Then to what do you ascribe the readiness with which those sittings are often taken when those in the Church of England are not?
—I think one reason is that they have more offices in the dissenting chapels; they have deaconships and visitors, and tract distributors: and in these ways the dissenting chapels manage to employ their people very much better than the church in general does. This is an attraction to small shopkeepers and mechanics, who find that they are looked upon as somebody in their congregations, and they are not an unheard of unit as they are in the church congregations.

62   Nonconformist migrations, 1859

An extract from the evidence of the Rev. A. Hume to the House of
Lords Select Committee on Church Rates: *H.C. 1859, Sess. 2*, v,
pp. 155–6.

One of the strongest defences of Church Rates was the obligation of
the Church of England to maintain its parish churches whether the
parish was rich or poor: Nonconformists, on the other hand, were
free (and sometimes forced) to leave the poor areas when the
wealthier supporters migrated. The Rev. A. Hume of Liverpool was
a notable exponent of this view, and in this extract combines a
defence of Church Rates with a vigorous attack on Dissenters for
their desertion of the poor.

1282   . . . When a district becomes poor, the Dissenting congregation
generally migrates; the chapel is given up, and it is replaced in a better
district of the town. In my pamphlet I mention nine Dissenting chapels
which have occupied 26 different sites. That is to say, there have been
17 migrations; whereas, a church is a permanent building for various
grades of the population, and when all the richer part of the population
leave the neighbourhood it is left finally surrounded by paupers, for
whom it should still make provision.

1283 [Lord Bishop of *London*]   Do you consider that Dissent as a
system is able to supply the wants of a poor population, and to act in
that Missionary character which you say the Church is obliged to
assume in the poorer neighbourhoods?
    Dissent, as a system, does not supply the poorer classes. It supplies
the middle classes; sometimes the better portion of the middle classes,
but more usually the lower section of the middle classes. In all our large
hives of industry in England the action of Dissent, jointly with that of
the Church, has utterly failed to evangelise the people; and it has come
to this that, in several instances, the non-worshipping community quite
outnumbers the worshipping community of all kinds.

1284 [*Chairman*]   So that, in fact, one of the chief reasons for the maintenance of church rates is in order to enable the Church of England to meet the wants of the poorer part of the population?

Yes; I put it almost exclusively on Missionary grounds. The abandonment of church rates is the abandonment of the poor.

63   The causes of Quaker decline, 1859

An extract from J. S. Rowntree, *Quakerism; Past and Present* (1859), pp. 27–8, 30–1, 174–6, 180–3, 185.

The Quakers continued to decline in numbers throughout the nineteenth century. In the later 1850s a prize was offered for the best essay on the subject which was won by J. S. Rowntree, a leading evangelical Friend. He stressed the Quaker peculiarities, their lack of evangelical character, but most of all their marriage policy in giving his explanations.

We believe the peculiar form of public worship adopted by the Friends has not a little to do with their declining numbers. In the desire to abstain from all 'forms', they meet together for the purpose of public worship in silence, and should no minister be present (now often the case in many meetings) not a word will be spoken, and the worshippers, after sitting an hour or two in silence, disperse. . . . There will be few spiritually minded men of any persuasion, who will affirm that true worship may not be rendered to Almighty God in meetings conducted in this manner; and that it is so rendered, the experience of the Friends for two hundred years warrants us in affirming. . . .

The mistake of the 'early Friends' was, we apprehend, that of supposing that the one form of worship which corresponded most closely, in their judgment, with the spiritual nature of this exercise, was the only one acceptable to God, or worthy the adoption of his Church; whereas . . . more truly would they have advanced the cause of spiritual religion in the world, by uniting the practice of silent worship with those other arrangements which, though not worship itself, do at times prepare the way for it; as the audible reading of Holy Scripture, the teaching of Christian truth, etc.; not now to recount the arguments which may be adduced on behalf of congregational singing. . . .

The contracted, legal use of the Scriptures by the Puritans, explains why the 'early Friends', deeply conversant with the sacred volume themselves, and constantly appealing to it, were yet so jealous in maintaining its inferiority 'to the Spirit that gave it forth'; and though this mode of speaking might be harmless to them and not without its use to their Puritan opponents, yet, when it became part of a traditional phraseology—when the Bible was not read in meetings for worship, nor regularly in the domestic circle—the consequences, by allowing a wide-spread ignorance of scriptural truth, were most hurtful to the growth of vital religion. . . .

We unite in the opinion expressed by writers of that period, that to the want of careful religious education, much of the loss of members in the eighteenth century may be attributed. In the present century education has been greatly improved in quality, and extended in amount, and we drew attention to the economic facts, that this diffusion of intelligence had lessened the number of poor, stimulated the emigration of young men from the agricultural districts, diminished the frequency of marriage, and the consequent frequency of births; and had thus, whilst conferring immense benefit on the Society at large, been the unlooked for cause of lessening its numerical strength. . . .

Great numbers of disownments took place between 1760 and 1780; some for acts of flagrant immorality, but many others for breaches of the Society's 'testimonies', for the payment of tithes, for marriage 'contrary to rule', etc., acts not immoral, and not even necessarily errors of judgment. From the period now under review, the Society of Friends has occupied a more contracted and a more sectarian basis, and its 'testimonies' have been negative rather than positive. The renovators of 1760 . . . created a public opinion which enforced conformity to a costume in dress and to the use of a set phraseology—'peculiarities' which, having originated in the endeavour to maintain those legitimate requirements of religion, simplicity in dress and truthfulness of language, degenerated into agents for maintaining an ascetic isolation from the rest of mankind.

Much spiritual loss, we apprehend, was sustained in many districts, during the eighteenth century, from the great doctrine of Justification by faith in Christ being inadequately set forth; and in a previous page of this volume, it has been stated that the gloomy, mystical view of religion not unfrequently presented to the young, coupled with unreasonable requirements respecting matters of behaviour and attire, had alienated the affections of many young persons from the Society of Friends, and induced them to leave it on attaining years of maturity. But the most influential of the *proximate* causes of decay, mainly introduced into the Society's practice in the middle of last century, were its marriage regulations. . . . As the Friends declined in numbers, and as merely nominal members were retained amongst them, it became increasingly difficult to confine marriage within their own limits. . . . Within a considerable portion of the present century, the Society of Friends in England has disowned nearly one-third of all its members who have married, a total of not less than four thousand persons! From this and other causes already referred to, marriage has become increasingly rare; and not merely has the Society lost its four thousand adult members, but their removal has occasioned the deaths to exceed the births, so that while in the general population of England there have been since 1810 three births to every two deaths, in the Society of Friends during the same period the deaths have exceeded the births by two thousand four hundred. . . .

Whilst we are thus unable to say what proportion of decline is due to *this* cause, and what to *that*, the sum total of their effects can be accurately determined. Not merely can it be shown that there is now only one in every eleven hundred of the population of the United Kingdom professing with the Friends, and that there was once one in every one hundred and thirty, but we can also ascertain that in spite of the annually increasing population, the Friends are still declining at the rate of nearly one hundred per annum, and that the number of members in England, which in 1800 was about twenty thousand, is now reduced to less than fifteen thousand.

64   Description of believer's baptism, c. 1860

An extract from E. Gosse, *Father and Son* (1907), pp. 212–16.

A number of denominations as well as the Baptists practised believer's baptism by total immersion, instead of infant sprinkling: they included the Brethren, Churches of Christ and the Mormons. It is not easy to convey an impression of what it means to those who have not seen it, and descriptions are rare. This one comes from Edmund Gosse's account of his upbringing, *Father and Son*. Gosse was baptised as a member of the Brethren, and although he left them his description is a powerful one.

In the centre of the chapel-floor a number of planks had been taken up, and revealed a pool which might have been supposed to be a small swimming-bath. . . . The whole congregation was arranged, tier above tier, about the four straight sides of this pool; every person was able to see what happened in it without any unseemly struggling or standing on forms. . . .

Mr. S . . . proposed to the congregation a hymn, which was long enough to occupy them during the preparations for the actual baptism. He then retired to the vestry, and I (for I was to be the first to testify) was led by Miss Marks and Mary Grace into the species of tent of which I have just spoken. . . . Part of my clothing was removed and I was prepared for immersion. A sudden cessation of the hymn warned us that the Minister was now ready, and we emerged into the glare of lights and faces to find Mr. S. already standing in the water up to his knees. Feeling as small as one of our microscopical specimens, almost infinitesimally tiny as I descended into his Titanic arms, I was handed down the steps to him. He was dressed in a kind of long surplice, underneath which—as I could not, even in that moment, help observing—the air gathered in long bubbles which he strove to flatten out. The end of his noble beard he had tucked away; his shirt-sleeves were turned up at the wrist.

The entire congregation was now silent, so silent that the uncertain splashing of my feet as I descended seemed to deafen me. Mr. S., a little embarrassed by my short stature, succeeded at length in securing me with one palm on my chest and the other between my shoulders. He said slowly, in a loud, sonorous voice that seemed to enter my brain and empty it, 'I baptize thee, my Brother, in the name of the Father and of the Son and of the Holy Ghost!' Having intoned this formula; he then gently flung me backwards until I was wholly under the water, and then—as he brought me up again, and tenderly steadied my feet on the steps of the font, and delivered me, dripping and spluttering, into the anxious hands of the women, who hurried me to the tent—the whole assembly broke forth in a thunder of song, a paean of praise to God for this manifestation of his marvellous goodness and mercy.

65   A congregation of Brethren, c. 1860

An extract from E. Gosse, *Father and Son* (1907), pp. 139, 141–2.

As well as the established denominations there were a large number of small, independent congregations around the country, often consisting of quite humble folk. Some were Calvinists, others were the local followings of a particular preacher lasting only as long as the preacher was present: all were based on direct study of the Bible. In the second half of the century, some of these congregations associated in the smaller denominations. The largest of these was the Brethren, and this description is of a congregation in Devon.

Before our coming, a little flock of persons met in the Room, a community of the indefinite sort just then becoming frequent in the West of England, pious rustics connected with no other recognised body of Christians, and depending directly on the independent study of the Bible. They were largely women, but there was more than a sprinkling of men, poor, simple and generally sickly. In later days, under my Father's ministration, the body increased and positively flourished. It came to include retired professional men, an admiral, nay, even the brother of a peer. But in those earliest years the 'brethren', and 'sisters' were all of them ordinary peasants. They were jobbing gardeners, and journeymen carpenters, masons and tailors, washerwomen and domestic servants. . . .

My Father preached, standing at a desk; or celebrated the communion in front of a deal table, with a white napkin spread over it. Sometimes the audience was so small, generally so unexhilarating, that he was discouraged, but he never flagged in energy and zeal. Only those who had given evidence of intelligent acceptance of the theory of simple faith in their atonement through the Blood of Jesus were admitted to the communion, or, as it was called 'the Breaking of Bread'. It was made a very strong point that no one should 'break bread'—unless for good reason shown—until he or she had been baptized, that is to say, totally immersed, in solemn conclave, by the ministering brother. This rite used, in our earliest days, to be performed, with picturesque simplicity, in the sea on the Oddicombe beach, but to this there were, even in those quiet years, extreme objections. A jeering crowd could scarcely be avoided, and women, in particular, shrank from the ordeal. This used to be a practical difficulty, and my Father, when communicants confessed that they had not yet been baptized, would shake his head and say gravely, 'Ah! ah! you shun the Cross of Christ!' But that baptism in the sea on the open beach *was* a 'cross', he would not deny, and when we built our own little chapel, a sort of font, planked over, was arranged in the room itself.

66   Middle-class Nonconformity in the 1860s

An extract from A. Birrell, *Things Past Redress* (1937), p. 38.

Augustine Birrell, Liberal Member of Parliament and son of a
Baptist minister, was also brought up in a Baptist background, like
John Clifford (document 49). But his was a middle-class home in
Liverpool. His description does, however, illustrate the social gulf
which was fixed between Nonconformity and the Church of
England.

Things may have greatly changed since the sixties of the last century,
and must I am sure have done so, but in those days to have been born
a Nonconformist in England entailed many consequences of a 'separa-
tist' nature. Like Offa's dyke, it marked a boundary, hard to jump over.
Not only different places of worship—but different friends, different
schools, different books, different habits of life. The great public
schools, the Universities, Scholarships, Fellowships, etc. lay as much
out of the ordinary track of the Nonconformist as the Opera House in
Paris, or a Court Ball at the Palace of St. James, or other suchlike places.
The Church of England, at the time I have in mind, was not at its best
in Liverpool. The prevailing type was that of the Rev. Hugh McNeile,
afterwards Dean of Ripon, an Ulster Protestant, whilst the then Rector
of Liverpool was a mere Erastian not unsuspected of Simony. It is not
too much to say that in those days my Father, the Rev. Hugh Stowell
Brown (a brother of T. E. Brown, the man's poet), Dr Raffles, the
Rev. James Kelly and Dr Martineau, Father Nugent, to name no other
'Dissenters', were better representatives of Christian culture and
Christian zeal than any of the then Anglican Clergy; but it made no
difference—there the dyke was, broad, deep and practically impassable,
cutting clean through social life. The Unitarians, owing to their wealth,
mercantile positions and civic activity were somewhat differently
situated—but in their case their more obvious unorthodoxy still kept
them apart.

67   The mission of Congregationalists, 1861

An extract from Joshua Wilson's paper to the Congregational Union Assembly of 1861 on the bicentenary celebrations: *Congregational Year Book, 1861*, pp. 63–5.

Joshua Wilson was the energetic secretary of the Congregational Home Missionary Society. He was a wealthy layman and had a hand in most of the new projects of Congregationalism in the mid-nineteenth century. His paper to the Congregational Union Assembly of 1861 made a number of proposals for the celebration of the bicentenary of the Great Ejectment of 1662, the main one of which was for the building of one hundred new chapels.

It is unquestionable fact, that our strength as a denomination lies in the large cities and towns, as our special vocation is to the middle classes of the people, who form the chief portion of their inhabitants. . . .

Our watchword should now be 'London and the large towns!' If we act wisely, we shall strengthen our position in these, and by means chiefly of churches gathered *in them*, provide pecuniary means for the building of rural chapels, and for the supporting of evangelistic agencies to act on the village population and the small agricultural towns. I earnestly hope that the year 1862 will be signalized and rendered memorable by a great advance in the work of chapel-building. May we not expect that *one hundred* will be added to those now existing in England, Wales, and Ireland: fifty to be opened on or before the 24th of August, 1862, and the foundation-stones of fifty more to be laid on that day? I must, however, take leave to express my decided opinion, that of this total number, fifty, at least, should be erected in towns having a population of 5,000 and upwards, and the buildings be sufficiently capacious to furnish accommodation for from 600 to 800 adults. Nor, I submit, should many of the others be built in places of smaller population than 8,000, nor any of them of less dimensions than to be capable of seating 400 adults. . . .

While maintaining that our immediate and most pressing duty is to provide respectable chapels in large towns, I cannot refrain from asking—Have we not too much neglected the poor, who should have the Gospel preached to them, who need the consolations of religion most, and would open their hearts to receive the truth were it presented in a familiar and simple form, especially that most interesting class—the working men and their families? We have made very small provision for these in our town-chapels; would not it be a proper and becoming arrangement, in all the larger chapels that may be built next year, to leave the galleries free, only asking for free-will weekly contributions? And should we not, in the towns in which the working classes are very numerous, provide at least one plain, simple, but commodious building for their special use and benefit? . . .

68 The bicentenary of the Great Ejectment, 1862

An extract from J. Waddington, *Congregational History, 1850–1880* (1880), p. 374.

A central committee consisting mainly of Baptists and Congregationalists was formed to organise the commemoration of the bicentenary. An address was circulated over the names of Samuel Morley (chairman), S. Morton Peto (treasurer) and Samuel Cox (secretary). This extract shows the differences in belief that had developed over two hundred years.

For us, fellow-Dissenters, there are additional and special reasons for commemorating the Bicentenary of that event. True, suffering for conscience' sake is no uncommon fruit of the religion we profess; nor, unhappily, have eviction from the pulpits of the Church Establishment, the violent rupture of pastoral ties, and the sudden exposure of ministers of the Gospel to want, disabilities, and hardships been confined to one religious party. Equally true is it that the two thousand, although, for the most part, they bore testimony to Christian truths to which we attach importance, held views regarding the relation of the civil power to the Church which we deem irreconcilable with both the letter and the spirit of the New Testament. But it becomes us gratefully to acknowledge that the legacy they bequeathed us far transcends in worth their own estimate of it, and that the irresistible logic of their deeds swept away the fallacies and errors which adhered to their ecclesiastical policy. They vindicated for themselves the right of private judgment—the foundation of all the religious rights we possess or claim. They preserved from destruction the germ which, since their day, has expanded into the forms of beauty in which we take increasing pride. They handed to us, at the expense of all that they held dear, the sacred fire at which we kindle our lamps. We receive not our opinions from them—but we do recognize in their united confession one of the grandest illustrations contained in history of the singular unsuitableness of secular authority and power as an agency for building up the Church of the living God, and of the all-conquering might of simple truthfulness and godliness as weapons wielded for spiritual ends. If Dissent may be rightly regarded as the protest of religious Individualism against Multitudinism, we, as Dissenters, have abundant reasons for a thankful commemoration of Sunday, August the 24th, 1662—when that protest was so solemnly and impressively given in to the ruling powers of this country.

69 A Nonconformist deacon defends the minister against the congregation, 1862

An extract from Mrs M. O. W. Oliphant, *Salem Chapel* (1863), chapter XXXVI.

Mrs Oliphant's novel is a good evocation of Nonconformist life in mid-century, despite one or two lapses (e.g., the use of 'the connection' in a supposedly Congregational chapel). The story is somewhat sensational, but the defence of the minister (Mr Vincent) by one of the deacons (Mr Tozer) contains several home truths about the kind of attitudes found in many congregations.

'My friends, the pastor as is the subject of this meeting'—here Tozer sank his voice and looked around with a certain solemnity—'Mr Vincent, ladies and gentlemen, as has doubled the seatholders in Salem in six months' work, and I make bold to say, brought one-half of you as is here to be regular at chapel, and take an interest in the connection —Mr Vincent, I say, as you're all collected here to knock down in the dark, if so be as you are willing to be dictated to—the same, ladies and gentlemen, as we're a-discussing of to-night—told us all, it ain't so very long ago, in the crowdedest meeting as I ever see, in the biggest public hall in Carlingford—as we weren't keeping up to the standard of the old Nonconformists, nor showing, as we ought, what a voluntary church could do. . . . Now, I ask you, ladies and gentlemen, what is the reason? It's all along of this as we're doing to-night. We've got a precious young man, as Mr Tufton tells you, and a clever young man, as nobody tries for to deny; and there ain't a single blessed reason on this earth why he shouldn't go on as he's been a-doing, till Salem bein' crowded out to the doors (as it's been two Sundays back), we'd have had to build a new chapel, and took a place in our connection as we're never yet took in Carlingford! . . .

'But it ain't to be,' said Tozer, looking round him with a tragic frown, and shaking his head slowly. 'Them as is always a-finding fault, and always a-setting up to dictate, has set their faces again' all that. . . . It's not his preaching as he's judged by, nor his dooty to the sick and dyin', nor any of them things as he was called to be pastor for; but it's if he's seen going to one house more nor another, or if he calls often enough on this one or t'other, and goes to all the tea-drinkings. My opinion is,' said Tozer, suddenly breaking off into jocularity, 'as a young man as maybe isn't a marrying man, and any-how can't marry more nor one, ain't in the safest place at Salem tea-drinkings; but that's neither here nor there. If the ladies haven't no pity, us men can't do nothing in that matter but what I say is this,' continued the butterman, once more becoming solemn; 'to go for to judge the pastor of a flock, not by the dooty he does to his flock, but by the times he calls at one house or another, and the way he makes hisself agreeable at one place or another, ain't a thing to be done by them as prides themselves on being Christians and Dissenters. It's not like Christians—and if it's like Dissenters the more's the pity. It's mean, that's what it is,' cried Tozer, with fine scorn; 'it's like a parcel of old women, if the ladies won't mind me saying so. It's beneath us as has liberty of conscience to fight for, and has to set an example before the Church folks as don't know no better. But it's what is done in our connection,' added the good deacon with pathos, shaking his forefinger mournfully at the crowd. 'When there's a young man as is clever and talented, and fills a chapel, and gives the connection a chance of standing up in the world as it ought, here's someone as jumps up and says, "The pastor don't come to see me," says he—"the pastor don't do his duty—he ain't the man for Salem." And them as is always in every flock ready to do a mischief, takes it up and there's talk of a change, and meetings is called, and—here we are! . . . We've called a meeting, all in the dark, and give him no chance of defending himself; and them as is at the head of this movement is calling upon us to dismiss Mr Vincent. But let me tell you,' continued Tozer, lowering his voice with dramatic intuition, and shaking his forefinger still more emphatically in the face of the startled audience, 'that this ain't no question of dismissing Mr Vincent; it's a matter of disgusting Mr Vincent, that's what it is—it's a matter of turning another promising young man away from the connection, and driving him to throw it all up. . . . It's what we're doing most places, us Dissenters; them as is talented and promisin', and can get a better living working for the world than working for the chapel, and won't give in to be worried about calling here and calling there—we're a-driving of them out of the connection, that's what we're doing! I could reckon up as many as six or seven as has been drove off already; and I ask you ladies and gentlemen, what's the good of subscribing and keeping up of colleges and so forth, if that's how you're a-going to serve every clever young man as trusts hisself to be your pastor? I'm a man as don't feel no shame to say that the minister, being took up with his family affairs and his studies, has been for weeks as he hasn't crossed my door; but am I that poor-spirited as I would drive away a young man as is one of the best preachers in the connection, because he don't come, not every day, to see me. No, my friends! . . . It shall never be said in our connection as a clever young man was drove away from Carlingford, and I had part in it. There's the credit of the denomination to keep up among the Church folks—and there's the chapel to fill, as never had half the sittings let before—and there's Mr Vincent, as is the cleverest young man I ever see in our pulpit, to be kep' in the connection; and there ain't no man living as shall dictate to me or them as stands by me! Them as is content to lose the best preaching within a hundred miles, because the minister don't call on two or three families in Salem, not as often as they would like to see him,' said Tozer with trenchant sarcasm, 'can put down their names again' Mr Vincent; but for me, and them as stands by me, we ain't a-going to give in to no such dictation: we ain't a-going to set up ourselves against the spread of the Gospel, and the credit o' the connection, and toleration and free-dom of conscience, as we're bound to fight for! If the pastor don't make hisself agreeable, I can put up with that—I can; but I ain't a-going to see a clever young man drove away from Salem, and the sittings vacant, and the chapel falling to ruin, and the Church folks a-laughing and a-jeering at us, not for all the deacons in the connection, nor any man in Carlingford. And this I say for myself and for all as stands by me!'

Notes

1 A. Miall, *Life of Edward Miall* (London, 1884), pp. 91-8; Waddington, *Congregational History: continuation to 1850* (London, 1878), pp. 568-76.
2 B. L. Manning, *The Protestant Dissenting Deputies* (Cambridge, 1952), pp. 90-1.
3 Evidence of Samuel Courtauld to the House of Commons Select Committee on Church Rates, 1851, *H. C. 1851*, ix, pp. 85-6.
4 See J. Vincent, *The Formation of the Liberal Party, 1857-68* (London, 1966), pp. 70-5.
5 The standard work on the Quakers is now E. Isichei, *Victorian Quakers* (Oxford, 1970).
6 B. Gregory, *Side Lights on the Conflicts of Methodism, 1827-52* (London, 1898), pp. 444-75; R. Currie, *Methodism Divided* (London, 1968), pp. 67-76.

7 H. B. Kendall, *Origin and History of the Primitive Methodist Church* (2 vols, London, n.d.), ii, pp. 456–65.

8 See particularly the paper by Algernon Wells, *Congregational Year Book, 1848,* pp. 83–90.

9 B. Harrison, 'Religion and Recreation in Nineteenth-Century England', *Past and Present,* no. 38 (1967).

10 F. Engels, *The Condition of the Working Class in England in 1844* (ed. W. H. Chaloner and W. O. Henderson, Oxford, 1958), p. 55.

11 *Minutes of the Wesleyan Conference, 1855,* collected edition, xiii (1859), pp. 124–6.

12 G. S. R. Kitson Clark, *The Making of Victorian England* (London, 1962), pp. 187–9.

13 J. Waddington, *Congregational History, 1850–1880* (London, 1880), p. 355

14 A. Miall, *Life of Edward Miall,* pp. 242–3, 251–2.

15 T. B. H. Stenhouse, *An Englishwoman in Utah* (1880), p. 48.

16 C. Ricks, *The Poems of Tennyson* (London, 1969), p. 1059.

Four   The golden age

From the bicentenary to the Home Rule split,
1863–86

When Matthew Arnold attacked Puritanism in his book, *Culture and Anarchy*, published in 1869, he chose Miall's newspaper, the *Nonconformist*, with its proud motto, 'The Dissidence of Dissent and the Protestantism of the Protestant Religion', as its typical example (71). This shows the impact which that paper had made on the public, and in particular the kind of people that Arnold met in his work as an inspector of schools. Matthew Arnold's criticism of the narrow outlook of Nonconformity is very similar to that of his father nearly thirty years before (40). Doubtless in many cases the criticism was justified: but it was rather unfair to hold up Oxford as the ideal at a time when Dissenters had only been able to attend the university since 1854, and when they were still barred from college fellowships; and it is surprising that Arnold made little mention of the provincial literary societies, in which Nonconformists frequently took a leading part and which often offered the only cultural life available. Miall was not slow to ask whether the countryside abounded in 'sweetness and light' where the parish priest ruled supreme (73). More serious was the charge of Llewellyn Davies that the 'gathered church' in Nonconformity encouraged an unchristian air of moral superiority (70)—a criticism to which ministers such as R. W. Dale were sensitive.[1]

Arnold's fear was that the extension of the franchise in 1867 would increase the political power of the uncultured middle classes. The election of 1868 returned sixty-three Dissenters and Gladstone came to power as prime minister of a Liberal government.[2] He had already carried his Bill to abolish compulsory Church Rates against Disraeli's government.[3] He was able to settle other grievances, for example, by abolishing religious tests in the universities in 1871. The first major Bill of his government was the disestablishment of the Church of Ireland (1869). The reasons for this lay in Irish politics, but it encouraged Nonconformists to think that disestablishment in other parts of the United Kingdom might be a possibility. It was in this context that Edward Miall, now a Member of Parliament again, moved his motion on disestablishment in the

House of Commons in 1871 (73). The motion was unsuccessful, as Miall expected, but the divisions in the Church of England over ritualism in the 1870s made even Lord Shaftesbury think that disestablishment would come in twenty years.[4] Nonconformists, with the possible exception of Joseph Chamberlain, consistently underrated the depth of Gladstone's opposition to disestablishment in England.

The disputes over education, however, ruined the Nonconformist–Liberal alliance. The Education Act of 1870 came as a shock to Nonconformists. Some, indeed, in the 1860s had come round to the view that State intervention in education was inevitable, including Joseph Chamberlain (a Unitarian) and the Rev. R. W. Dale (a Congregationalist). These two founded the Education League in 1869 to campaign for a government system of education that would be compulsory, unsectarian and free. The government would not go so far. The Education Bill underwent considerable changes before it reached the statute book, but its essential features were two: instead of a new State-financed system, there were to be two—the existing voluntary schools and new rate-supported schools where voluntary provision was inadequate; and by the famous Cowper-Temple clause rate-aided schools were forbidden to use 'catechisms or religious formularies distinctive of any particular denomination'. Nonconformists were divided over religious instruction: some, like Edward Miall, accepted the logic of a secular system and declared for no religious instruction at all; others, like Spurgeon, probably the majority, believed in Bible teaching. Neither was satisfactory to Anglicans or Roman Catholics. But the main objection of Nonconformists was to the fact that where a voluntary (Church) school was adequate for the neighbourhood it was almost impossible to establish a school board, and this meant that very little change would take place in the countryside (72). Furthermore, it was possible in such cases for aid to be given from the rates, and thus, Nonconformists argued, denominational instruction was being supported at public expense. The government was unresponsive to Nonconformist protest, and the reputation of Forster, the education secretary, was permanently damaged in Nonconformist eyes (75). In January 1872 a conference of Nonconformists decided to veto any Liberal candidate who did not express support for their point of view (74), and this was probably one of the reasons for Gladstone's defeat at the polls in 1874.[5]

But it was clear that the Nonconformists could not get a better deal from Disraeli, and the relationship with the Liberals was recreated while they were in opposition. In particular, Gladstone's links with Nonconformity were strengthened by their common cause over the Bulgarian massacres in 1876 (80). The foreign and colonial policy of Disraeli was another point of common hostility, and the Nonconformists threw themselves whole-heartedly behind Gladstone for the general election of 1880 (87). Even so there were voices which protested against too great a preoccupation with political affairs (83). Gladstone's second ministry ended the dispute over the right of Nonconformists to be buried in parish churchyards with their own service (88)—the last of the old Dissenting grievances.

But Ireland split the Liberals, and in doing so it also split the Nonconformists. A majority of them remained loyal to Gladstone over Home Rule: but others, notably Spurgeon, Dale, Bright and, of course, Chamberlain deserted him. The consequences were grave: no longer did Nonconformity have a united voice, and personal relationships were deeply affected (92).[6] It may also be that by this split, the Nonconformists lost the chance of disestablishment in England (91, 102c). The Home Rule split marked the end of an era.

In many ways the atmosphere of Nonconformity seemed the same. Now the papers carried reports of Nonconformist services, whether in the main stream, like the Presbyterians, or out of it, like the Sandemanians (77). Spurgeon had become an institution at the Metropolitan Tabernacle (86): Primitive Methodism was still firmly identified with the working classes (76, 82): the Salvation Army (as it was known after 1878) began as the Christian Mission in the East End of London, but its methods were traditional. Even Moody and Sankey differed from their predecessors more in the scale of their meetings than in their message (81). Beatrice Webb found traditional Nonconformity thriving on her visits to Bacup in the 1880s (89).

But underneath, there were changes. These were seen most strikingly in the countryside where the pressure of a revived Church of England was keenly felt (84). The Nonconformists had supported Arch's Agricultural Labourers' Union in the 1870s—a Congregational minister was editor of their newspaper, and Primitive Methodists were very active in it (76).[7] The nascent trade unionism was hit by the depression in the later 'seventies, which increased the rate of migration from the countryside and emigration (78, 84).

In the towns, continued growth and movement within towns was making the suburban problem more common (79). The movement of more prosperous people to the suburbs reflected a social mobility that sometimes carried people out of Nonconformity altogether. In 1872, three years before it declared its belief in its mission to the working classes (82), the Primitive Methodist Conference noted that 'intelligence, wealth and respectability are becoming increasingly characteristic of us as a community'.[8] The 1870s saw a renewal of interest in the problem of why the working classes did not come to church, and in class divisions in the churches.

Moreover, although the *Nonconformist* published a series of supplements on the statistics of religious accommodation in 1872 which showed that Nonconformists had increased their church room more rapidly than Anglicans since 1851,[9] some at least were aware that they were not keeping pace with the growth of population (85). It was little comfort to them that the Church of England was falling behind as well. The various unofficial censuses of attendance produced in 1881-2 generally confirmed that although church attendance had increased in absolute terms since 1851, relatively it had fallen behind.[10]

The rise in the standard of living and the existence of new, alternative social institutions began to erode traditional Nonconformist strength. Beatrice Webb noticed that the younger generation were beginning to look elsewhere (89). There was also an increasing interest in social questions (89, 90). Attempts were made to mobilise this social concern in the development of the 'institutional church' and the Methodist mission. John Clifford, the Baptist, and Hugh Price Hughes, the Wesleyan, were both leaders in this attempt to involve the church in the whole life of the community by making a centre for all kinds of social and educational activities (99).[11] Some Nonconformists were becoming interested in socialism, such as Clifford, but generally they were no better prepared than the Church of England for this change in the social mood.

70 Criticism of the Voluntary Principle, 1868

An extract from 'The Voluntary Principle' by J. Ll. Davies in *Essays on Church Policy* (1868), ed. W. L. Clay, pp. 70–2, 77–8.

The Rev. J. Ll. Davies was rector of Christ Church, Marylebone, and a leading Broad Churchman. His criticism of Nonconformist narrowness is similar in some ways to that of Matthew Arnold (see document 71), but is theologically more penetrating. Davies was very much influenced by F. D. Maurice, and this extract advances an argument similar to that in Maurice's *Kingdom of Christ*.

'The Scriptural idea of a Christian Church' undoubtedly implies that all its members should be, if they conform to the idea, unworldly disciples of Christ. But whether the policy of Christian Churches, as we find it illustrated in the New Testament, was to labour always to exclude the undevout and irreligious, is another question. . . .The perpetual appeals to the high ideal of a Christian society which recur in the Apostolic writings have led our nonconformist friends to the fallacious conclusion that the first Christians attempted to realize this ideal by a policy of separation,—a conclusion which is wholly disproved by the character of those writings. 'These be they who separate themselves' was not said of the spiritual members of the Church.

But the policy of forming a select society,—a close corporation,—of devout believers, and excluding the unbelieving and undevout, though it does not find any real support in the practice of the New Testament age, is undoubtedly a plausible and attractive one. To the sect-spirit it commends itself as the only religious policy. If we ask, What, on this hypothesis, is to become of the undevout?—the first and most natural answer might be, 'That is their concern, not ours. Our business is to keep ourselves unspotted from the world.' But it may also be argued that the fact of being themselves excluded, and the spectacle of a body which is like a light shining in a dark place, are calculated to exert the best possible influence upon those who do not

make a profession of religion. That this effect may be produced, it is
necessary that the Free Churches should be very visibly distinguished
by a more heavenly spirit and conduct from the rest of the world.
The policy of separatism fails altogether unless it is carried to an
extreme; and no religious community dreams now of carrying it to
an extreme. To realize the idea of a Christian Church by separation,
the members ought to go on cutting off one questionable member
after another till the residue are like flawless gems; in practice, the most
zealous Nonconformists aim at no such selection of the best, and lay
claim to no peculiar Christian perfection. But the theory, though it
will not work where it has its proper work to do, is held fast where it
flatters the sect-spirit. 'The Church' delights to prove that it is not 'the
world' by governing its affairs in its own way and for its own ends.
Zeal and activity are thus developed; religion flourishes. And to 'a
Church' it seems the ultimate good that religion should flourish;
whether the religion is of a good kind or a bad is a question which
seldom occurs to those who are animated by the ecclesiastical spirit. . . .

Against the acknowledged difficulty of introducing new adjustments
into the machinery of the National Church must be set such evils as
belong to small and free religious societies. It is possible to exaggerate
and to misrepresent those evils. The satire which has revelled in the
description of the internal history of little Nonconformist Churches
has taken a scarcely fair advantage of the fact that the persons described
are petty shopkeepers, whose speech and manners are naturally not
those of the cultivated class, and can be made by humorous rendering
to appear ridiculous to the readers of satire. Vulgarisms are not always
signs of an essential vulgarity. But if justice and good sense would
restrain us from adopting the satirical estimate of the deacons and the
Church-meetings of the Free Churches, it may also be expected that
those who are familiar with the actual working of these small republics
should shrink from speaking of them as if purity of Christian motive
found in them an ideal shrine. It is evident that in these Churches the
direct and daily government, in the sphere of all that is most subtle
and delicate and difficult, is put into the hands of ignorant persons.
And in the history of religion, the most ignorant have always been
the most narrow, and the most inclined to apply other than spiritual
pressure in the interests of faith. Persecution has always found its real
motive power in the fears of the religious laity. It seems absolutely
inevitable that a congregationalist 'Church' should consider itself
bound to guard the traditional and popular doctrine of the sect, and
therefore to be watchful in measuring the sermons of the pastor by

that standard. The pastor has—for good, if you will, but for evil also—
the strongest inducements to make his preaching acceptable to his
employers. Where a premium is put upon self-will by the worship of
the Voluntary Principle and of the power of the majority, it would be
singular if there were no development of the evils of self-will. Impress
upon a society that it is a glorious thing to say, 'I am of Paul, and I of
Apollos, and I of Cephas, and I of Christ,' and it will be unaccountable
if such teaching should not result in envying and strife and divisions.
And where these fruits are found, a society may be perfectly religious,
and yet, in the judgment of an Apostle, thoroughly carnal. Moreover,
Congregationalist Churches are subjected to the influence of the principle of competition in all its severity. Each Church is naturally anxious
to prosper. It is essential that the pews should be let. Competition is a
powerful stimulant, but it is not the most spiritualizing of influences.
What will 'draw' and what will edify are not always the same thing.
A successful Congregationalist therefore deserves especial esteem, if he
resists the temptations to claptrap, buncome, and jocularity, which
beset him, and preserves in his bearing, not unction, but high-minded
spiritual dignity.

71 Matthew Arnold's attack on Nonconformity, 1869

An extract from M. Arnold, *Culture and Anarchy* (1869), pp. 26–31.

Matthew Arnold's famous attack on the narrow-mindedness of
Nonconformity was based on his experience as an inspector of
schools. His attack is similar to that of his father (document 40), but
goes further in its idealisation of culture—'sweetness and light'.

. . . The impulse of the English race towards moral development and
self-conquest has nowhere so powerfully manifested itself as in
Puritanism. Nowhere has Puritanism found so adequate an expression
as in the religious organisation of the Independents. The modern

Independents have a newspaper, the *Nonconformist*, written with great sincerity and ability. The motto, the standard, the profession of faith which this organ of theirs carries aloft, is: 'The Dissidence of Dissent and the Protestantism of the Protestant religion.' There is sweetness and light, and an ideal of complete harmonious human perfection! One need not go to culture and poetry to find language to judge it. Religion, with its instinct for perfection, supplies language to judge it, language too which is in our mouths every day. 'Finally, be of one mind, united in feeling,' says St. Peter. There is an ideal which judges the Puritan ideal: 'The Dissidence of Dissent and the Protestantism of the Protestant religion!' And religious organisations like this are what people believe in, rest in, would give their lives for! Such, I say, is the wonderful virtue of even the beginnings of perfection, of having conquered even the plain faults of our animality, that the religious organisation which has helped us to do it can seem to us something precious, salutary, and to be propagated, even when it wears such a brand of imperfection on its forehead as this. And men have got such a habit of giving to the language of religion a special application, of making it a mere jargon, that for the condemnation which religion itself passes on the shortcomings of their religious organisations they have no ear; they are sure to cheat themselves and to explain this condemnation away. They can only be reached by the criticism which culture, like poetry, speaking a language not to be sophisticated, and resolutely testing these organisations by the ideal of a human perfection complete on all sides, applies to them.

But men of culture and poetry, it will be said, are again and again failing, and failing conspicuously, in the necessary first stage to a harmonious perfection, in the subduing of the great obvious faults of our animality, which it is the glory of these religious organisations to have helped us to subdue. True, they do often so fail. They have often been without the virtues as well as the faults of the Puritan; it has been one of their dangers that they so felt the Puritan's faults that they too much neglected the practice of his virtues. I will not, however, exculpate them at the Puritan's expense. They have often failed in morality, and morality is indispensable. And they have been punished for their failure, as the Puritan has been rewarded for his performance. They have been punished wherein they erred, but their ideal of beauty, of sweetness and light, and a human nature complete on all its sides, remains the true ideal of perfection still; just as the Puritan's ideal of perfection remains narrow and inadequate, although for what he did well he has been richly rewarded. Notwithstanding the mighty result of the Pilgrim Fathers' voyage, they and their standard of perfection are rightly judged when we figure to ourselves Shakespeare or Virgil, —souls in whom sweetness and light, and all that in human nature is most humane, were eminent,—accompanying them on their voyage, and think what intolerable company Shakespeare and Virgil would have found them! In the same way let us judge the religious organisations which we see all around us. Do not let us deny the good and the happiness which they have accomplished; but do not let us fail to see clearly that their idea of human perfection is narrow and inadequate, and that the Dissidence of Dissent and the Protestantism of the Protestant religion will never bring humanity to its true goal. As I said with regard to wealth: Let us look at the life of those who live in and for it,—so I say with regard to the religious organisations. Look at the life imaged in such a newspaper as the *Nonconformist*,—a life of jealousy of the Establishment, disputes, tea-meetings, openings of chapels, sermons; and then think of it as an ideal of a human life completing itself on all sides, and aspiring with all its organs after sweetness, light, and perfection!

Another newspaper, representing, like the *Nonconformist*, one of the religious organisations of this country, was a short time ago giving an account of the crowd at Epsom on the Derby day, and of all the vice and hideousness which was to be seen in that crowd; and then the writer turned suddenly round upon Professor Huxley, and asked him how he proposed to cure all this vice and hideousness without religion. I confess I felt disposed to ask the asker this question: and how do you propose to cure it with such a religion as yours? How is the idea of a life so unlovely, so unattractive, so incomplete, so narrow, so far removed from a true and satisfying ideal of human perfection, as is the life of your religious organisation as you yourself reflect it, to conquer and transform all this vice and hideousness? Indeed, the strongest plea for the study of perfection as pursued by culture, the clearest proof of the actual inadequacy of the idea of perfection held by the religious organisations,—expressing, as I have said, the most wide-spread effort which the human race has yet made after perfection,—is to be found in the state of our life and society with these in possession of it, and having been in possession of it I know not how many hundred years.

72   Effects of the Education Act in the countryside, 1870

An extract from a paper by the Rev. T. W. Davids on 'The Position of Congregationalism in Rural Districts' read to the Congregational Union Assembly in 1870: *Congregational Year Book, 1871*, pp. 120–1.

Nonconformist opposition to the Education Act of 1870 centred particularly on the Act's failure to provide an alternative to the Church of England school in most rural parishes. This Congregational comment is typical.

In the great majority of our rural parishes school-boards will be impossible. What schools will be provided for them by the Act will therefore be 'denominational'; but seeing that our Churches are, with few exceptions, much too poor to secure such schools for themselves, a denominational school in rural parishes generally means a school that is dependent on the local clergyman. The Act, indeed, provides a 'conscience-clause', which some suppose will be a most effective one. The opinion that prevails, however, in the rural districts is, that where it is most required, fewest parents will avail themselves of the protections which it seems to offer them. Nor would any conscience clause whatever meet the case in its entirety. Our people in the rural districts also naturally want to have the education of their children under their own control. It would be so, at least, to some extent, in the case of schools established by a local board; but in the case of denominational schools, things being as they are, the education of their children must come under that of the parochial clergy. What, then, can be done to help them? Is it possible to raise a fund which shall enable them to claim State-aid for schools established by themselves? If not, then there is every reason for alarm lest Mr Forster's Bill should but enhance an influence which in our rural districts is already far too great for either the religious or the social interests of the people, and in that, as well as in other ways, add others to the many and the very serious difficulties that we have to meet with there, that we can hardly hope to overcome—not, certainly, for many years.

73   Edward Miall on disestablishment, 1871

Extracts from *Parliamentary Debates* (third series), ccvi, cols. 475, 480–1, 487–90.

Miall's speech of 9 May 1871 in the House of Commons was not the only one he made on disestablishment, but it was the most famous. Both Disraeli and Gladstone praised it.[12] It should be remembered that disestablishment was always assumed to involve the secularisation of Church property, though opinions varied as to the extent of this. Some argued that all pre-Reformation property should be seized, as not having been intended for the Church of England; others argued that all property granted before 1662 should be taken because prior to that date there was only one legal Church and its property should be regarded as belonging to the nation.

The object I have in view is a perfectly practical one, namely, to ascertain how far the House is disposed to apply to other parts of the United Kingdom a policy sanctioned by Parliament in its application to Ireland. In seeking to gain that object I earnestly and honestly disclaim all feeling of hostility to particular Churches, as well as to particular Church parties. . . . I shall not assail either the Church of England or the Church of Scotland as a spiritual organisation, but I shall attempt to show that the relationship they sustain towards the State, and the position which the State assigns to them, are condemned by experience as well as by reason, and ought to be put an end to as soon as possible. . . .

The Church of England is not now in fact, whatever she may be in profession, the Church of the whole people of England. She is the largest of the denominations into which the Christian people of this country are divided, comprising, we will say, half the population as her voluntary adherents and members, and that half, for the most part, the upper, the less dependent, and the better-to-do half of society. She can lay claim, with truth, to the bulk of the wise men, the mighty men, and the noble of this land. She lives in the esteem of the wealthy and the respectable. But it can hardly be said with truth that she has taken a proportionate hold upon the far more numerous classes beneath them. She has never—and probably less than ever in our times—overtaken the work which she arrogates exclusively to herself. She claims the whole ground for spiritual cultivation; but at least a moiety of that which comes under cultivation at all, is cultivated by Churches which she will not recognise. She is never likely to cover the whole ground now. She is not therefore a National Church for she neither does nor can comprehend within her ministrations, her sacramental and tuitional agency, the entire body of the nation. All the resources, it is true, which the nation, as such, has given for religion she appropriates to herself. All the worldly honours by which it means to mark its appreciation of religion, she keeps in her own hands. But she is not the National Church in the sense of being the accepted or adequate organ of the whole people of England, for quickening, nurturing, or giving expression to, their religious sentiments. . . .

I shall be asked, no doubt, what there is in the State–Church policy, as carried out in these days and in this country, which meddles with a man's freedom of conscience, or places him in an exceptional position, on account of his religious profession. . . . Take a survey of the operation of this State–Church policy in its amplest breadth—what does it show you? It shows you a nation sharply divided by law in regard to their religion into two great sections—the one privileged, the other tolerated. . . . It shows you the lesser half (we will say) of the community beholden to the greater half for their liberty to worship God as conscience may direct them—and, whilst they do so witnessing the appropriation of resources common in both, to the exclusive support of the religious institutions of the stronger of the two. . . . It is, perhaps, difficult to say which has been most injured in this respect by the law's partiality and injustice—the party on which it lavished the sunshine of its smiles, or the party which it has driven out into the cold shade. The moral damage each has sustained differs in kind, no doubt, from that suffered by the other. But the country is the main loser by this kind of thing. With those who look upon it from a foreign standpoint, it loses in reputation, it loses in influence, it loses in the weight of its counsels, it loses in the force of its example—while it has to lament among its own people the absence of that unity of feeling and spirit which would give the cohesion, force, and *verve*, needed to grapple effectually with the monstrous forms of social evil which are rearing their heads in the present day. . . .

But this is not the whole extent of the injustice perpetrated by the Church Establishment system. Its exclusive appropriation of property belonging to the nation as a whole, in providing for the spiritual need of but a part of it, under whatever specious pretexts it may be done, cannot be made consistent with what is due to equity in the employment of national resources. The working men of England and Scotland, for example—what share have they in the proceeds of that large estate which has been appropriated to the religious teaching they decline? It should be borne in mind that when we speak of Church property, we speak of the property set aside by the nation for its ecclesiastical affairs—the Church being the ecclesiastical, as the State is the political, phase of the entire community. . . . I say you are doing, not merely Dissenters, but the perhaps still larger class which, I am afraid, may be more accurately styled Absenters, an enormous injustice when you abstract from the common fund a revenue which, when capitalised, would amount to from one to two hundred millions sterling, to provide religious means for the upper and the richer half of the community. For, really, it comes to this in the main. Divide society in this country into three sections—the upper, the middle, and the lower—and I think it will be admitted that it is to a far greater extent with reference to the lower section, than to the middle and the upper, that the machinery of the Church Establishment has become of no avail. You will say that the machinery provided by the Nonconformists has also failed in regard to this class. I must admit it. . . . There is this great difference, however, in the position of the two: the non-established communities, in all that they attempt for the evangelisation of the lower stratum of society, employ none but their own resources; the State-Church—so far at least as it acts as a State-Church—employs the resources of the nation. . . .

From the political injustice inflicted by the system, I pass on to notice the social mischief which it works. The tendency of legislation for some time past has been, slowly, it may be, but progressively, to sweep away class distinctions, and, as far as law can do it, to remove the causes of social divisions and discords. We all profess to lament them. We have reason to do so. An immense work of social amelioration is waiting to be done in this country. The plague-spot of pauperism calls for all our vigilance and skill to check its spread, and the abject and helpless poverty which lies immediately contiguous to pauperism has little chance of resisting its inroads by the help of a wisely-organised system of beneficence. Outside the action of the law there is almost unbounded scope for the action of voluntary zeal and generosity. One of the great needs of the day is a thorough systematisation of the efforts prompted by good-will—and thorough systematisation pre-supposes unity of feeling in order to unity of organisation. . . . Almost every village of any size has two distinct sets of apparatus for doing good—the one worked by Churchmen, the other by Dissenters. Every town has its exclusive circles of social intercourse—the one appropriated to Churchmen, the other to Dissenters. Every section of society is thus split up into incoherent parts. Many are the useful schemes that have had to be abandoned owing to the absence of good feeling between the favoured and degraded sects. Still more numerous are those which, from the same cause, are worked inefficiently. All parties must take their share of blame for permitting it to continue. But the State is really the most responsible party. By its injudicious meddlings with religious opinions, it has thrown the torch of discord into every corner of the kingdom—and, to an immense extent, has transmuted simple differences of belief into personal alienation and bitterness of feeling.

I come now to the last main consideration of the question to which I shall advert—I mean the very serious disadvantage which the system inflicts upon the Church itself. . . . Sir, she cannot be at once free and established. So long as she remains in connection with the State, the people of this country will always, and wisely, insist upon determining in the last resort what she shall teach, and how she shall worship. There cannot be a Church Establishment—at any rate, there is never likely to be—without some distinct dogmatical basis. The dream of compre-hending in one national and State-supported Church all religionists of all denominations, and of providing out of national resources for the authorised teaching of all creeds, and perhaps of no creed, is but a vain dream—'the baseless fabric of a vision'—a beautifully many-tinted bubble, which bursts and disappears as soon as it is touched by the finger of practical statesmanship. As I said before, the Church cannot remain one of our political institutions without acknowledging the doctrinal and ritual conditions which the law imposes on her. Nor can it be forgotten that recent judgments in the highest court of appeal have narrowed rather than widened those conditions. I venture to predict, moreover, that as the law defines itself more precisely, the authorised exponents of religion who are subject to the law will necessarily become more and more cramped in their position, and more and more interfered with in their work. The system cannot go on much longer. The relationship of the clergy to the civil power is becoming intolerable to those of them who are most in earnest, and is felt by them to paralyse their spiritual power. It will be real mercy, I think, to do by legislation, and therefore simultaneously for the entire body of the clergy, what will require an immense amount of moral courage in any of them to do individually, or even as Church parties— namely, sever the bond which, even on their own showing, fatally restricts their freedom of action.

Sir, I will not trespass much longer upon the forbearance of the House. . . . But I wish to say something of the rural parishes of the kingdom. In each of these, we are told, the clergyman, maintained by national endowment, is a living link between the highest and the lowliest of the parishioners—is a cultivated gentleman, located just where there is, if not the greatest need, at any rate the best opportunity, for diffusing both 'sweetness and light'—is the fixed centre in the parish of civilisation, of education, of charity, of piety—and I am told that I propose to abolish him and leave the people to fall back again into ignorance and Paganism. . . . These rural parishes have been in the undisturbed spiritual occupation of the clergy of the Church of England for generations past. Indeed, the clergy have all but undisputed religious sway in them. Ecclesiastically speaking, they can do pretty much as they like. Well, what, on a large scale, has been the result? What are the most conspicuous characteristics of our labouring agricultural population? Do they include 'sweetness and light'? Do they include fairly-developed intelligence? Do they include a high state of morality? Do they include affectionate veneration for religion? Are these the most prominent features by which the character of our agricultural population is distinguished, and in respect of which they bear away the palm from the inmates of towns? And the discouraging and painful answers to these queries—are they not to be found in blue-books, verified as they may be by minute personal observation? . . . But is it fair or reasonable to assume that the abolition of the parochial endowments in these rural districts will be tantamount to the abolition of the clergy? Does the House really believe that it would? If so, I must say that its faith is in direct opposition to most of the facts which bear upon the case. Take the Principality of Wales, for instance, where very few persons besides land-owners prefer the State-Church, where the bulk of the population is poor, and in many cases thinly scattered over the face of the country; surely no one will be bold enough to contend that it is by the endowments possessed by the Church Establishment that the Welsh people are kept from a relapse into heathenism. . . . England is reputed to be the richest country in the world. English land-owners and occupiers enjoy at least a fair proportion of that wealth. For the most part, they profess devoted attachment to the Church of England. Well, Sir, it seems most extraordinary to me that the right rev. prelates of that Church should so loudly and so frequently proclaim their distrust of the readiness of those among whom they ordinarily mingle, and to whom they minister, to do what most other people do—namely, make some sacrifice for the maintenance of their religious faith. . . . My conviction, on the contrary, is, that the disappearance of State-endowments would be instantly followed by a rush of voluntary efforts to fill up the vacuum. Depend upon it, that faith in Christianity is not yet at so low an ebb in this country as to suffer a single village community to remain destitute of the means of religious instruction and Divine worship. It would not be for lack of means, or of liberality, that a deficiency of spiritual provision could befall our villages—it would be, if at all, merely for want of proper organisation. . . .

74   The Nonconformist conference on education, 1872

An extract from A. Miall, *Life of Edward Miall* (1884), pp. 339–40.

In January 1872 a conference of Nonconformists was held in Manchester, and 1,900 delegates from the Congregationalists, Baptists, Unitarians, Primitive Methodists, Calvinistic Methodists and United Methodist Free Churches attended. Only the Wesleyans were unrepresented. The subject of the conference was the political relations of Nonconformists to the leaders of the Liberal party in the light of the government's refusal to amend the Education Act of 1870. The resolution here described was an attempt to exercise a local veto on Liberal candidates.

The practical outcome of the Conference was a resolution which, after affirming that 'the educational policy unfortunately adopted by Her

Majesty's Government is hostile to the interests of religious liberty' for reasons then detailed, went on to recommend to the Nonconformists of Great Britain that 'they should not accept as a satisfactory representative any candidate for a seat in the House of Commons, who would not pledge himself to the amendment of the Education Act, in the sense and to the extent of the propositions adopted by this Conference; and further, to make it clearly understood that, except under the pressure of good national exigencies, they will not give any such candidate their support.'

75 Political consequences of the education controversy for Nonconformists, 1870–80

Extracts from J. G. Rogers, *An Autobiography* (1903), pp. 173–4, 220–2.

The Rev. J. Guinness Rogers, a Congregational minister who was active in the education controversy, here describes the consequences for relations between Nonconformists and the Liberal party. The first extract discusses relations with Forster, and the second the effects on the choice of a Liberal leader.

a.

. . . It is possible that unwise words were spoken, and charges brought, against Mr Forster at that time by those who were intensely disappointed in relation to a measure which, as coming from a professed Radical, might have been expected to have so different a character. The Nonconformists who had done so much to place the Government in power had a right to expect very different treatment from what they received. It was not surprising that they should regard the author of the measure as a traitor to what they supposed was their common cause. But so far as Dale and myself were concerned, I do not believe that we had anything to regret in the spirit and mode of our advocacy. At the Education Conference in Manchester indeed, I, with his full sympathy, emphatically declared that Nonconformists would never be satisfied while Mr Forster remained Minister of Education. The scene that followed was a remarkable demonstration of the intensity of Nonconformist feeling on the subject. The excited assembly rose *en masse*, and made it abundantly manifest that in its view Mr Forster and his policy must, at all costs, be resisted. I did not believe then that Mr Forster was influenced by any unworthy motive. But, in common with Dale, I held that the measure was contrary to true Liberal principles, and would be unfriendly to the development of a national system of education worthy of the name. Beyond this, we objected to the violation of the rights of conscience involved in any scheme of religious instruction supported out of the public exchequer, over which the State exercised a certain control, and for which, to that extent, it necessarily accepted responsibility. With this view Mr Forster had no sympathy, and it was probably the surprise of finding one, who had been regarded as the representative of Radicalism in the Cabinet, so decided a supporter of an Erastian policy in education that provoked such keen indignation. That indignation, in truth, never abated. Our attitude in that controversy was misunderstood by Anglicans, and especially by those of the narrow-minded order. There are Anglicans who seem unable to get the faintest conception as to the grounds on which Nonconformists object to the special kind of teaching which Churchmen desire given in National schools. They have been so ready to identify their Church with Christianity and to regard Dissent as in some way deficient in fundamental principles, that they were not deterred from making the suggestion that our action was due to a failure to appreciate a necessity for religious instruction. It is strange that the facts which must have been patent to them should not have led them to a different conception. We are not only spending money freely on Christian work both for the adult population as well as the children, but we are accepting a position of civic disadvantage solely because of our religious convictions. All this, however, was left out of sight in the education controversy of 1870, and is certainly forgotten still by a certain section of Anglicans. . . .

b.

At one point in the education controversy the 'Nonconformists' Revolt' was very pronounced, and threatened serious disaster to the Liberal Government. It is impossible, even were it desirable, to re-call all its incidents, but it is necessary to emphasise the fact of the dis-content which was strongly manifest in various ways, both in Parliament and the constituencies, during the years immediately preceding the dissolution of 1874, because it supplies a conclusive answer to the charge so often brought against Nonconformists, that they were blind followers of Mr Gladstone. . . . There were times when it threatened the permanent alienation of the advanced section from the Liberal Party altogether. To some of us it seemed that this would be a serious shock to the cause of progress, and, therefore, while firmly maintaining our own principles, we were careful to treat the question as a domestic affair to be settled within the party itself.

The differences between Mr Forster and the recalcitrant Nonconformists were irreconcilable. . . . The simple fact was that our religious affinities were much closer with the Premier than with the Education Minister. Erastianism was distasteful to both Mr Gladstone and ourselves, and the intensity of his own convictions made him the more capable of understanding and respecting ours.

This episode had a most potent influence on the politics of the times. The first effect was to introduce the element of dissension into a harmonious party, whose unity had accomplished so much and promised still more. The prestige of Mr Gladstone's first ministry was materially lowered and was never afterwards regained. Mr Forster's own position was seriously damaged. This was seen when a new leader had to be chosen in 1875, on the temporary withdrawal of Mr Gladstone from the active life of the party. It was the displeasure of a large body of Nonconformists and Radicals which made the election of Mr Forster impossible. But it cannot be forgotten that it was this issue which first brought Mr Chamberlain into political prominence. During the education struggle he was one of the Nonconformist leaders to whom the confidence of political Dissent was gradually attracted. This told for much in the troublous time which followed during the Ministry of 1880. Those who had acted with Mr Chamberlain in the educational controversy were, in general, sympathetic with him in the new difficulty that arose out of the Kilmainham negotiation. Perhaps it would be more accurate to say they judged Mr Forster's Irish Secretariat under the influence of feeling engendered by their recollection of his action as Education Minister. They had no sympathies with Mr Parnell and his party, but they distinctly leaned to the policy of Mr Chamberlain, who at that time was understood to be the prominent champion of the Irish cause in the Cabinet in opposition to Mr Forster. . . .

76   Early days of a Primitive Methodist local preacher, 1872

An extract from G. Edwards, *From Crow-Scaring to Westminster* (1922) pp. 32–6.

George Edwards began life as an agricultural labourer in Norfolk, became a Trade Union organiser and was eventually returned as a Member of Parliament. He here describes some of his early experiences as a Primitive Methodist local preacher. This is typical of what Nonconformity did for many thousands of working people, though obviously not all of them went so far.

The September Quarterly Meeting of 1872 of the Aylsham Primitive Methodist Circuit decided that my name should appear on the preachers' plan as an 'Exhorter', and I was planned to take my first service on the third Sunday in October of that year.

Up to this time I could not read, I merely knew my letters, but I set myself to work. My dear wife came to my rescue and undertook to teach me to read. For the purposes of this first service she helped me to commit three hymns to memory and also the first chapter of the Gospel according to St. John. . . .

My first three were good old Primitive Methodist hymns. The opening verse of the first hymn I learned was:—

> Hark, the Gospel news is sounding,
> Christ has suffered on the tree,
> Streams of mercy are abounding,
> Grace for all is rich and free.
> Now, poor sinner,
> Look to Him who died for thee.

The second hymn was:—

There is a fountain filled with blood,
     Drawn from Immanuel's veins;
And sinners plunged beneath that flood,
     Lose all their guilty stains.

The third hymn was:—

     Stop, poor sinner, stop and think
          Before you further go.
     Will you sport upon the brink
          Of everlasting woe?
     On the verge of ruin stop,
          Now the friendly warning take,
     Stay your footsteps or you'll drop
          Into the burning lake.

   The last hymn does not appear in the present-day Primitive Methodist hymnal. Needless to say, I have long ceased to use the hymn. It
was too horrible for my humanitarian spirit. I might say that at my
first service I was not quite sure that I held the book the right way up,
as I was not quite certain of the figures. I had, however, committed the
hymns to memory correctly, and also the lesson, and I made no mis-
takes. In those days we used to give out the hymns two lines at a time,
as very few people could read, and they could possibly remember the
two lines. There was no musical instrument in many of the small
village chapels at that time. . . . My first text was taken from the first
chapter of John: 'Behold the Lamb of God which taketh away the
sin of the world.' . . . I made rapid progress with my education under
the tutorship of my wife, who would sit up very late at night to teach
me. She would sit on one side of the fireplace and I on the other. I
would spell out the words and she would tell me their pronunciation. . . .
Having once learned to read, I became eager for knowledge. Until
then I possessed only a Bible and hymn-book and two spelling-books.
But I had no money to buy other books. My wife and I talked it over,
and I decided I would give up smoking and purchase books with the
money saved. I was then smoking 2 oz. of tobacco a week, which in
those days cost 6d. This did not seem much, but it was £1 6s. a year.
It was a great sacrifice to me to give up smoking, for I did enjoy my
pipe. I had, however, a thirst for knowledge, and no sacrifice was too
great to satisfy my longing. My first purchase was Johnson's Dictionary, two volumes of *The Lay-preacher*, which contained outlines of

sermons, Harvey's *Meditations among the Tombs* and *Contemplation o the Starry Heavens*, a Bible dictionary, and a *History of Rome.* . . .

Although my preaching efforts did not give me entire satisfaction, still I can look back with pleasure at some of the results of my labours. Although uneducated and not well informed and although I used such phrases and put the Gospel in such a way that I should not think for one moment of doing to-day, still it had its effect. I can recall instances of ten and twelve of my hearers at my Sunday services making a stand for righteousness. Many of them in after years became stalwarts for truth.

They also soon began to be dissatisfied with the conditions under which they worked and lived. Seeing no hope of any improvement they migrated to the North of England, and found work in the coal-fields, and never returned to their native county. When in Newcastle last December I met several of my old converts and friends.

With my study of theology, I soon began to realize that the social conditions of the people were not as God intended they should be. The gross injustices meted out to my parents and the terrible sufferings I had undergone in my boyhood burnt themselves into my soul like a hot iron.

Many a time did I vow I would do something to better the conditions of my class.

77 Presbyterians and Sandemanians in London, 1873

Two extracts from C. Maurice Davies, *Unorthodox London* (1873), pp. 307–11, 285–8.

The Rev. C. Maurice Davies was an Anglican clergyman who became a free-lance journalist in the 1870s. The essays originally appeared as articles in the *Daily Telegraph*. The Presbyterians described in (a) belonged to the Presbyterian Church in England (in communion with the Church of Scotland) which united with the United Presbyterians in 1876. The Sandemanians described in (b) are included to represent the many small Nonconformist denominations, which are usually ignored in studying English Nonconformity.

a.

I was attracted to Edward Irving's old church in Regent Square, one Monday evening in May, by an announcement that the Scottish Synod for England would commence its annual sitting there, when the Rev. Donald Fraser would preach; and on bending my steps thither found a large congregation assembled, or rather assembling, for they dropped in by detachments during the entire evening, the service commencing at the unusually early hour of six.

I was handed to a seat by a tall verger in a dress-coat, with the most unmistakably Caledonian visage, who smiled blandly as familiar members of Dr. Dykes's congregation took the seats he assigned them, many of the front pews being separated by a red cord from the rest of the church to accommodate the impending Synod. Precisely at six o'clock Dr. Fraser ascended the pulpit, habited in gown and bands, his snow-white hair looking from the distance almost like a forensic wig, and giving him the appearance of a barrister. A curious oak canopy surmounts the pulpit, probably by way of sounding-board, but it looks very much as though it would topple over and precipitate the preacher from its dizzy height into the pew below.

The service, which was striking from its utter simplicity, began with the singing of a metrical psalm to one of the quaint old Scottish tunes. This was followed by an Old Testament reading from Ezekiel, in which Dr. Fraser's well-known powers of elocution were admirably displayed. An extempore prayer bearing on ministerial duties came next, and then one of the hymns following the psalms in the collection used at the Church, and specially adapted 'for ministers'. The singing was of course unaccompanied, and led by a precentor with powerful voice, who occupied a position below the pulpit. Then Dr. Fraser read 1 Peter v., and immediately proceeded to the exposition, which was to form his sermon for the evening. The chapter commences, it will be remembered, with the words—'The elders'—that is, the presbyters—'which are among you I exhort, who am also an elder'—or presbyter; but in nearly every instance Dr. Fraser used the term bishop as equivalent in its sense of overseer to that of presbyter. The Episcopate was needful now as then, he said. It was necessary that each congregation should have its group of bishop-presbyters, and that these should meet in Presbyteries and Synods. Peter had an overwhelming claim to personal authority, but it was, said the preacher, only little men who stood on official importance. Real heroes like Peter and Paul put themselves on a level with their fellow-men. Feed the flock—'episcopize' the flock—was the command. (It is perhaps impossible for those out of the Anglican Church to understand how strangely these 'episcopal' terms sounded coming from such a source.) This shepherding of the sheep was the crucial question of the day. It was no use to say that all presbyters are bishops, unless the Christian episcopate could be recognised in the presbyters above the chaos of system, anti-system, over-system, and under-system. Then, again, they were not to lord it over God's heritage. They were not 'lord bishops'. So, when the chief-shepherd, the archbishop (and there was no archbishop but Christ), should appear they should receive a crown of glory at the great day of coronation!

Another hymn called 'Pressing on' followed, and then Dr. Fraser descended from the pulpit, and, occupying the Moderator's chair, 'constituted the Synod by prayer'. Names were called over, and Dr. Fraser proposed as his successor in the office of Moderator for the ensuing year one who had been thirty years in the ministry, and nine years in his present charge, the Rev. John Mathieson, minister of Hampstead. The name was received with much applause; and Mr.

Mathieson, being fetched from the vestry by the smiling man in the dress-coat, passed to the Moderator's chair, and read from MS. his inaugural address.

In broad Scottish accent quite different from Dr. Fraser's diction, which had not the suspicion of a 'brogue', Mr. Mathieson eloquently dwelt on the present aspects of Presbyterianism in England. He congratulated his co-religionists on their unity, while they were, he said, 'broad' enough to embrace different opinions on minor matters. He threw in a word of commendation on the American evangelists, 'who have moved the myriad-peopled city', he said, 'as it has never been moved before'. It might have been that their own ministers had relied too much on intellect, and that God was teaching them a lesson in these men, whose lips had been touched by a live coal from the altar. In the last ten years the English congregations had increased from 106 to 160, and that not chiefly in the North, where such increase might have been expected, but in the South, where they were more scattered. Perhaps the state of the Church of England might lead people to look at Presbyterianism as the safeguard against Romanism under the form of Ritualism. He concluded a most interesting excursus by dwelling on the prospects of Church extension, of union with the United Presbyterians, and eventually of a complete unanimity which might once more make people say, 'Behold, how these Christians love one another!'

b.

When I set out on my voyage of discovery to Barnsbury Grove one Sunday morning, I really knew little more of the Sandemanians or Glassites than what the general public had probably learnt from the fact of the late Professor Faraday having been a member of the body— a circumstance which alone did much to rescue them from otherwise inevitable obscurity. I had heard that they carried to its extreme point the doctrine of 'faith without works', and that a love-feast, very like an ordinary early dinner, formed part of their cultus. I had heard sly hints that the 'kiss of peace' was literally retained among them too; but a somewhat prolonged experience had led me to discount considerably popular rumour on these matters. How far I had to do so in this case will by-and-by appear.

To Barnsbury Grove, Islington, then, I bent my way, and found the Sandemanian Chapel externally very like other chapels. Entering, I made one of a moderate congregation, composed of all grades and both sexes, who had commenced worship by singing a psalm. At the farther end of the chapel were two rows of raised seats, one above the other;

and in these were seated seven gentlemen, four in the lower and three in the upper bench, who were apparently the ministers for the day. The person who occupied the centre of the upper row was evidently the chief minister; while the middle of the lower was filled by one who acted as sort of precentor, giving out the psalms and leading the singing. The version of the Psalter in use was unrhymed; and at the conclusion of the first portion the Lord's Prayer was said by the chief minister, in a strange nasal voice, which may have been either natural or assumed. Singularly enough, this presiding minister bore a strong personal resemblance to the late Professor Faraday—a fact which I should have certainly noticed even had I not known of Faraday's connection with the community. After the Lord's Prayer came another portion of psalmody, this time from the lugubrious 69th Psalm, sung to a melancholy tune, as slowly as possible; then another prayer; then another portion of Psalm 69th, followed by still another prayer, and still another portion of the same psalm. This went on until every gentleman on the two rows of seats had prayed, and a selection from the peculiarly mournful psalm had been sung over each. The effect was to me monotonous in the extreme. During the whole period, however, people kept dropping into the chapel, so that comparatively few underwent the whole ordeal.

After this remarkable exordium, which took up much time—for the prayers were long, and the psalms slow—four chapters were read in succession by the same person, without any break at all. These chapters were Numbers 13th, Ezra 8th, Psalm 37th, and St. John 9th. Thus, with so little variety, did the service make progress for one hour and fifty minutes; and just when the Islington people were coming out of their churches, and I must plead guilty to being at the very nadir of depression, the most melancholy of the seven gentlemen got up and began a sermon which lasted more than half an hour. He took for his subject an exposition of that most penitential Psalm, the 77th, 'I cried unto God', etc; and, though there really was nothing particular to cry about in his sermon, he kept weeping and almost losing his voice from emotion—nay, more than that, he made many of his congregation cry too, out of mere sympathy, for the discourse was rather critical than pathetic. I could not pretend to sketch its subject. The only definite idea which I could clearly trace was, that thoughts of sin in the night were not to be explained away next morning by merely physical causes; but when the preacher arrived at this point he broke down from sheer emotion, and passed on to some other topic, which gradually worked up to the same lamentable climax. I never remember under-

going such a protracted process of depression in my life. I am not
exaggerating when I say that, throughout the whole service and sermon,
the words kept ringing in my ears, as though I had really seen them
forming a motto over the doorway, 'All hope abandon, ye who
enter here'. And yet—let me make an honest confession of my fault—
when I did, now and then, look round the congregation, I could not
help for a moment marvelling at the substantial and intellectual
appearance of many of its members; and wondering still more to see
many pretty girls near whom I felt I should like to sit at the love-feast
if the φιλημα really were still an institution. However, the service was
over; the good people fell to talking; and I was quite glad to see the
gloom disperse. I saw something else, too: that, as a stranger, I was
expected to take my departure; so, not without a feeling of relief, I
made my exit, leaving them to their love-feast, with a pious wish that
it might prove more cheerful than their service.

78   The effects of emigration, 1873

An extract from the Baptist Union Committee Report, 1873, *Baptist
Handbook, 1874*, p. 42.

In the second half of the century emigration was ever more
frequently cited as an explanation for reductions in membership in
Nonconformist churches. This extract applies to Baptists, but
references could be produced from each denomination. The 1870s
marked the beginning of an increase in emigration which was later
accentuated by the agricultural depression.

There were special reasons, moreover, why the last year should have
been marked by a diminished increase in our membership. Emigration,
which has been carried on upon an unusual scale of magnitude, has
affected the rural churches, of which so many are Baptist, to a very
appreciable extent. No fewer than *nine* Baptist ministers have left
the parent country for the Colonies or the United States; and it is by no
means a solitary instance of the degree to which church membership

suffers, when one pastor reports the loss of from twenty to thirty
from his own congregation. Every year are our churches despoiled of
the hope and flower of the flock; and no doubt the inequalities in
our annual returns of increase are considerably due to the rise and fall
of the tide of emigration.

79   The effects of the growth of suburbs, 1873

An extract from the address of the Wesleyan Conference to the
societies: *Minutes of the Wesleyan Conference, 1873*, pp. 278–9.

Nonconformists were not unaware of the effect of social changes on
religious observance in the towns, particularly caused by the
movement of population from the centre to the suburbs. The
Wesleyan Conference had first drawn attention to this in 1855, and
this extract from 1873 is one of several references to the problem.

We have evidence of alteration in the increase of population, in the
growth of cities and towns, in the development of industrial resources,
in the augmentation and wide distribution of wealth, in methods of
locomotion, in the general spread of physical comforts, and in the
unintermitting stimulus applied to the public mind by a cheap press.
The result is, that men live at so rapid a rate, the mind is so constantly
excited by the endless succession of subjects hurrying through it, that
habits of reflection can scarcely be formed, and a thoughtful, meditative
piety becomes difficult. The high pressure at which business is carried on,
and the multiplication of all kinds of engagements, are unfavourable to
devotional retirement and attendance on the week-night means of
grace. . . . Many institutions, never designed to come into competition
with our week-night services, nevertheless do present counter-attrac-
tions which draw away from chapels and class-rooms not a few of the
lukewarm and the young. Need we add, beloved brethren, that the
plea of promoting intellectual culture, or even philanthropic work,
cannot justify the 'forsaking the assembling of ourselves together, as
the manner of some is'?

Amongst the altered customs of the people, that of the removal of their residence by influential families from the centre to the suburbs of large towns, however excusable or even commendable in itself, has acted in some instances prejudicially to the interests of religion. Old chapels, some of them of hallowed associations, have been left struggling with diminished congregations, and these made up largely of one class—the very poor. On the other hand some suburban congregations are so distant from the quarters inhabited by the indigent, that wealthy members of them have little opportunity of showing kindness to fellow-worshippers in poverty, and of spreading amongst the poor, by efforts of their own, the blessings of the Gospel,—a work which the Lord Jesus referred to as one proof of His own Messiahship. Not a few families, moreover, have been lost to us altogether by this modern custom. Drawn to pleasant neighbourhoods by such considerations as salubrity and respectability, they have suffered serious spiritual loss in passing from localities where religious advantages abound to places where there are few or none. Is it not deplorable and strange that families professing godliness should not, in selecting a new home, consider first and foremost the soul's health? And yet, in the migratory tendencies of the age, an aggressive evangelism should find an incentive to zeal and liberality in chapel-extension and Home-Missionary work; so that it may become difficult for any of our members, be they merchants, artisans, miners, or agriculturists, to find themselves wherever they go, at a considerable distance from a Methodist chapel and a Methodist class.

80   Nonconformists and the Bulgarian massacres, 1876

An extract from J. G. Rogers, *An Autobiography* (1903), pp. 210-11.

The Rev. J. Guinness Rogers discusses the view that it was the Nonconformist reaction to the Bulgarian massacres which led to the close links between Gladstone and the Nonconformists, but leaves unanswered the question why this should have aroused so much public indignation.

It has been said that it was this Eastern Question which more than any other cemented the bonds of attachment between Nonconformists and the great Liberal statesman. Personally, I never had any hesitation as to the course which, as a Christian man, I ought to take in relation to the Bulgarian atrocities.   When the first report of them reached this country, I happened to be spending a quiet vacation time at Whitby. The story at once touched the imagination and the hearts of the towns-people, as well as of a great many visitors who happened to be at that delightful watering-place at the time. A meeting was held—the fore-runner of many—and the enthusiasm in opposition to the Turk was intense. Shortly after my return to London, a friend came to me and said that Mr Gladstone, with whom I was then but slightly acquainted, had said that the Nonconformists might, if so disposed, help very materially in awakening the opinion of the country upon the question, and my friend had therefore come to me in order to consider what was possible to be done. I immediately, in co-operation with two or three others, convened a meeting of well-known Nonconformists, and to them I submitted a series of resolutions on the subject. The proposals were at first received with some doubt and hesitation, for though they were not violent, they were certainly sufficiently decided. One able doctor of divinity, an excellent Presbyterian, at once pronounced upon them his condemnation. I quietly asked that they should be read clause by clause and *verbatim et literatim*. When the discussion closed, and the document had been adopted. I had the satisfaction of finding that my original resolution had been passed with the alteration of one single word—'bloody' for 'sanguinary', or it may have been the reverse. A Vigilance Committee was appointed, which acted quietly and vigorously throughout the whole of the agitation. We held no great public meetings at that time except one at Cannon Street Hotel, the only one held in London during the height of the excitement and which passed off without disturbance. But the Committee was what it professed to be—a Committee of Vigilance. Not a step of importance was taken in Parliament upon which it was not summoned and did not express an opinion. It was commissioned to act on every emergency, and it took care to let none escape. I venture to think it did some service to the cause of Liberty, Christianity, and Humanity at an extremely severe crisis.

It is not easy to understand the real secret of the intensity of passionate excitement prevailing during the Bulgarian agitation. The Home Rule controversy, and the schism which succeeded, produced more division and consequent estrangement in Dissenting circles, but the public feeling was hardly so intense as in relation to this Eastern Question. Why London citizens should have taken upon themselves the championship of the Turks is a point which I have never been able to comprehend.

81   The Moody and Sankey Mission, 1874-5

An extract from N. Hall, *An Autobiography* (1898), p. 233.

The American evangelistic team of Dwight L. Moody (who preached the sermons) and Ira D. Sankey (who sang the solos) made their first extended visit to England in 1874–5. The denominations remained officially uncommitted on the new style of mission, but individual ministers often joined in enthusiastically, as did Newman Hall, the famous Congregationalist.

January 26th—Telegram from Moody to help him at Birmingham. A convention at Bingley Hall, 6,000 present in afternoon. I spoke on

'How to Reach the Masses'. In the evening Moody preached to 15,000, and multitudes vainly tried to enter. Hundreds rose in token of a desire to be prayed for. Afterwards I addressed a crowd of young men in a neighbouring church.

February 1.—Again summoned by Moody, and addressed 7,000 the following night. Kindly entertained by Dr. and Mrs Dale. Much impressed with his strength of character, learning, genius, and piety.

February 5th—Moody invited all the London clergy to meet him at Freemasons' Hall, which was crowded. Among many questions, a clergyman said: 'Please tell us what your object is?'—'*To preach the Gospel.*' 'What do you do with converts?'—'*Leave them with Christ to take care of.*' 'Would it not be well to print your views of the Gospel, that we might know?'—The evangelist replied, '*They're in print already; you'll find them in the Fifty-third of Isaiah.*'—Ritualists, Evangelicals, and Nonconformists of all sorts crowded the hall.

March 15th—To Moody and Sankey's service at the Agricultural Hall. 20,000 present. Till nearly midnight busy with him in the 'Enquiry Room' trying to guide anxious seekers to Christ.

82   The mission of Primitive Methodism, 1875

An extract from the Address to the Societies, *Minutes of the Primitive Methodist Conference, 1875*, pp. 92–3.

The Primitive Methodists always regarded themselves as having a special mission to the working classes. This reassertion of that belief came at a time when the social composition of Primitive Methodism was beginning to change, and some of its members were beginning to prosper.

Wesleyan Methodism has sprung from the bosom of the Church of England; the leading Nonconformists of our country have sprung from Puritan forefathers, who also came from the bosom of the same Church. But Primitive Methodism has no ecclesiastical pedigree of which to boast. It has sprung from a root out of a dry ground—the lowly working classes of English society. The other churches of our country have been, and are, more or less, identified with the upper or middle classes of society. Among the sons of toil we see the rock whence we were hewn, and the hole of the pit whence we were digged. Such an origin is neither a matter of boasting nor of humiliation. It is simply a matter of fact. But facts, historical facts, belong to God—they are the utterances of his mouth, the disclosures of his purposes. Other churches have their respective characteristics—let them preserve them; they have their appropriate work—let them perform it. We shall not envy them, however, nor repine at their success. . . . We think that Primitive Methodism, being a distinct denomination, having sprung from a distinct and independent root, must have a separate existence if it is to answer the purpose for which God has brought it into being. As a distinct denomination, it has certain germs of power, and possibilities of excellence, on the cultivation of which, not amalgamation with others, depends its usefulness and success. It has been from the beginning the people's Church; it is now; and wherever and whenever it shall cease to sustain this peculiarity, its career is ended, and its glorious possibilities prevented.

83   Secular and spiritual priorities in Congregationalism, 1876

An extract from a paper on 'Organised Congregationalism' by the Rev. Dr Joseph Parker, read to the Congregational Union Assembly in 1876: *Congregational Year Book, 1877*, p. 88.

The political preoccupations of Nonconformists did not go unchallenged, but the contrast posed here is between secular and spiritual, not Liberal and Conservative. Joseph Parker was minister of the City Temple and one of the most famous preachers in late nineteenth-century Congregationalism.

Another effect of a too highly organised Congregationalism is to turn the Congregational Union into a politico-religious debating club and board of directors. What an amazing amount of so-called 'business' we have to do! We have to disestablish the Church, modernise the Universities, rectify the policy of School Boards, clear the way to burial-grounds, subsidise magazines, sell hymn-books, play the hose upon Convocation, and generally give everybody to understand that if we have not yet assailed or defended them, it is not for want of will, but merely for want of time. Let me be clearly understood here, if you please. All the points I have mentioned are more or less important, some of them supremely so. Occasional and emphatic reference ought to be made to them; but I contend that they ought not to form the very staple and substance of our discussions, that we have other work to do, and that such work as I have referred to can be better done by the great and vigorous societies which have already undertaken to do most of it. I want to know what we ourselves are doing for the spiritual enlightenment and progress of the world? What are we doing in foreign missions? in missions home and colonial? in chapel building? in Sunday schools? These I should make the main, the necessary, the cital questions, and leave other subjects to be treated incidentally, and vollaterally as time might allow.

84   Rural Nonconformity, 1876

An extract from a paper by the Rev. John Clifford on 'Religious Life in the Rural Districts of England' read to the Baptist Union Assembly in 1876: *Baptist Handbook, 1877*, pp. 108–10.

The difficulties faced by rural Nonconformity in the 1870s, both as a result of social and economic change, and traditional social pressures, are here described by the Rev. John Clifford. His experience as secretary of the New Connexion of General Baptists brought him into direct contact with many of the situations he describes.

. . . These small Christian Republics feed the fires of loyalty to truth, maintain the rights of conscience, build up invisible but real barriers against enervating tyrannies and degrading superstitions, and, in many cases, keep village life from becoming a monotonous and disgusting corruption. As a matter of fact and figures, they have as strong a hold upon the men as the women, and, compared with churches in small towns, have twice as large a proportion of males to females and three times as many as the churches in such towns as Nottingham and Birmingham. . . .

Still, as everybody who knows anything about our village churches is aware, theirs is a troubled and increasingly perplexed life. . . . Letter after letter has come to hand assuring me that the struggle for existence is becoming more and more keen, because men and women are becoming more scarce. Science is improving man out of the agricultural village, and substituting machines which do his work better and in less time. The most popular, and, in some districts, the only available solution of the labour question is that unfortunate one of England— the emigration of men and women to Canada and Australia, in order to retain devastating hares and rabbits, pheasants and partridges. The gains of manufacturing Lancashire, New South Wales, and the Canadas are due to the depopulation of the counties of Lincoln and Berks, Wilts and Somerset.

And our churches are the first to suffer from this exhaustive process, and they suffer the most. Only villagers who have a soul venture in them, the best brains, and the most resolute will, are ready to leave the traditions and associations of the old home for the risks of the sea and the hazards of a crowded town; and these are precisely the men and women who have had courage enough to think for themselves, to mark out an independent path, and in fidelity to conscience join the conventicle in the village back street; and, therefore, by their removal, there are not only fewer hearers of the Gospel message, but also fewer members of our churches, fewer local preachers and Sunday-school teachers, fewer new books on the ministers' shelves, and, therefore, less freshness in his sermons and brightness in his work; in a word, there is in too many quarters the slow and painful weakening of the village church.

Nor is it less distressing to find that, whilst the population is being gradually thinned of its best members, the foes the remnant has to fight are more and more desperate every day. It is a trifle that 'Society' in its superior enlightenment treats 'Salem Chapel' as a vulgar impertinence. That can easily be borne. But it is intolerable that landowner and squire, justice of the peace and priest of the Church, should form a confederacy to close the chapel doors, and stamp out the hated pestilence

of Dissent, not minding what mud they put their feet into if they only
succeed. 'Protestant' clergymen resort to the arts of the theatre for a
Christian liturgy, and to the tricks of the Confessional for a ritual, that
they may save men from the perils of schism. They empty our chapels
with the lever of parochial charities, forge fetters for human minds out
of the beneficence of our forefathers, muffle the parental conscience
with the garments of a clothing club, and use the whip of the magistrate
to lash an unwilling people to church. . . .

85   The need for church extension, 1876

An extract from a paper by the Rev. C. Clemance on 'The Evangelisation of England' read to the Congregational Union Assembly in
1876: *Congregational Year Book, 1877*, pp. 79–80.

Although the second half of the century has been called a period of
religious boom, Nonconformists were as keenly aware as the Church
of England that relatively they were falling behind. The Rev.
Clement Clemance, a Nottingham Congregational minister, lists
the areas of priority if the churches are to keep pace with new
developments.

It is, we think, too often forgotten that the growth of our Churches
cannot be considered satisfactory (in neighbourhoods where the population is increasing) if they remain numerically the same, nor is it
satisfactory if, in such localities, they merely show a numerical increase.
In no place can our position in 1876 be satisfactory, unless our Church
membership bears a proportion to the population equal to that which
it had, say twenty-five years ago—and not even then, unless that
proportion to the population twenty-five years ago, was such as it
then behoved our Churches to have exhibited and maintained. A
Church of 300 members in a town of 5,000, has declined proportion-
ably if it remains 300 while the town has been growing to 10,000.
Its membership is just what it was. Its strength is *one-half* what it was in
relation to the town. . . . In looking for an answer to the question—

In what direction shall we extend?—there are at least three kinds of districts whose welfare we have to study. There are thinly-populated districts, where villages lie scattered, in none of which are there enough inhabitants for a considerable place of worship, but which may be grouped around one centre of evangelising zeal. Call these Class A. There are growing neighbourhoods, composed once of rural populations, but which, through the opening up and development of mining and manufacturing operations, are not only changing their character, but are so on the increase that they are rapidly becoming large towns. Call these Class B. There are our large centres of population, in which the tendency must be to a withdrawment of the people from the centre to the suburbs, and in many cases the cities and towns may even decrease in population, in which case the population is sent out afar, and is, therefore, in the suburbs increasing in a double ratio, because the suburbs are receiving two streams of population. They are receiving one stream of population from the very heart of these towns, and they are receiving another stream of population from the people who are leaving the thinly-populated districts, and drifting towards the great centres of industry; and it is most important that we should know just how this matter stands, how it affects the growth of our Congregational Churches. Call these Class C. . . . Thinly-populated districts are in many cases over-supplied with religious accommodation; rapidly-increasing districts are as yet inadequately met; the greatest need of all is in the county town; and where a town is largest the need is greatest.

86   A service at the Metropolitan Tabernacle, 1878

An extract from W. Y. Fullerton, *C. H. Spurgeon: A Biography* (1920), pp. 150–5.

C. H. Spurgeon continued to fill his church regularly until his death in 1892. Periodically the regular congregation stayed away on a Sunday evening so that outsiders might have a chance to hear him, and it is one of these services that is described in this report in *The Hornet*.

At 6.15 we find ourselves in Newington, opposite the most stolid and matter-of-fact-looking place of worship. Nothing can be more practical-looking than this vast edifice. Not an inch of space is devoted to idle ornament, not a ton of stone is sacrificed to effect. There is a Greek portico, no doubt; but the portico of the Greeks was useful to keep the sun from the philosophers who taught, and the portico of the Tabernacle is useful to keep the rain off those who come to learn.

People are crowding in at about the rate of two hundred a minute, quite as fast as the business-like doors can swallow them up. Tram-cars and omnibuses come up to the gates, set down their swarm of serious-looking folk and pass away empty. Now and then a hansom cab rattles up, drops a commonplace bride and bridegroom, or a common-place elderly couple, and departs. But the vast majority of those who come arrive on foot, and toil up the steps with laggard feet, as though they had walked from a great distance. We do not observe any of the very poor. The waifs and strays of many shires remote from London, and the usual visitors from the two cities, twelve towns, and the one hundred and forty-seven villages that go to make up the metropolis, appear all to be in the social zone between the mechanic and the success-ful but not fashionable tradesman. We find no one as low as a working man, no one who follows any liberal or learned profession. . . . There is a steady persistence in the way these people come up these steps, as though they were quite sure of finding within exactly what they seek. There is no hesitancy or loitering. Each one has come to hear Spurgeon preach, and each one is resolved to get as good a seat as possible. The congregation does not look super-spiritualised or super-depraved. It is Sunday, and its worldly work for the week is over, and this day has been laid aside for rest and the business of the other world, and this congregation has come to look after its work for the other world or to rest.

At twenty minutes past six we enter. All places on the floor have been occupied for some time; all seats on the first tier are full, so we climb up the steep, high stone steps through the square, desolate-look-ing stair-well. Everything here, as outside, is practical, except the steps, which are so high as almost to be impracticable. In a moment we are in the spacious body of the church. Beyond all doubt, this is one of the most novel sights in London. The vast lozenge-shaped space is paved with human heads and packed 'from garret to basement' with human forms. 'Over the clock' there is a little room to spare, but in less than five minutes the seats there are appropriated, and for fully five minutes before the hour at which the service is announced to begin there is not a vacant seat in the church.

Inside, too, all is practical and business-like in the arrangements. The light is capital, the colour is cheerful, the seats are comfortable and commodious. There is no attempt to produce a dim religious light, no subduing or dulling of spent tertiary colours, no chance of any one posing as a martyr because of occupying one of the seats. When the acoustical properties of the building are tested they are found to be most admirable. The place was evidently designed and built that the congre-gation might sit in comfort, and hear and see without strain to the senses.

Fortune favoured me, and we got a place in the first row, about half-way down the left-hand side of the platform. Upon the seat to be occupied by each person is a half-sheet of paper, printed on one side, and bearing the heading 'Hymns to be sung at the Metropolitan Tabernacle on Lord's Day evening, August 11, 1878.' Under the head-ing comes the following paragraph preceding the hymns: 'It is earnestly requested that every sincere worshipper will endeavour to join in the song, carefully attending to time and tune; and, above all, being con-cerned to worship the Lord in spirit and in truth. The hymns are selected from "Our own Hymn Book", compiled by Mr Spurgeon. It is a special request that no one will attempt to leave the Tabernacle until the service is quite concluded, as it creates much disturbance, and renders it difficult to hear the preacher.' For the present, each person has the half-sheet of paper folded up, or is studying it, or using it as a fan.

On a level with the first tier of seats is Mr Spurgeon's platform. It protrudes into the well of the amphitheatre, so that it is visible from all parts of the church. Upon it are a table, chair and sofa. On the table rests a Bible. From the platform to the floor runs down each side a semi-spiral flight of stairs leading to a lower platform, situated immediately under and in front of the higher. The carpet of the platform and the cover of the sofa are of the same hue—deep red, approaching plum colour.

Precisely at thirty minutes past six several men come down the passage directly behind the platform. First of these is a stout, square-built, square-jawed man of between forty and fifty. Although most of those present this evening are strangers, there is no commotion upon the entry of the famous preacher. There are two reasons for the apparent insensibility, one physical, one mental. The physical reason is that the building is so admirably constructed, so successfully focussed upon the small patch of platform, that every man, woman and child in the house can see the preacher from the moment he reaches the parapet of his balcony. The mental reason is that at the root of the attendance of this vast concourse here this evening lies the business idea. There is no personal enthusiasm toward the preacher. The people have come on business, and are too good business people to jeopardise their business-like calm by a disturbing interest in anything whatever but the subject-matter of the evening's service. It is rarely that a preacher of such wide and lasting popularity exercises so little personal magic over a congregation.

The service opens with a prayer. Looking down from the height at which we sit, the great number of bright-coloured hats and bonnets of the women on the floor of the house look like a parterre of flowers, and, higher up, the first tier, sloping from the back to the front, presents the appearance of flowers on a vast stand. At the beginning of the prayer the whole multitude bend forward with one impulse, the bright hats and bonnets and bald and grey heads are lost to view, and in their stead appears a dark grey surface, made up of broadcloth-clad backs of the men and dark shoulder articles of the women.

When the prayer is concluded there is a faint rustling sound, and looking down again we see the heads are now uplifted, and close to each head a half-sheet of paper held at a convenient distance for reading. We glance carefully round, and as far as we are able to see no one is without a paper and every one seems studying his own. There are four hymns in all, and one is about to be sung. Mr Spurgeon gives it out slowly and with enormous distinctness. The effect of his voice in giving out the hymn is very peculiar. The words come separately and individually, and take their place, as it were, with intervals between them, like men who are to assist at a pageant, arriving one by one and marching to their posts. The first stanza having been read over and the first line repeated, all rise to their feet by one act of accord. The choir start the hymn (a special band of singers for this particular evening), and between five and six thousand voices take it up with great precision as to time and great accuracy as to tune. The vast volume of sound does not deafen or disgust. It is mild and suppressed. You know it has the strength of a giant, but you feel it is not using it tyrannously. At our back is a poor, slender-looking man with a red-brown beard. He is like a shoemaker out of work. His voice comes in with clear, sharp edge, a counter-tenor. By our side is a woman, a maid-of-all-work we guess her to be. She strikes in only now and then with a few low contralto notes she is sure of; she never risks a catastrophe up high. She has only about three and a half notes, but she never loses a chance of contributing them when the occasion offers. On our other side is a fresh-coloured schoolgirl home for the holidays. Her voice is a thin soprano, and seems to roughen the edges of the counter-tenor's. But when this happens there floats in upon our exercised ears the dull, low boom of a rolling bass. Who the owner of the bass is we cannot find out. We look around vainly endeavouring to discover. Now we fix on one, now on another, but this *ignis fatuus* of a voice eludes our most exhaustive efforts to run it to—flesh. Meanwhile abroad in the hollow roof of the building the confluent concord of five thousand voices swells the hymn to an imperial pæan.

87   Condemnation of the government, 1879

Resolution of the Baptist Union Assembly, 9 October 1879, *Baptist Handbook, 1880*, pp. 99–100.

The political resolutions of the Nonconformist assemblies became increasingly specific in the 1870s and early 1880s. Resolutions condemning the Conservative government and upholding the Liberal opposition were passed by Baptists, Congregationalists, the Methodist New Connexion and the United Methodist Free Churches, both nationally and locally. The resolution of the Baptist Union is typical.

That the present condition of the country demands the serious consideration of the Christian community; that in the judgement of this Assembly the policy of the Government has been the cause of needless wars, has involved the nation in grave financial difficulties, and has failed to ameliorate by domestic legislation the social and moral evils under which the country suffers; that this meeting, therefore, urges upon all members of the Baptist Union the duty of active and united efforts to return members to Parliament pledged to oppose that policy.

88   Burials Act, 1880

Public General Acts, 43 & 44 Vict., *c.* 41.

Gladstone's Burials Act of 1880 solved the grievance which
Dissenters had felt over burials in parish churchyards for more than
fifty years. Most of the Act is concerned with the procedure by
which Nonconformist burials are to be notified to the incumbent,
but the crucial clause 6 which provided for a non-Anglican service
at the graveside is given here.

6   At any burial under this Act all persons shall have free access to
the churchyard or graveyard in which the same shall take place. The
burial may take place, at the option of the person so having the charge
of or being responsible for the same as aforesaid, either without any
religious service, or with such Christian and orderly religious service at
the grave, as such person shall think fit, and any person or persons who
shall be thereunto invited, or be authorized by the person having the
charge of or being responsible for such burial, may conduct such
service or take part in any religious act thereat. The words 'Christian
service' in this section shall include every religious service used by any
church, denomination, or person professing to be Christian.

89   Nonconformity in Bacup, 1883-6

An extract from B. Webb, *My Apprenticeship* (1946), pp. 138-42.

Beatrice Webb visited some of her distant cousins in Bacup in the early 1880s in disguise, to see how the working classes lived. In her diary and letters to her father she describes her impressions of Nonconformity. The shift towards social issues is interesting, as is the suggested rivalry of new institutions, like the 'Co-op'.

I have spent the day in the chapels and schools. After dinner, a dissenting minister dropped in and I had a long talk with him; he is coming for a cigarette this evening after chapel. He told me that in all the chapels there was a growing desire among the congregation to have political and social subjects treated in the pulpit, and that it was very difficult for a minister, now to please. He also remarked that, in districts where co-operation amongst the workmen (in industrial enterprise) existed, they were a much more independent and free-thinking set.

There is an immense amount of co-operation in the whole of this district; the stores seem to succeed well, both as regards supplying the people with cheap articles and as savings banks paying good interest. Of course, I am just in the centre of the dissenting organisation; and as our host is the chapel keeper and entertains all the ministers who come here, I hear all about the internal management. Each chapel, even of the same denomination, manages its own affairs; and there are monthly meetings of all the members (male and female) to discuss questions of expenditure, etc. In fact each chapel is a self-governing community, regulating not only chapel matters but overlooking the private life of its members.

One cannot help feeling what an excellent thing these dissenting organisations have been for educating this class for self-government. . . .

Certainly the earnest successful working man is essentially conservative as regards the rights of property and the non-interference of the central government; and though religious feeling still has an immense hold on this class, and forms a real basis for many lives, the most religious of them agree that the younger generation are looking elsewhere for subjects of thought and feeling. . . .

[Letter to her father, November 1883.]

In living amongst mill-hands of East Lancashire (I reflect a few months later) I was impressed with the depth and realism of their religious faith. It seemed to absorb the entire nature, to claim as its own all the energy unused in the actual struggle for existence. Once the simple animal instincts were satisfied, the surplus power, whether physical, intellectual or moral, was devoted to religion. Even the social intercourse was based on religious sympathy and common religious effort. It was just this one-idea'd-ness and transparentness of life which attracted my interest and admiration. . . .

[MS. diary, 16 March 1884.]

Old Bacup remained unaltered among the bleak high hills. The mills, now working busily overtime, nestled in the valley, long unpaved streets of two-storied cottages straggled irregularly up the hills. The old coaching inn, with its air of refined age, still stood behind the new buildings representing municipal life; a 'Co-op.' shop asserted its existence with almost vulgar prominence. The twenty chapels of all denominations, the parish church, and the 'gentry-built' new church, stood on the same ground and are as yet unemptied. Bacup life is still religious—the book of science, insinuating itself into the mill-hand's cottage, has not yet ousted the 'book of life'. The young man goes to chapel, but he will not teach in the Bible class or the Sunday school. The books from the free 'Co-op.' library interest him more; his talk about God is no longer inspired by the spirit of self-devoting faith. But Bacup, in spite of municipal life and co-operative industry, is spiritually still part of the 'old world'. . . .

I was interested in the mill-hand's life. So long as the hours do not include overtime, the work is as healthful to body and mind as it well could be. Sitting by the hands at work, watching the invigorating quickness of the machinery, the pleasant fellowship of men, women and children, the absence of care and the presence of common interest— the general well-being of well-earned and well-paid work—one was tempted to think that here, indeed, was happiness—unknown to the strained brain-worker, the idle and overfed rich, or the hardly pressed very poor. Young men and women mix freely; they know each other as fellow-workers, members of the same or kindred chapels; they watch each other from childhood upwards, live always in each other's company. They pair naturally, according to well-tested affinity, physical and spiritual. Public opinion—which means religiously guided opinion—presses heavily on the misdoer or the non-worker,— the outcasting process, the reverse of the attracting force of East End life, is seen clearly in this small community, ridding it of the ne'er-do-weel and the habitual out-o'-work. There are no attractions for those who have not sources of love and interest within them; no work for those who cannot or will not work constantly. On the other hand, ill-success and unmerited failure are dealt with gently—for these people are, in the main, thinking of another world, and judge people not according to the position they have scrambled into in this, but according to their place in a future Heaven—won by godliness and self-renunciation. . . .

[MS. diary, October 1886.]

90   Congregational resolution on economics, 1885

Resolution of the Congregational Union Assembly, 15 May 1885: *Congregational Year Book, 1886*, p. 17.

All churches were slow to criticise the accepted political economy, but from the 1880s such criticisms began to appear. The resolution of the Congregational Union quoted here is obviously cautious, but reflects concern over the land question, popularised by Henry George.

That this Assembly, while deprecating all action that would lessen the sanctions of the rights of property, and recognising the conditions which at the present time control the markets both of labour and material, affirms it to be the duty of every Christian citizen to seek by all means in his power to diminish the inequalities which unjust laws and customs produce in the conditions of those who are common members of the State, to endeavour to bring about such changes in the modes of property in land as shall lead to a fairer distribution of it

among the people, to a more profitable employment of it in the pro-
duction of the common food of the people, and to the better housing
of the poor, and the relief of the overcrowding of the cities; and,
further, that it calls upon every Christian man and woman to remember
that the so-called laws of trade and economics are not the only rules
which should direct the transactions of manufacturers, traders, labourers
and purchasers.

91 Gladstone, Nonconformists and the Liberal party, 1876–86

Extracts from J. G. Rogers, *An Autobiography* (1903), pp. 214–15, and
J. Amery, *Life of Joseph Chamberlain*, iv (1951), pp. 511–12.

Although Nonconformist Liberals mostly regarded Gladstone as their
hero, it could be argued that it was his leadership which at critical
points prevented the Liberal party implementing Nonconformist
demands. The Rev. J. G. Rogers (a) took a charitable view, but
Joseph Chamberlain (b) was more cynical in an interview he had
with R. W. Perks, a prominent Liberal Member of Parliament, at
the height of the Education Bill controversy in autumn 1902.

a. (Rogers)
. . . Unquestionably there were two separate occasions when Mr.
Gladstone's policy did seem to check the Nonconformists' hopes. The
first was in that passionate movement on the Eastern Question which
began in 1876, and which, for the time, occupied the public mind
almost to the exclusion of every other question. At that time, Dr. Dale
and myself had just completed our Disestablishment campaign, and it
is not too much to say that there was an amount of interest and excitement on the subject which led us to hope, not certainly for immediate
action, but for greater prominence being given to it both inside the
circle of Dissent and in the Liberal Party itself. The agitation on the
Bulgarian atrocities effectively prevented any movement of the kind.

But, as has been seen, the Nonconformists, so far from regarding Mr. Gladstone as responsible for this unhappy *contretemps*, were among his most loyal and vigorous supporters. The same thing occurred in 1885. At that time the enfranchisement of the labourers had introduced an entirely new element into the county constituencies, which hitherto had been regarded as the preserves of rabid Toryism. I was myself at a great many meetings in the county elections at the time, and nothing struck me more than the intense feeling against the Establishment which was displayed by newly enfranchised electors. There was nothing which seemed to excite more enthusiasm than a reference to Disestablishment, and when any rustic speaker appeared on the platform he was pretty certain to make a vigorous onslaught upon the parson. The Disestablishment spirit was undoubtedly strong, as no one understood better than Mr. Chamberlain, the author of 'the unauthorized programme' of that time. Unfortunately, the Irish question appeared above the horizon at the critical moment. I cannot forget the feeling of intense disappointment with which I myself threw down the newspaper after reading one of Mr. Gladstone's Edinburgh speeches. 'Ah,' I said, 'Mr. Gladstone seems ready to do anything for the Irish; what is he going to do for his best friends, the English Nonconformists?' No doubt his action on this subject alienated a great many of his old Nonconformist supporters, and yet again it was amongst us that he found some of his most enthusiastic friends. Let me add that those who, like myself, steadily adhered to him, never for a moment suspected that the Irish question was introduced to evade the demands of the Nonconformists. Circumstances were unfortunate, that was all. . . .

b. (Chamberlain)
He then said, 'You Nonconformists, Perks, made a great mistake in 1886 when they followed Mr. Gladstone and refused to listen to me. Had they supported me, they would have had Disestablishment long ago. Now they have got nothing'. He then added, 'When Mr. Gladstone suddenly sprang his Irish policy upon the country after consulting Morley, it was not so much to satisfy Ireland that he did so, as to prevent me placing the Disestablishment of the Church of England in the forefront of the Liberal programme, as Mr. Gladstone knew and feared I meant to do', and then he repeated what he said before, 'You Nonconformists have got nothing—nothing'.

Notes

1 See A. W. W. Dale, *Life of R. W. Dale* (London, 1905), pp. 394–7.
2 H. S. Skeats and C. S. Miall, *History of the Free Churches of England, 1688–1891* (London, 1891), p. 599.
3 Text of Act in G. M. Young and W. D. Handcock, *English Historical Documents, 1833–74* (London, 1956), pp. 395–6.
4 N. Hall, *An Autobiography* (London, 1898), pp. 223–4.
5 M. Cruickshank, *Church and State in English Education* (London, 1964), pp. 14–37.
6 E.g., that between Dale and other Congregationalists: J. G. Rogers, *An Autobiography* (London, 1903), pp. 169–70.
7 See the Countess of Warwick, *The Life of Joseph Arch* (London, 1898); M. K. Ashby, *Joseph Ashby of Tysoe* (Cambridge, 1961).
8 Address to the Societies, *Minutes of the Primitive Methodist Conference*, 1872, p. 79.
9 'Statistics of Religious Accommodation in the Large Towns of England and Wales', the *Nonconformist*, November 1872 (supplements).
10 A. Mearns, *The Statistics of Attendance at Public Worship, as published in England, Wales and Scotland, by the Local Press, between October 1881 and February 1882* (London, 1882).
11 J. Marchant, *Dr John Clifford* (London, 1924), p. 42; D. Price Hughes, *The Life of Hugh Price Hughes* (London, 1904), pp. 190–208.
12 There is a description of the debate by Henry Richard, M.P., in A. Miall, *The Life of Edward Miall* (London, 1884), pp. 316–17.

Five   Ebb tide

From the Home Rule split to the First World War,
1886–1914

The 1890s began with a striking example of the new importance
attached to the social question—the publication of *In Darkest
England* in 1890, in which General William Booth of the Salvation
Army announced his conversion to the value of social work (93).
The details of Booth's social plan of salvation are not very important,
partly because they were not novel (particularly in the idea of self-
supporting farm colonies and emigration), but mainly because they
were never fully implemented. It was only the first stage of social
relief work for the poverty-stricken, the drunkards and the
prostitutes that was started. It is interesting that the Salvation Army
should have become so closely associated in the popular mind with
a feature of its work that was not adopted until more than twenty
years after its foundation.

1890 was also the year when the phrase 'the Nonconformist
conscience' was coined. It arose directly out of the Nonconformist
reaction to Parnell's involvement in the O'Shea divorce case. Hugh
Price Hughes was the Nonconformist spokesman on the issue (94),
and the irony of the situation in view of Nonconformist support for
Parnell and Home Rule was not lost on him. Nonconformist
pressure was important in determining Gladstone to declare that the
Liberals could no longer work with an Irish party led by Parnell.
But Parnell was not the only victim. Sir Charles Dilke's political
career was ruined through his involvement in a similar kind of
scandal. But it would be unfair to suggest that Nonconformists had
a monopoly of indignation on these occasions.

It was, in fact, becoming increasingly difficult for Nonconformity
to speak with a united voice on political issues. The Irish question
had begun the process, separating men like R. W. Dale from the
rest (92). Hugh Price Hughes, though a notable Wesleyan Liberal,
was cautious about identifying the Church collectively in party
politics,[1] perhaps because Wesleyan Liberals had always had to live
with Wesleyan Conservatives. Now Dale advanced a similar view
(95) and others too rejected the idea of a natural alliance between
Nonconformity and Liberalism (104). But on an issue like the Boer

War even Liberals were divided. Clifford opposed the war: Hughes favoured it, but more interesting than his support is his view that as Nonconformists were divided on the matter, it should not be discussed (98).

There was no let up in the problems facing Nonconformity in this period either. Agriculture remained depressed, affecting the Primitive Methodists with their strength among agricultural labourers (96b) and also the Baptists and Congregationalists with their strength among small farmers (96a). Both denominations felt that if the number of small farmers could be increased in some way, they would benefit. It may be misleading to speak of a general agricultural depression; but it should be noted that Baptists, Congregationalists, and Primitive Methodists were all strong in East Anglia where the depression was bad.

In the towns, the suburbs remained a challenge to church extension: the Congregationalists formed a new Church Extension Committee in the early 1890s, which presented a report in 1895 suggesting that there was a need for new churches in London and twenty-four other towns.[2] Other denominations too were concentrating their efforts in the suburbs, particularly the Wesleyans in London (100), who seemed to suffer more than other denominations from inner city drift (103 *Wesleyans*, cf. 62). The various missions, tabernacles, etc., were still very much in favour, and met with some success (99, 103 *Baptists*).

The Congregational Union in 1895 provided a pithy summary of the problems facing Nonconformity:[3]

> . . . In the rural districts, which are being rapidly denuded of their yeomanry, once our chief supporters, the struggle for existence grows increasingly severe. In the centres of population the out-of-town drift of the middle classes strains the resources of those who yet remain in the city churches; and meantime the rapid growth of suburban districts has created a clamant need for church extension. . . . If Congregationalism is to discharge its vocation it must be by proving its adaptation to the wants of the age. The time has gone by when any order of churches can flourish simply by its polity.

The last sentence was an almost unnoticed time bomb under traditional Nonconformist assumptions, for polity still lay at the heart of their differences from the Church of England.

It was perhaps a sign of these changes that the movement for

Free Church unity was a product of these years, as well as some
actual unions, in particular, the union of General and Particular
Baptists in 1891, and the union of the Methodist New Connexion,
the Bible Christians and the United Methodist Free Churches to form
the United Methodist Church in 1907. The Free Church unity
movement (97) began with a Free Church Congress on the lines of
the Anglican Church Congress in 1892. In order to make this a
representative gathering without committing the denominations to
send national representatives, it was decided in 1894 to invite
representatives of local councils of Free Churches. In 1896 the name
was changed to the National Council of the Evangelical Free
Churches. Quite as important as the institutional development and
the increasing claim of the Council to speak for the Free Churches
as a whole in the twentieth century is the theological development
that was its precondition, namely the development of a more
catholic doctrine of the Church among Nonconformists.
Relationships between leading Nonconformists and Anglicans were
improving; social divisions between the two groups were beginning
to disappear and it is interesting to speculate whether social or
theological factors were really more important in these changes.

Charles Booth's series of volumes on the religious influences in
the *Life and Labour of London* provides a useful picture of the state
of Nonconformity at the turn of the century. When taken with
the *Daily News* religious census of 1903-4,[4] it gives a survey of
unrivalled detail. It is true that it is confined to London, and
therefore it is in many ways untypical of the rest of the country,
particularly Nonconformity in the north. But in many ways the
style and pace of life in London was prophetic of twentieth-century
developments. Booth's picture (103) shows the effects of change but
also the diversity that still existed despite a certain 'convergence'
that had taken place over the previous century. What the surveys
showed more than anything else was the prevailing background of
indifference. The Anglican, Charles Masterman, summed up the
situation:[5]

> The tide is ebbing within and without the Churches. The drift is
> towards a non-dogmatic affirmation of general kindliness and
> good fellowship, with an emphasis rather on the service of man
> than the fulfilment of the will of God. Most modern activities of
> the great religious bodies are coming more and more to enlarge
> themselves into efforts towards social or humanitarian reforms.

Even the noisy warfare between the various denominations may be interpreted less as a sign of secure vitality than as evidence of uncertain position; a struggle excited less by confidence than by foreboding.

This illustrates how anachronistic the battle over the Education Bill of 1902 was. This was the last great battle between Nonconformity and the Church of England, and if it was won by anyone it was not by Nonconformity. It was not unimportant: there were grave issues of principle at stake. But, as Chamberlain saw, it was crassly handled so as to reunite the Nonconformists (101), a fact not lost on Lord Rosebery (102f). Divisions over the Boer War were soon forgotten. Education was the last area where discrimination against Nonconformists was still obvious, as Dr Macnamara pointed out (102b), but despite government concessions the main demands of Nonconformists were left untouched. In the country, out and out opposition was led by Clifford, and some Liberal Members of Parliament feared that a compromise might weaken this movement.[6] After the Bill became law, however, only a minority of Nonconformists followed Clifford into the Passive Resistance Movement which was modelled on the Church Rate agitation: members withheld their school rates.

The education battle rallied the Liberal ranks and sank the separate Liberal Unionist group among the Conservatives. It was probably partly responsible for the Liberal landslide of 1906, which produced the largest number of Nonconformist Members of Parliament in British history. But the Liberal government of 1906 was not the promised land. Birrell's Education Bill was dropped after hostile amendments in the House of Lords, and the only real gain for Nonconformists was the disestablishment of the Church in Wales, which became law under the Parliament Act in 1914. One minor triumph for Nonconformity was the election of the Rev. C. S. Horne to Parliament in 1910 (105). His description of the work of the House of Commons in the following years is a reminder that religious issues still lay below the surface of parliamentary business, even if they did not form the great issues of the day.

The First World War swept away nineteenth-century England for good, and with it went nineteenth-century Nonconformity. For those with eyes to see, the slowing down of Nonconformist expansion had been apparent long before. But the war produced a new crisis of faith, and dissolved many traditional values. After the war, John Clifford rejoiced that the presence of the king and queen at the Nonconformists' Thanksgiving Service confirmed a status that had been slighted when they were not invited to take part in the national service at Westminster Abbey (106). Clifford himself was made a Companion of Honour while Lloyd George was prime minister. But at the point when the status of Nonconformists was recognised, as Clifford saw it, the basis for that status in membership terms was slipping away; and the social changes transforming twentieth-century Britain were working against Nonconformity rather than for it.

92   R. W. Dale, the Congregational Union and the Irish question, 1888

An extract from A. W. W. Dale, *The Life of R. W. Dale* (1905), pp. 587–8.

After an embarrassing scene at the Congregational Union Assembly at Nottingham in 1888, the Rev. R. W. Dale of Birmingham, a friend and supporter of Joseph Chamberlain, decided to stay away from meetings of the Union in future. In this letter of 20 October 1888 to his friend, the Rev. J. Guinness Rogers (who supported Gladstone), he explains his reasons.

You will not wonder that I was just a little amused at your saying that we must take care not to sever religion from politics. I can sever religion from no political question; it does not follow that every political question is the proper concern of the Union. There are many grave things into which religion enters with which the Union has nothing to do. . . .

I have done very little for the Union for a great many years, and never did much, but I trust it will become more and more a real spiritual force. And if I drop out for a time I want to drop out quietly. I cannot at present see any other course. To discuss the Irish question either in general or special meetings seems to me a course full of danger; and my judgment today, therefore, is my judgment of last week—to be no party to the discussion of it. But how I can be present and yet silent I do not see. Put the case the other way. Suppose that the Union passed a resolution congratulating the Government on the remarkable diminution of boycotting and on the letting of derelict farms, and transmitted it to Mr Balfour, could you, with your views, be present at the discussion leading up to that resolution and be silent? If you felt it a duty to be silent, could you with a quiet conscience be present at the Union meetings?

I have been very unhappy about the whole business. It was a painful thing to separate myself from the Liberal Association; it is infinitely more distressing to have the conviction forced on me that I must for a time isolate myself from the Union and from other Nonconformist assemblies of a kindred sort.

93   'In Darkest England', 1890

The preface to W. Booth, *In Darkest England* (1890).

William Booth's book, *In Darkest England*, marked a change of policy for the Salvation Army by introducing social relief work as a prelude to evangelism. The preface explains and justifies the change of policy, while the book outlines an elaborate scheme of social relief, only the first stage of which was ever implemented on a large scale.

The progress of The Salvation Army in its work amongst the poor and lost of many lands has compelled me to face the problems which are more or less hopefully considered in the following pages. The grim necessities of a huge Campaign carried on for many years against the evils which lie at the root of all the miseries of modern life, attacked in a thousand and one forms by a thousand and one lieutenants, have led me step by step to contemplate as a possible solution of at least some of those problems the Scheme of Social Selection and Salvation which I have here set forth.

When but a mere child the degradation and helpless misery of the poor Stockingers of my native town, wandering gaunt and hunger-stricken through the streets droning out their melancholy ditties, crowding the Union or toiling like galley slaves on relief works for a bare subsistence, kindled in my heart yearnings to help the poor which have continued to this day and which have had a powerful influence on my whole life. At last I may be going to see my longings to help the workless realised. I think I am.

The commiseration then awakened by the misery of this class has been an impelling force which has never ceased to make itself felt during forty years of active service in the salvation of men. During this time I am thankful that I have been able, by the good hand of God upon me, to do something in mitigation of the miseries of this class, and to bring not only heavenly hopes and earthly gladness to the hearts of multitudes of these wretched crowds, but also many material blessings, including such commonplace things as food, raiment, home, and work, the parent of so many other temporal benefits. And thus many poor creatures have proved Godliness to be 'profitable unto all things, having the promise of the life that now is as well as of that which is to come'.

These results have been mainly attained by spiritual means. I have boldly asserted that whatever his peculiar character or circumstances might be, if the prodigal would come home to his Heavenly Father, he would find enough and to spare in the Father's house to supply all his need both for this world and the next; and I have known thousands, nay, I can say tens of thousands, who have literally proved this to be true, having, with little or no temporal assistance, come out of the darkest depths of destitution, vice and crime, to be happy and honest citizens and true sons and servants of God.

And yet all the way through my career I have keenly felt the remedial measures usually enunciated in Christian programmes and ordinarily employed by Christian philanthropy to be lamentably inadequate for any effectual dealing with the despairing miseries of these outcast classes. The rescued are appallingly few—a ghastly minority compared with the multitudes who struggle and sink in the open-mouthed abyss. Alike, therefore, my humanity and my Christianity, if I may speak of them in any way as separate one from the other, have cried out for some more comprehensive method of reaching and saving the perishing crowds.

No doubt it is good for men to climb unaided out of the whirlpool on to the rock of deliverance in the very presence of the temptations which have hitherto mastered them, and to maintain a footing there with the same billows of temptation washing over them. But, alas! with many this seems to be literally impossible. That decisiveness of character, that moral nerve which takes hold of the rope thrown for the rescue and keeps its hold amidst all the resistances that have to be encountered, is wanting. It is gone. The general wreck has shattered and disorganised the whole man.

Alas, what multitudes there are around us everywhere, many known to my readers personally, and any number who may be known to them by a very short walk from their own dwellings, who are in this very plight! Their vicious habits and destitute circumstances make it certain that, without some kind of extraordinary help, they must hunger and sin, and sin and hunger, until, having multiplied their kind, and filled up the measure of their miseries, the gaunt fingers of death will close upon them and terminate their wretchedness. And all this will happen this very winter in the midst of the unparalleled wealth, and civilisation, and philanthropy of this professedly most Christian land.

Now, I propose to go straight for these sinking classes, and in doing so shall continue to aim at the heart. I still prophesy the uttermost disappointment unless that citadel is reached. In proposing to add one more to the methods I have already put into operation to this end, do not let it be supposed that I am the less dependent upon the old plans, or that I seek anything short of the old conquest. If we help the man it is in order that we may change him. The builder who should elaborate his design and erect his house and risk his reputation without burning his bricks would be pronounced a failure and a fool. Perfection of architectural beauty, unlimited expenditure of capital, unfailing watchfulness of his labourers, would avail him nothing if the bricks were merely unkilned clay. Let him kindle a fire. And so here I see the folly of hoping to accomplish anything abiding, either in the circumstances or the morals of these hopeless classes, except there be a change effected in the whole man as well as in his surroundings. To this everything I hope to attempt will tend. In many cases I shall succeed, in some I shall fail; but even in failing of this my ultimate design, I shall at least benefit the bodies, if not the souls, of men; and if I do not save the fathers, I shall make a better chance for the children.

It will be seen, therefore, that in this or in any other development that may follow, I have no intention to depart in the smallest degree from the main principles on which I have acted in the past. My only hope for the permanent deliverance of mankind from misery, either in this world or the next, is the regeneration or remaking of the individual by the power of the Holy Ghost through Jesus Christ. But in providing for the relief of temporal misery I reckon that I am only making it easy where it is now difficult, and possible where it is now all but impossible, for men and women to find their way to the Cross of our Lord Jesus Christ. . . .

94   Hugh Price Hughes and Parnell, 1890

Two extracts from D. Price Hughes, *The Life of Hugh Price Hughes* (1904), pp. 347–8, 351–3.

The Rev. Hugh Price Hughes, a Wesleyan minister, is probably best known for his remark that 'what is morally wrong can never be politically right', made at the time of the O'Shea divorce case in which C. S. Parnell, the Irish Nationalist leader, was cited as co-respondent. These extracts from Hughes' biography describe his heart-searching on the matter on the day the court decision was announced, 17 November 1890, and give a few paragraphs from his address at St James's Hall the following Sunday.

a.
The current caricatures of my father always represented him with something of a distracted appearance—eyebrows knit to excruciation, and the look of one who was fighting foes within as well as those without. Certainly he was thus that afternoon every line and movement betraying that distress which the popular imagination had accorded him. As he paced up and down, his eyes fixed on the carpet, he repeated with almost dirge-like monotony a phrase which was soon to become general. 'Parnell must go. We cannot help it, but he must go.' From time to time he stopped at the window, surveying the opposite houses with unseeing gaze and lost apparently in prayer. Full well this time he saw the enemy charging, for there was that in his humanity which charged with them—so he prayed. Men of heart and conviction do not give their support—moral or active—to a man

and a party without sharing in the dismay that accompanies their sins and calamities. Tragedies are great in so far as they engulf those who are not immediately concerned with them. What men would say he already heard, and he wrestled with them in advance. Of Ireland as yet he scarcely dared to think, save that the cup of her sorrow was one drop the fuller. 'Parnell,' said his companion, 'will fight to the last. He will never retire.' 'What, what?' said he, and stood facing the window again. Then, as he paced, came a repetition of the dirge, 'He must go; it is terribly distressing, but he must go.' As he walked, it was observed that he gained in collectedness, in determination, as if, despite the distress which still devoured him, he was increasingly able to articulate his thought. 'If necessary,' he said quietly, 'everything must go. What are parties and causes compared to an issue like this— the establishing of Christ's kingdom? If we once let this principle go, and allow men convicted of these sins to assume honourable and leading positions, what is to happen to us, our youth, or anybody? The whole atmosphere will become vitiated, and righteousness an impossibility. Unless we speak out plainly now there will be loss untold, the social atmosphere more vitiated even than it is at present.' That entity which few understand, but which is so powerful in life, the social atmosphere into which men and women are born, was the goal of many of his endeavours. The leader who must go stirred compassion greater than the public divined, but the thought of the public life, the public tradition, which mould men and women from their youth up, heartened him for a thankless task, one of those tasks that men get through somehow, and then never refer to again. Many considered his action at this crisis the most striking of his whole life, and would refer to it with pleasure; but he never did.

b.
. . .'No one can suppose that I have any pleasure in dealing with this case. I have stood on this very platform at Mr Parnell's side rejoicing at the vindication of his character from the infamous charge of Pigott the forger; and if he had been able to vindicate it now, we all should have rejoiced more than we did then. Further, if he had retired quietly and promptly from public life, we would have spread the mantle of silence over him, and not uttered a word to add to his humiliation. I have a right to speak as a friend of the Irish people. I have made sacrifices for their cause; and although I have never declared myself on this debated issue on this platform, it is a matter of public notoriety that I have been for some years past an enthusiastic Home Ruler.

'I do not underestimate the immense and unique services which Mr Parnell has rendered to the Irish race. I say that it is to their credit that they should be grateful to him, that it would be truly disgraceful if they were not grateful, and that they should show their gratitude in every legitimate way. But there ought to be two limits to their gratitude. It ought not to exceed their patriotism, and it ought not to exceed their faith in God. . . .

'Suppose Mr Parnell died tomorrow, Home Rule would not die. A cause so legitimate and so sacred does not depend upon the life of any man. Put your trust in God, and not in Parnell. . . .

'We love Ireland. We passionately desire her well-being; but our first obedience and our highest devotion must be to God. We have sacrificed much for Ireland. She is entitled to many sacrifices at our hands; but there is one thing we will never sacrifice, and that is our religion. We stand immovably on this eternal rock; what is morally wrong can never be politically right. . . .'

95   R. W. Dale warns the Birmingham Free Church Council against political involvement, 1892

An extract from A. W. W. Dale, *The Life of R. W. Dale* (1905), p. 649.

The Rev. R. W. Dale was a supporter of co-operation between Nonconformists for religious purposes, but he did not regard social and political reforms, however desirable in themselves, as legitimate objects of the churches' activity. In this extract from a speech at the conference called to discuss the formation of a Free Church Council in Birmingham, he explains his view.

. . . we have come to the conclusion that the interference of organised churches with organised political societies has proved after all a false method of effecting the great objects of the Christian gospel. . . . I have always felt that the line to be taken is this: that the churches should do all they can in the power of the grace and truth of Christ to renew and sanctify all whom they reach; and that then Christian men—as citizens, not as members of churches—should appear in the community to discharge their duties to it, under the control of the spirit and law of Christ. . . .

You will not be able to stop with pronouncing an opinion on questions that are practically before Town Councils and Parliament. I believe that you will be bound to interfere in local elections, both municipal and parliamentary, if you carry out the principles which led to the formation of such a council as is now proposed. I believe that we shall not hasten the triumph of the principles for which we care—shall not hasten the securing of the ends on which our hearts are set—by any such organised interference of churches with municipal and political life. I do not want to see a Nonconformist party in Birmingham touching municipal elections. I do not want to see a Nonconformist party in Birmingham touching political elections. . . .

I look back upon the history of this town. Some twenty years ago, I remember, there was a great and successful movement for reforming our administration and ennobling it. The men that took part in that movement had learnt the principles on which they acted, and caught the spirit by which they were inspired, very largely in the Nonconformist churches of Birmingham. . . . I do not believe that if the Nonconformist churches of Birmingham had been organised to secure the results which were achieved by that municipal reform, their organised efforts would have been half as effective as the efforts of their individual members as citizens in the community.

96 Nonconformist losses in the countryside, 1893–6

Extracts from the special report of the Baptist Union Council on the village churches: *Baptist Handbook, 1894*, p. 77; and the Address to the Societies: *Minutes of the Primitive Methodist Conference, 1896*, pp. 183–4.

Both the Old and the New Dissent suffered reverses in the countryside in the 1890s. The Baptist Union Council Report of 1893 (a) suggests some socio-economic causes, and the Congregational Union stressed the role of smallholders in rural Nonconformity in 1897. The Primitive Methodist address of 1896 (b) shows that a church based on rural labourers was suffering too.

a.

... V.   With that very serious question of the law of social economics —the depopulation of the villages—of course no religious body, as such, can deal. Those who remember the state of our churches many years ago can recall the fact that the tenant farmers of this country were the backbone of religious Nonconformity. That class of supporters may to-day be looked for almost in vain among our village churches. The condition of things from this point of view can be remedied only by such altered relation between the people and the land as will create a class of small-holding proprietors, and so check in some measure the deportation of the villagers from their natural homes. The proposed appointment of Parish and District Councils, and the enfranchisement of religious thought with the ennobling spiritual results of disestablishment when it comes, will bring about changes in our rural districts that will undoubtedly tend to restore to the churches which hold our distinctive denominational principles in those districts, the vitality which, through causes already referred to, is now so seriously diminished. This is therefore a function pertaining to wise and progressive legislation. ...

b.

. . . The condition of our work in the villages has for several years occupied the serious attention of the Conference, but this year the question took a new departure. Two years ago inquiries were set on foot which have resulted in the collection of a mass of statistics which bring to light certain facts demanding the serious and immediate attention of our people. They show, for instance, that to a much larger extent than was generally thought, we are a village church. Nearly 75 per cent. of our chapels and a large proportion of our 'preaching places' are in the villages. And this circumstance adds greatly to the significance of the startling fact, also brought to light by these statistics, that during the last twenty-five years we have abandoned 516 places, and only succeeded in opening up 236 new ones, thus showing a decline of 280 in our country societies.

There can be no doubt that at many of the abandoned places our cause would be very small, and it is probable that in connection with very few of them was there a Sunday school; but in spite of such considerations it would be foolish to attempt to disguise the serious import of these figures. The declining population of the villages, and the increasing hostility of a certain section of the clergy of the Established Church, are, in fact, creating difficulties with which many of our country circuits are unable to successfully deal. Owing to the loss of local preachers by removal, they are so seriously undermanned that many of their village pulpits are unsupplied Sunday after Sunday. We have often a superabundance of local preachers in the towns and larger villages; but, without conveyances, it is in many cases scarcely possible for these brethren to reach the outlying hamlets. . . .

97   The Free Church Unity Movement, 1897

An extract from an article by Hugh Price Hughes on 'Free Church Unity: The New Movement', *Contemporary Review*, March 1897, pp. 441, 447–52.

The 1890s saw a new move towards united action by the Free Churches in the form of the National Council of the Evangelical Free Churches. This was the first grouping fully to include the Wesleyans, largely because of the initiative and support of Hugh Price Hughes. In this article Hughes describes the history, principles and potential of the movement.

As Dr. Guinness Rogers had foreseen, the responsible national assemblies of the various Evangelical Churches could not possibly commit themselves to any movement of this kind, the ideals and scope of which were realised only by a very few. Moreover, it was extremely important that such a gathering should be entirely free from the embarrassing and hampering responsibility of committing great historic Churches on any question which they had not had the opportunity of deliberating and deciding for themselves. At the same time it was increasingly evident that the movement would have no force and no value unless it were really representative of the convictions of Evangelical Free Churchmen. The problem, therefore, was to discover some method by which Evangelical Free Churchmen, as such, could express themselves freely on various issues of common interest to them all, without embarrassing or committing their several communions and without the least interference with the internal autonomy of their respective Churches. The happy suggestion of a territorial basis of representation achieved the great object in view. In consequence of this happy inspiration, England is already covered by a network of local councils. All the Congregationalists, Baptists, Methodists, Presbyterians, and Quakers in a given area are requested to select, in such a way as they think best, representative ministers and laymen to constitute the local council. In that council they meet, not as Congregationalists or Baptists, or Presbyterians or Methodists, or Quakers, but as Evangelical Free Churchmen. They do not and they cannot attempt to interfere at any time or in any way with the internal organisation or discipline of their represented communities, either locally or nationally; but at the same time, by their coming together in this spontaneous manner, they are able to demonstrate their unity and to act together for mutual defence, and for a common attack upon the forces of evil. The more this method of representation is pondered, the more it will be felt that it secures unity without uniformity, and all the practical advantages of unity without sacrificing any of the indisputable advantages of denominational organisation. . . .

There is no doubt that in a very short time the local organisations will be so perfected that the annual Council will be a veritable parliament of Evangelical Free Churches—that is to say, of a majority of the Christian public in this country. The Evangelical communities have been so split and divided and isolated that even they themselves have not realised how numerous they are. It is not surprising, therefore, that outsiders, and especially other communions, should underestimate their strength. The Free Churches represent at this moment a majority of the English people who actually attend places of worship and take a real interest in Christianity. It appears from a Parliamentary Blue Book, prepared in 1882, under the auspices of the Local Government Board, that the number of our sanctuaries registered and licensed for public worship largely exceeded that of the Anglican Church. It would also appear from an article published in this REVIEW last month, entitled 'Religious Statistics of England and Wales', that the Evangelical Churches directly or indirectly represented in the National Council have 1,807,723 communicants; the Church of England in her latest returns claims only 1,778,351. We have 373,685 Sunday school teachers; she has 200,596. We have 3,103,285 Sunday scholars; the Church of England has 2,329,813; that is to say, we have an excess of more than three-quarters of a million Sunday scholars. The sitting accommodation of the associated Evangelical Churches is 7,610,003; that of the Church of England is 6,778,288. We therefore provide nearly a million more sittings than the Church of England, although at the beginning of this century, out of 5,171,123 sittings, the Church of England provided 4,289,883. This is an astounding revelation of the immense growth of Evangelical Dissent during the present century. Any one who has grasped the significance of these figures will realise the importance of a Council which represents the views of a majority of the Christian people of England.

The important features of the constitution adopted at Nottingham are, first (for reasons already assigned) the title; secondly, the objects. The title is 'The National Council of the Evangelical Free Churches.' 'The Churches constituting the local councils entitled to representation on the National Council are the Congregational and Baptist Churches, the Methodist Churches, the Presbyterian Church of England, the Free Episcopal Churches, the Society of Friends, and such other Evangelical Churches as the National Council may at any time admit.' With respect to the title, I need call attention only to the clause which asserts that the Council will heartily welcome the co-operation of any Episcopal Church which is not subject to the authority of the secular power, and which enjoys that complete self-government which is essential to the full discharge of Church duties. This movement, there-fore, does not represent any antagonism whatever to Episcopacy as such. The true nature of modern Dissent as expounded by Dr. Guinness Rogers, Dr. Berry, and others, is very much larger, more compre-hensive, and more catholic than views which have sometimes pre-vailed. The promoters of this movement will be only too glad to co-operate and to combine heartily with any Churches, however con-stituted, which are absolutely loyal to the Head of the Church, and which are faithful to what we regard as the fundamental ecclesiastical idea of the New Testament—namely, the real, uninterrupted, and perpetual presence and supremacy of Jesus Christ in the midst of His own Church.

The Constitution defines the objects of the movement in the follow-ing terms: '(a) To facilitate fraternal intercourse and co-operation among the Evangelical Free Churches. (b) To assist in the organisation of local councils. (c) To encourage devotional fellowship and mutual counsel concerning the spiritual life and religious activities of the Churches. (d) To advocate the New Testament doctrine of the Church, and to defend the rights of the associated Churches. (e) To promote the application of the law of Christ in every relation of human life.' . . .

In our own time we are known mainly by three names—Protestant, Nonconformist, Dissenter. We are proud of all three. We still claim and vindicate all three. But they are all negative. No doubt they present certain aspects of positive truth. We are Protestants, because we protest against any one coming between us and our Lord Jesus Christ. We are nonconformists, because we refuse to conform to a schismatical Act passed in the degraded reign of Charles II., which would have placed us in a position of schismatical isolation from the majority of our fellow Christians. We believe that there is a sin of schism, and that the very worst form of schism is to pledge ourselves never to enter the pulpits of our fellow-Christians, never to recognise them, and never to meet them at the communion table of our Lord. We are also Dissenters because we dissent from the strange and anti-scriptural doctrine that the Church should be subject to the authority of the State. It seems to us as monstrous that the State should domineer over the Church as that the Church should domineer over the State. It would be thought monstrous if we proposed that the President of the Methodist Conference should nominate the members of her Majesty's Government. But surely it is equally and more monstrous that the members of her Majesty's Government should nominate the President of the Methodist Conference. The Church has the same right as the State to be self-governed. Both are of God, both have their own sphere, and the only Christian doctrine of their relation is expressed in the famous formula of Cavour, 'A free Church in a free State.' . . . We quite admit, however, that after we have thus vindicated our title to those three names we are open to the criticism that each of them is a negative one, and that we are bound not only to inform the public what we are not, what we do not, and what we will not, but also to state positively what we are. We now agree to say in the first place that we are 'Churchmen'. It is an injustice to state that the original Congregationalists came out of the Church of England because they were capricious and wilful and self-assertive, and because they put the whim of the lawless individual before the authority of the Church. They came out because they were 'Churchmen', and Churchmen so pronounced and so strong that they suffered the loss of all things rather than tolerate any arrangement by which it seemed to them that the authority of Christ and the rights of the Church were sacrificed. The unit of this movement is not the individual Christian but the Church. Therein it differs *toto caelo* from the Evangelical Alliance, which is merely a fortuitous concourse of Evangelical individuals who meet together occasionally to say that they love one another, and who also render some excellent service in speaking a kind word for persecuted Protestants on the Continent. All honour to those who started that Alliance half a century ago; it was all of which men were then capable, and it was very much more than any of their predecessors could have done since the sixteenth century. But it falls far short of the union which we desire. We seek not the occasional co-operation of individual private Christians, but the constant co-operation and fellowship of fully organised Churches. We are, therefore, as I have said, Churchmen,

1

and we are 'High Churchmen', so High that, as I have explained, we can no more tolerate the interference of the secular power than could the Popes of the Middle Ages. On that side of the protest and struggle we wholly agree with the Popes; we differ from them when, having vindicated their right to be free from the tyranny and interference of the State, they proceed to commit a similar offence and attempt to dominate the State.

Lastly, we are 'Catholic High Churchmen', for we do not hold ourselves in schismatic separation from our fellow Christians of other communions differently constituted from our own. We do not boycott or excommunicate any body of our fellow Christians who recognise the divine supremacy of Jesus Christ, the Head of the Church. They may fall short of what we desire or they may exceed it, but we are in love and charity with them all. . . . We do not attempt to escape from practical difficulties by arguing that the Church is an invisible body. There is, of course, an invisible body, and the majority of the members of the Church being in heaven, they are invisible to us; but we hold as strongly as any that Christ came into this world, not merely and not mainly to save individual men, but to establish a Church, and the Church He established is obviously a visible Church. Baptism, the sacrament of initiation, cannot be administered by or to an invisible Church. The Holy Communion, the perpetually renewed sacrament of membership, is equally inapplicable to an invisible Church. We repudiate the modern dangerous delusion that religion is simply a matter between a man and his Maker. The Christian religion has at every stage relation to our fellowmen as well as to our God and Saviour. The highest and richest blessings of personal sanctification are offered, not to the individual who isolates himself from his brother Christians, but to the Christian Church. It is only when we are in full communion with our fellow Christians, it is only when we are actually enjoying the 'communion of saints', that we have any scriptural right to expect Christian blessing for ourselves. . . .

98 Hugh Price Hughes on the Boer War, 1900

An extract from D. Price Hughes, *The Life of Hugh Price Hughes* (1904), pp. 573-4.

Nonconformists were divided over the Boer War, some following the 'Imperialist' line, and others being 'pro-Boer'. Hugh Price Hughes was an 'Imperialist', as can be seen from this letter to his friend Dr Lunn, dated 12 February 1900. Once again, however, the view is expressed that where the Free Churches are divided on an issue, it should not be discussed. The reference is to a meeting of the National Council of Evangelical Free Churches.

I am very sorry the South African War is to be discussed at Sheffield. Excellent Free Churchmen differ so deeply about that, that if I had been at the Committee I should have done my utmost to induce them to leave the subject severely alone. The War, Home Rule, and all topics on which we are not agreed, should never be touched. The one great peril of the moment is the perpetual attempt to drag such burning questions into our midst. Our business is to keep to the deep theological and ecclesiastical issues on which we are agreed.

So far as the war is concerned, I wish you and all who agree with you could see the blissful results of British rule in Egypt, and could realise the effect abroad of the incessant nagging at your own great country, and the even more pestiferous whitewashing of one of the most cruel and mendacious military oligarchies that ever enslaved black men and outraged white men. . . .

99   Programme of a Congregational church mission, c. 1900

Quoted in C. Booth, *Life and Labour of the People in London,* third series, *Religious Influences* (1903), vii, pp. 172–3.

This extract from the manual of a Congregational chapel in a wealthy suburb, quoted by Booth, gives a good idea of the scale of the weekly programme of activities promoted by such a mission.

LIST OF MEETINGS

Sunday—9 a.m., Men's adult school; 11 a.m., Sunday school service; 3 p.m., Sunday school and Bible-classes; 3 p.m., Women's adult school; 3.30 p.m., Open-air service (summer months); 7 p.m., Service.

Monday—11 a.m. to 1 p.m., Metropolitan Association for Befriending Young Servants; 2.30 p.m., Mothers' meeting; 7.30 p.m., Boys', girls' and men's clubs; 8 p.m., Girls' brigade; 8.30 p.m., Library.

Tuesday—10.20 a.m., Ladies' prayer meeting; last Tuesday in the month; 11 a.m., Work-room; 11 a.m., Visitors' meeting; 3 p.m. Women's sick benefit and sharing-out society; the first Tuesday in the month, Mothers' union; 4 p.m., Library; 6.15 to 7.30 p.m., Band of Hope; 7 p.m., Men's club; 7.30 p.m., Boys' club; 8 p.m., Gymnasium, Girls' club; 8 p.m., Girls' brigade; 8.30 p.m., Miss ★ ★ ★ ★ ★'s class.

Wednesday—11 a.m. to 1 p.m., Metropolitan Association for Befriending Young Servants; 2.45 p.m., Women's adult school; 7 p.m., Sunday school Bible-class; 7.30 p.m., Boys', girls' and men's clubs; 7.30 p.m., Men's gymnasium; 8 p.m., Girls' brigade; 8 p.m., Total abstinence society.

Thursday—7.30 p.m., Boys', girls' and men's clubs; 7.30 p.m., Boys' brigade, gymnasium and drill; 8 p.m., Wood carving (men); 8 p.m., Girls' brigade; 8.30 p.m., Men's chess club.

Friday—11 a.m. to 1 p.m., Metropolitan Association for Befriending Young Servants; 3 p.m., Class for ex-members of the girls' club; 7 to 8 p.m., Girls' gymnasium and drill; 7.30 p.m., Evening classes for men; 7.30 p.m., Boys', girls' and men's clubs; 8 p.m., Girls' brigade; 8 p.m., Boys' brigade; 9 p.m., Ambulance class.

Saturday—7.30 p.m., Boys', girls' and men's clubs; 8 p.m. Concert (in winter months); 8.30 to 10 p.m., Men's sick benefit and sharing-out club; 8.30 to 9.30 p.m., Savings bank; 8.30 p.m., Men's debating society.

100   A new suburban church, c. 1900

Quoted in C. Booth, *Life and Labour of the People in London*, third series, *Religious Influences* (1903), vii, pp. 200–2.

This is an extract from a church leaflet, quoted by Booth, which illustrates the development of new suburban churches at the turn of the century.

There has been a wonderful transformation. Mr. Cameron Corbett, M.P., waved his magic wand over Hither Green in the year 1896, and houses began to spring up in place of farmers' crops. Street after street spread across the fields, and, so rapid has been the influx of population, that by the end of the year (1900) nearly two thousand houses, mostly of the middle-class type, will be occupied. . . .

Early in 1898 the Lewisham Wesleyan Mission Band began to hold open-air services in the neighbourhood, and in November a workman's dining hall was secured, where regular services began to be held, and a Sunday school was started. This was the first home of the Hither Green Wesleyan Church. . . .

Meanwhile the Lewisham Quarterly Meeting had approached Mr Corbett with a view to securing land for a church, and being first in the field, they secured the finest site on the whole estate. . . . They did this without the slightest expectation of being able to build for many years to come. . . .

In May, 1898, on the recommendation of a representative London Methodist Committee, and at the request of the Lewisham Quarterly Meeting, the case was taken up by the Third London District Synod. Then matters went ahead. . . .

Building operations commenced in June, 1899. . . . A personal appeal to a number of friends in the district raised £1000. A further £360 was obtained when the memorial stones were laid on July 22nd. This stone-laying ceremony was most successful in every way, and a happy augury for the future of the church.

The conference of the same year (1899) appointed the Rev. ★ ★ ★ ★ to take charge . . . he entered on his duties at the beginning of September, and found a congregation of thirty worshipping in the 'dining hall'. There were three members, a society steward, a Sunday school secretary, and two or three teachers. . . . All else had to be sought, and until the right men were found the minister must take the various duties himself.

It was a novel experience to preach in such a place as the 'dining hall'. Scores of flies buzzing around, an occasional cockroach straying over the Bible, the scurrying rush of a startled mouse . . . and on one famous night the marvellous acrobatic performance of a frenzied cat, made it no light task to hold the attention of the congregation. . . . Yet the congregation grew till the room was quite filled, so eager were the people for the Word of Life. Dingy and repulsive though their surroundings were, the presence of the Saviour made the place glorious with the salvation of sinners. The people proved the blessed truth—

> Jesus where'er Thy people meet
> There they behold the mercy seat;
> Where'er they seek Thee, Thou art found,
> And every place is hallowed ground.

Still they looked forward to the completion of the new church with an eagerness bordering on impatience. After every service the congregation went to count the rows of bricks. . . .

The day of deliverance came at last. On April 26th (1900) the handsome new church was opened. . . .

Looking at the whole situation, one can only exclaim, 'What hath God wrought.' He has far exceeded the most daring expectations, and has blessed His Church at Hither Green not only with large increase, but with every spiritual blessing in Christ Jesus.

101 Joseph Chamberlain on the Education Bill, 1902

An extract from J. Amery, *Life of Joseph Chamberlain*, iv (1951) p. 495.

Joseph Chamberlain, as leader of the Liberal Unionists, was embarrassed by the government's Education Bill, and found many of his own speeches in the 1870s quoted against him by his political opponents. In this letter to Balfour, dated 4 August 1902, he refers to the revival of a Nonconformist electoral interest hostile to the Conservatives.

. . . To my mind it is clear that the Bill has brought all the fighting Nonconformists into the field and made of them active instead of merely passive opponents. Their representations and appeals to the old war cries have impressed large numbers of the middle and upper working classes who have hitherto supported the Unionist Party without joining the Conservative organisation. The transfer of their votes will undoubtedly have immense importance at a general election, and, after Leeds,[7] I do not think that any seat, where there is a strong Nonconformist electorate, can be considered as absolutely safe. . . .

102   Debates on the Education Bill, 1902

Extracts from *Parliamentary Debates* (fourth series), cv, cols. 866–7;
cvii, cols. 908–9, 911, 1110–11; cxv, cols. 984–5, 1007–16; cxvi, col. 419.

The Education Bill was fiercely fought through all its stages, and
was substantially amended, though not as much as some Liberals
would have wished. The extracts illustrate some of the main views.
Balfour, introducing the Bill on 24 March 1902, explained the
provisions which would directly affect denominational schools (a).
Dr Macnamara, speaking on the second reading on 6 May 1902,
showed the extent of discrimination against Nonconformists in the
appointment and training of teachers (b). Lloyd George, in the same
debate, on 8 May expressed Nonconformists' resentment at the Irish
Nationalists' support for the Bill (c). In the third reading debate on
2 December 1902, Mr Wanklyn put the Anglican view that the only
alternative to denominational religious teaching was none at all (d),
whilst Mr R. W. Perks listed the main Nonconformist objections to
the final form of the Bill (e). Perks was a Wesleyan and Member
of Parliament for Louth. Finally, Lord Rosebery, speaking in the
third reading debate in the Lords on 9 December, repeated the
remark he had made to a Nonconformist deputation that they
should now realise where their political interests lay (f).

a.

Mr. A. J. Balfour: . . . The militant denominationalists, I admit, lose
the complete control of their schools which they have hitherto enjoyed.
The school managers will no longer be free from responsibility to
anyone except His Majesty's Inspector of Schools and the Department
at Whitehall. They will have to fall into line, so far as secular instruction is concerned, with other schools, and take such part as they may
be ordered to take in the general scheme of education. But the strain
of maintenance will be removed. No longer will the unfortunate
supporter of voluntary schools [ironical opposition cheers] while

freely paying his rates for the rival school over the way, have to beg subscriptions in order to keep his own school going. . . . And lastly, the denominationalists will for the first time have a clear right to provide schools where the necessity for such schools can be shown to exist. . . .

Now for the militant anti-denominationalists. I admit that they may dislike this Bill. Nevertheless, they will also gain something by it. There are two grievances in the present position of the English Non-conformists which have given rise to complaints which seem to me unanswerable. I hope in practice they do not weigh very heavily on any portion of the population, but still in theory they are unquestion-ably grievances which we ought to remedy as far as we can. The first is what I may call the grievance of the single school. In some districts there is but one school within reach, and that school is not conducted, so far as religious education is concerned, on lines pleasing to the Nonconformists. I do not say that this grievance is wholly removed, but it is greatly mitigated by a plan which in cases of real need will allow a school to be built although there be adequate accommodation already in the district—a school to be built which may be satisfactory to the Nonconformist parents of the children who go to it. There is yet a second grievance which I have heard stated, of the exact weight of which I am unable to judge, but which, upon paper at all events, seems genuine enough. It is said that there are whole regions of the country where, as all the schools, or nearly all of them, are practically Church schools, the child of a Nonconformist parent anxious to enter the teaching profession finds it almost impossible to obtain the neces-sary facilities. Again, by creating a local authority which will certainly have it in its power to deal with the whole question of the education and provision of teachers, this grievance also, if not removed, will be very largely mitigated. So I might even say to the militant Noncon-formist that he also gets something out of the Bill—gets some of the grievances of which he has so long and so loudly complained dimin-ished or removed. He also, I trust, therefore, may be induced to look with less malevolent eyes on the present educational reform which the Government is attempting. . . .

b.

Dr Macnamara: . . . It is deplorable to the last degree that every time education comes under discussion in this country, the real issues are promptly obscured by theological disputants. It is a striking fact that substantially there is no religious difficulty in the schools themselves. I have been connected with elementary schools in one way or another

—as pupil, pupil teacher, assistant teacher, head teacher, voluntary school manager and School Board member—for the last twenty-five years or more, and in no capacity whatever have I ever heard of a single case of dissent on the part of a parent to any form of religious instruction. Of this I am quite certain, there are parts of the country in which the people would stand any form of religious instruction rather than pay a rate for it. The Vice-President is absolutely correct when he says there is no difficulty whatever in the schools. I was astonished, however, to hear him say there is no difficulty in regard to teacherships, and at his flat contradiction of the statement that there is a difficulty in regard to young Nonconformists who desire to become school teachers. . . . He must know that under the trust deeds of eight out of ten village schools it is impossible for the managers to appoint anybody but a member of the Church of England. If the Vice-President does not know that, he is singularly lacking in the knowledge of his office. But that is not all. The Vice-President must know that a great many young Nonconformists who are employed in our larger towns by the School Boards as pupil teachers, apart from their particular religious faith, when they get to the end of their apprenticeship and have won a Queen's—now a King's—scholarship, which qualifies them for admission to a training college, find the greatest difficulty in getting into a training college because of their religious faith. . . . Let me give one specific case. A girl passed—I think it was in 1891—in the first class, No. 237. That is a very high position. She applied for admission to the Stockwell Training College—one of the three un-denominational colleges. The Stockwell list was an exceptionally good one, and they had filled their sixty or sixty-five places before they reached this girl's position. She immediately wrote to the other two undenominational colleges, but they also had completed their number. I know, as a matter of fact, that that girl could have got into any number of Church of England colleges if she had cared to become a member of the Church of England. Does any Member of this House desire that? Nobody does. I am sure these facts are not sufficiently known, or the state of things would be remedied at once. What happened in this particular case? She had the alternative of either wasting a year or changing her religion for the time being. She wasted a year. In that very year the Truro Training College, which is a very excellent Church of England training college, took in a girl of the second class No. 2,681. Why we should spend our money on a second class girl No. 2,681, and refuse to train a first class girl No. 237, passes my comprehension. This Bill does nothing to mitigate that evil. . . .

c.

Mr Lloyd George: . . . We are in a minority—for one reason, and one reason only, and I am not ashamed of it. It is because we committed ourselves to the cause of Ireland. . . . In 1886, we threw over our most cherished leaders in this country—Spurgeon and Bright, Dr Allon, Dr Dale, and even the right hon. Gentleman, the Member for West Birmingham. We threw them over for one reason only; because we felt what was due to Ireland; and it is rather hard I think—if they will forgive me speaking candidly—to be put in this plight of being beaten down for the cause of Ireland, and that Irishmen of all people, should help our foes and theirs to make our defeat the more intolerable. Let them remember this. Who are the people who will benefit by this Bill? The people who benefit by it are the people who coerced Ireland, and supported every measure for throwing the leaders of the Irish people into prison, and for keeping Ireland down with soldiers and police. Who are the people who are hit by the Bill? The people of Wales. We were offered by the right hon. Gentleman the Member for West Birmingham, Disestablishment, if we would throw over Home Rule. We did not do it, and some of the men who declined to do it will be sold up for rates under this Bill, and probably imprisoned under the mandamus of this Bill. They will remember that the instrument under which that happened was forged partly by the Irish Members. . . .

d.

Mr Wanklyn: . . . One section of Gentlemen opposite advocate a purely secular system of education, another section advocate an undenominational form in national schools, and all sections are agreed that they would do their best to repeal this Bill. We on the Government side claim that we have been the pioneers in the cause of education, and we have always been in the past. Will hon. Gentlemen opposite question the fact that the Church of England rejected anything that might be called a national system, or deny that the great Liberal Unionist, Mr Forster, took the great step, or that we on the Government side have been pioneers in the cause of education? We believe with the late Dr Dale that undenominational teaching is positively dangerous. We believe that education, unless based on definite religious teaching, to use Dr Dale's words, is dangerous and mischievous. We hold that belief, and on these issues we are prepared to join and to fight to the last.

e.

Mr. Perks: . . . I have never used the phrase that this Bill will kill Nonconformity. I do not believe that it is the intention of the Government, in bringing forward this Bill, to kill Nonconformity, but I do believe it is the hope of a very important section of the Church of England that the measure will have the effect of materially increasing the number of the supporters of the Church throughout the country by getting hold of these little Dissenting children in the elementary schools. Indeed this has been avowed by Canon Pendleton, a well-known inspector of schools in Lancashire, who declared that the syllabus was always so arranged as to give distinctive denominational instruction to the children of Nonconformists. But to talk about killing Nonconformity is, I quite admit, to use a phrase which is absurd. It is manifestly impossible to kill Nonconformity. . . . But, . . . the Church of England authorities evidently regard the Bill as a measure which is of the very greatest importance to their own Church. The Archbishop of Canterbury, speaking early last year, said there were signs that the Government would listen to anything that was said because in a very great degree their own political position depended on it, and it would be rather awkward for them to face the Church if only its members were united on the subject of education. My right hon. friend the Member for Oxford University has appealed to Churchmen not to throw away the opportunity, which might never recur, of allowing the Church of England to continue to be, wherever her strength was equal to it, the religious instructor of the people. Surely these quotations justify in saying that this Bill is regarded as being directed by the King's Government against Nonconformists, and as a direct attack upon the religious tenets and the ecclesiastical position of English Nonconformists. We are told that it contains within it numerous concessions made to the Nonconformists. But why were not those who are responsible for the educational organisation of the Nonconformist Churches consulted with reference to the Bill before it was introduced? Why were not the Free Church leaders and the Wesleyans consulted? There were indications that the Roman Catholics were consulted, but then the children attending Roman Catholic schools formed but a very small proportion of the community. But there is a vast number of Nonconformist children in the Anglican schools, and inasmuch as the Nonconformist leaders were not consulted, it is rather extraordinary to expect us to accept with gratitude the scheme of the Government when not the slightest attempt has been made to bring them into line. My own conviction is that an attempt of that sort in the early stages of the question would possibly have succeeded. I think that the abolition of the Cowper-Temple Clause in all the schools would probably have been accepted by the Nonconformist Churches if it had been accompanied by a scheme for placing the whole of the elementary schools under real effective popular control. But the Nonconformist leaders were not consulted, and none of their organisations were taken into counsel for a moment. The Free Churches of this country—I am not speaking of the Roman Catholic Church, but the Wesleyan Church, the Congregationalists, the Baptists, and an organisation which for the last few years has exercised very great influence throughout the country (I mean the Federation of Free Churches) have laid down schemes of elementary education which distinctly define our position. We claim no authority; we ask for popular control. We claim that there should be no tests; and lastly, we ask for Christian Bible teaching to be given under the protection of the Conscience Clause by the teachers in the elementary schools. . . .

There are four grievances of which Nonconformists have to complain, and these, instead of being removed by this Bill are exaggerated and enforced by it. In the first place, there is to be no application of the Conscience Clause to the training colleges. We endeavoured to secure for the pupil teachers who went up from the provinces to these great colleges, supported almost entirely out of public funds, the protection of the Conscience Clause, but we failed. The second grievance we have to complain of—I am not going to elaborate it, it is perfectly manifest to anyone who knows anything about the Bill— is that in 12,000 public schools in this country, supported almost entirely out of public funds, Nonconformists are excluded from the positions of headmaster and headmistress. A concession has been made in the case of pupil teachers; and permission which will never, or hardly ever, be exercised, has been given in the case of assistant teachers; but it is a serious blow to educational efficiency in this country to exclude from 12,000 schools Nonconformist teachers. . . . The third grievance we have is that the bishops and clergy of the Anglican Church will have to settle what is to be the religious teaching of 700,000 Nonconformist children in Anglican elementary schools. In Lincolnshire—I refer to it because I know it better than any other county—in many cases 70 per cent., in some cases 80 per cent., and generally 50 per cent. of the children attending the public elementary schools belong to the Methodist or some other section of Nonconformity. It seems to us a great injustice that the parents of these children should have absolutely nothing to do with their religious education;

and that, in the event of any question arising as to religious instruction, the bishop of the diocese and the local clergy should be the people to deal with it. I am not able to say, I do not think the Government themselves can say, what is their interpretation of the Kenyon-Slaney Clause. I should like to know what would happen in this case which occurred at Plymouth or Portsmouth, and was brought before the House a few weeks ago. A sailor, on coming home from sea, found that his little girl had been caned several times in an elementary school because she would not bow down to some image in the church she was taken to. . . .

[The Secretary of the Board of Education intervened to say that the story had been absolutely denied.]

. . . I am glad to hear that. I pass from that to a case which occurred at Dorchester. There the clergyman has given some explanation. He says the children were ordered, not to bow to the altar, but towards the altar. Crucifixes were put up, the children were compelled to bow to them, and they were only removed on the protest of the local Nonconformists. What I wish to know from the Secretary to the Board of Education is, who will be responsible in such cases? . . . Will it be the managers or the clergyman of the parish? What is the interpretation of the Kenyon-Slaney Clause? Is it solely limited to an appeal to the Bishop as to the religious instruction which may be given, or to the text books to be used; or does it extend to things put up in the school, such as crucifixes or to little invocations such as I have mentioned. . . . I hope, and indeed I believe, that the construction which will be put on the Kenyon-Slaney Clause by the Courts of Law when it gets there . . . will be that the local managers will have absolute control as to the use of manuals of devotion, the putting up of little ecclesiastical symbols in the schools, and the arrangements for marching the children to church on the various festivals connected with the Church.

There is one other grievance which Nonconformists seriously complain about, and that is that the Bill perpetuates, to some extent, one of the grievances and inequalities of the Act of 1870—namely, facilities for the erection of new sectarian schools and the enlargement of sectarian schools; which are denied to the local public education authority, because a number of conditions are imposed which the Education Department in London will take into consideration on the appeal of ten agreed parishioners. The extra cost involved will be a grievous injustice to all who wish to see the extension of schools under public control, not the extension of sectarian schools, whether Wes-

leyan, Roman Catholic, or Anglican. I wish just to refer to a mis-
conception which is very current, and which has frequently been
referred to in this House. The Nonconformists have been charged with
wishing to teach what is called 'Nonconformist religion', and School
Board schools certainly, and some of our Nonconformist schools, have
been called Godless schools. The Colonial Secretary, speaking at
Birmingham, said that Wesleyans in their schools taught 'Wesleyanism', whatever that may be. There is no such thing as the teaching
of Wesleyanism in Wesleyan schools. I know nothing of the doctrines
of the Wesleyan Church which differs from the doctrines of the
Evangelical section of the Anglican Church, except the application of
the cardinal principles of Christian faith. . . .

I quite understand the Catholic principle, as now asserted, that the
clergy have the prescriptive right alone to teach religion; but that is a
doctrine which Nonconformists absolutely repudiate. The prescriptive
right of experts alone to criticise and teach is now going beyond the
province of religion and is invading even the province of literature.
But the Methodist Church, which ranks in number next to the Church
of England, and in the United States stands first as regards number,
depends for its doctrinal teaching on lay teaching, on lay interpretation
of the Scriptures, and lay deduction of the principles of Christian
faith from the Scriptures. Next Sunday, 25,000 sermons will be
preached in Methodist churches, mission halls, and class rooms,
throughout the country, and, of these, 20,000 will be preached by
laymen of all ranks of society. We entirely repudiate the notion that
you can only have a clerical expert to expound the Scriptures, and
enforce their teaching on children in elementary schools. Our object
is not secularism. We are as much opposed to secularism as hon.
Members below the Gangway can be. In fact, we hold in common
with them certain principles of Christian faith; it is only when we
come to their practical application that we differ from them; but we
are opposed to secularism just as much as we are opposed to clericalism
in the elementary schools. . . .

We have been asked by the right hon. Gentleman the Member for
the Forest of Dean and by the hon. Gentleman, the Member for Oldham to work this measure, and discourage, in every possible way, the
contention put forward that it is the duty of Nonconformists to resist
the payment of the rate. The question whether a Nonconformist will
be justified or not in resisting the rate is a matter for each individual
conscience, and, having settled that problem for himself, he will not
be likely to be influenced in the slightest degree by the fact that he may

lose his right as a citizen. I would remind the House that if the great Nonconformist communities take this serious step, they will, to some extent, be following the advice given by the Colonial Secretary in Birmingham in 1872, when he said—

> 'It had been said that he encouraged resistance to a law—at all events, he did not encourage active resistance to the law. They were not going to fight the bailiffs, they were going to submit in their way; but an alternative was provided for them—an alternative which landed them in great sacrifices, but still permitted them to make a protest. Whatever might have been the opposition brought against the old Church rate, let the majority not doubt for a moment that there would be just as stout an opposition against the new. . . .'

. . . It will be quite possible in the constitution of the County Councils and of the local bodies of management to use every exertion in public elections, in the Press, and on the platform, to secure an adequate representation, and possibly in many parts of the country an effective control, over these educational agencies; and if this Bill is likely to have, as I fear it will, a paralysing effect on education through placing the children of the country largely under clerical control, I think it will be the paramount duty of all these organised institutions of Nonconformity to put forth their utmost efforts to secure, in a way they have never yet done in the present generation, a control of or adequate representation on these educational bodies. But I ought to say that this is quite a distinct and separate question from the other, which is still more grave, namely; whether it will be the duty of the Nonconformist churches to recommend their followers to organise a resistance, passive or active, against the payment of the rate which may be charged for the maintenance of these local sectarian schools. Already there are manifest indications that the country is dividing itself into two great hostile camps. On the one side we have the Anglican Church working on the lines of the Roman Catholic hierarchy and the Roman Catholic clergy and laity. On the other side we have the representatives of labour. It is indeed a notable fact that not one single labour organisation, no trades union, has pronounced in favour of the Bill. Everyone of them has reprobated it; and, surely, it cannot be said that those who ought to know the true interests of the children are the clergy, the upper classes and the privileged sections of Society, and that they alone have a prescriptive and paramount right to tell the working classes how their children ought to be taught.

Have the working classes no knowledge in this matter? On the other side, therefore, we have the labour organisations of the country, we have the whole of the Protestant community, and we have the Nonconformists solid. We may find here and there a Nonconformist who is put up on a public platform by a bishop of the Anglican Church as a sort of exhibit of Nonconformist opinion. I remember a friend of mine who took a great interest in foreign missions but had never seen a convert. One day he went down to the docks, and got a little black boy from the captain of one of the steamers, put him on a platform and exhibited him as a triumph of missionary enterprise. The other day an Anglican Bishop put one of our Methodist Tory baronets on the platform of the Albert Hall as a specimen. The thing was ludicrous, because the overwhelming majority of the Tory section of the Methodist Church, the Wesleyan Church, had pronounced against the Bill. At last we have a united Party against the Bill. There is no schism; we have not had to form any league; there is absolute unity in our Party. I do not believe that we can be charged with being guilty of travesty and misrepresentation when we talk of the clerical control and clerical influence which will be exercised under this Bill. We believe it to be a serious danger. John Bright speaking in this House on the education question said: 'Nothing tends more to impede the progress of liberty, nothing is more fatal to independence of spirit in the public, than to add to the powers of the priesthood in the matter of education.' It is because we are anxious to defend liberty of thought, which, in our judgement, is at the root of commercial and political progress, that we are opposed to a measure which has been inspired by the clergy, and which has the stamp of ecclesiasticism over almost every section of it.

f.

Lord Rosebery: . . . I believe that of late the Nonconformists of this country have been strangely passive in regard to politics; they have been indifferent to their own Liberal alliances, and they have even, positively or negatively, supported the cause of Toryism. What I said . . . to the Nonconformists was that, if they desired to have justice done to them in the matter of education—which they certainly have not had done to them by this Bill—they must shake off this insidious sloth and resume the active political agitation which was in their old days the strength of the Liberal party.

103   The Free Churches in London, 1903

Extracts from C. Booth, *Life and Labour of the People in London*,
third series, *Religious Influences* (1903), vii, pp. 112–15, 122–3,
125–8, 131–3, 139–41, 143–7.

These extracts come from the final summary volume of Charles
Booth's massive work on *Religious Influences* in his series on the
Life and Labour of the People in London, and contain his
assessment of the Nonconformist churches. London is not, of course,
typical of Nonconformity as a whole, but there is no comparably
broad survey for any other area. The comments on polity and the
atmosphere of worship are in any case of more general application.

[The Congregationalists]
'Ours', said one of the Congregationalist ministers, 'is not the Church
of the poor.' He might have gone further and have said 'not of the poor,
nor of the working class, not of the rich nor of the fashionable'. The
Congregationalist Church is more than any other the Church of the
middle classes, its membership being practically confined within the limits
of the upper and lower sections of those included under that compre-
hensive title. Where these classes prevail Congregationalists are to be
found in force; where not, their churches lead a struggling existence;
and, when owing to some change in the social character of a neighbourhood, old supporters leave, the chapels fall into disuse and one by
one are either closed or pass into other hands.

'But', continues the minister already quoted, 'among our own people
the church is invaluable,' and to this we, too, have borne witness. The
wide aims and remarkable successes of this body in North London, as
well as the extent to which their general methods are repeated by
almost all the other religious bodies in that neighbourhood, or wherever
similar social conditions obtain, have been noticed in previous volumes.
These methods are very social in character and depend upon the presence
among the members of a certain degree of culture, and upon the

absence of any very wide class-differences between them. The result
is that with the Congregationalist Churches the development of the
social side of religious activity attains its highest point. In one case it is
even complained that 'there are too many societies and meetings, so
that many of the young people spend all their spare time in attending
them, and see nothing of their homes'. In these churches, too, the
value of the sermon is at its highest; they provide the greatest scope
for the power of the pulpit. 'The life of the Church depends upon the
sustained attraction of preaching,' says one of their ministers. . . .

Politics are rarely touched upon, and if the pastor feels it his duty
to do so, the congregation do not like it. One of the ministers we have
conferred with, recalled an occasion when a deputation from his
congregation remonstrated with him, saying, 'We share your views,
but politics are not what we come to hear from the pulpit.'

The form of the buildings used, the character of the services and the
whole organization of the work, tend to emphasize the leadership of
the pastor. The most typical shape of church is octagonal, with galleries
on all sides, and roof rising to a low dome. One gallery is occupied by
the organ and choir. In front of it is a high and roomy pulpit, at the
foot of which on a low platform stands the Communion table, with
seats at either side for the deacons. In the pulpit the minister, if seated,
retires almost out of sight, but when he stands forward to speak,
every eye can see and every ear hear him. The whole service is intensely
personal. The prayers are his. At times he truly leads the congregation,
speaking for them and carrying them with him to the throne of grace;
but at other times he seems rather to be addressing the Almighty in the
presence of the congregation, calling His attention to their needs, or
to be speaking to the congregation in the presence of God calling their
thoughts to the things of God. . . . Into the reading of the lessons from
the Bible he throws much special meaning, often pausing to reiterate
some phrase or to interject the expression of some thought suggested to
him by the words. Even of the hymns, by reading with expression the
first verse (as is customary) or some selected verses, he makes a vehicle
for his thoughts.

Before the sermon there is always a long string of notices concerning
the affairs of the congregation and the fixtures for the week. To these
also a strong personal flavour is imparted, even when they are of the
most simple and businesslike nature, the congregation being congratulated, beseeched, or rebuked, as the case may require. The tone
may be quite playful or very serious, or anything between. Then, when
this is over and he begins to preach to his people, it is with a con-

fidence in himself born of the certainty of their confidence in him. He can do his best, and his best is often very good indeed. His audience listen with close attention. Sometimes a hymn, or part of a hymn, is sung after the sermon, but more often the benediction, solemnly uttered, ends the service.

The people do not hurry out. A few may begin to move and greetings are exchanged and whispered words pass; but the greater number remain sitting quietly in their places. Meanwhile the minister, descending from his pulpit, traverses the aisle and speaks to this one or that in making for the main entrance, where there is further lingering and conversation and much handshaking. Outside friendly groups gather, and as the congregation slowly streams away it often seems to fill the street with its numbers. Surely these people may repeat the words of David, 'I was glad when they said unto me, "Let us go into the house of the Lord." ' . . .

[*The Baptists*]

. . . The 'Open' Baptists, as they are sometimes called, in contradistinction to the 'exclusive' character of the others, form the main body. They believe that Christ died for all, and that a man's salvation depends on his acceptance or rejection of Christ; and will permit any believers in the Lord Jesus to take the Communion. The strength of religious life in their large congregations has been noted again and again in the foregoing volumes. Their 'Tabernacles', always imposing structures, are placed in leading thoroughfares in or on the edge of the most populous districts, within easy access of people of every class but especially of the lower middle and upper working classes, from whom, together with some of strictly middle class, the congregations are drawn. On the whole they touch a lower grade than the Congregationalists, and where there is no difference of class between the adherents of these two bodies, there seems to be a divergence of character and disposition. . . .

The order of the service in Open Baptist Churches, and in those of the Congregationalists, is practically the same, that is: opening hymn, short prayer, lesson from scripture, second hymn, long prayer, and usually a second lesson, third hymn (during which the collection is taken up), notices given out from the pulpit or by one of the church officers, sermon, final hymn, and benediction. The sermon lasts from thirty-five to forty minutes, and the entire service fully an hour and a half. This order applies to both morning and evening service on Sunday. At some Baptist churches a hymn and sermonette, specially adapted for the children, are introduced before the sermon proper, and the minister may perhaps give the children some text to find and think over during the week. If they come with their parents they will stay till the end of the service, but those coming from the schools troop out when their portion ends. The children's service is liked by everyone. It answers to the family side of religious feeling, which among the Baptists is strong (as always when men are prominent); and may be welcomed, perhaps, as softening a little the prevailing sternness.

The singing of hymns is universal, but the introduction of a choir or of part-singing, or of any musical instrument beyond a tuning fork, has only been allowed after much hesitation, and still is far from universal. The Baptists, however, have felt the flow of the tide in these directions and do not fear so much as formerly the adoption of practices which have been associated in their minds with priestcraft and prelacy. Even anthems are occasionally sung, though, as a rule, hymns in which all can join are preferred. But, given an organ, an organist, and a choir; and music will surely make its way in any church. . . .

At all times members of the congregation take part in the services in a way unknown among the Congregationalists, sometimes it may be to read the lesson, at others to lead in prayer. This participation is usually suggested and at the same time made more practicable by the use of a platform confronting the congregation, which forms the base of the pulpit, and on which are seats set apart for the deacons; while their joint office with the pastor is further symbolized by the arrangement of the Communion table, at which the deacons seat themselves on his either hand, like the Apostles with the Lord in the centre, as so often depicted. . . .

It will thus be seen that the ideals and practices of the Baptists differ greatly from those of the Congregationalists. This is brought out still more distinctly with the smaller churches of the 'Open' community, and most of all with those of the Exclusives of whatever description.

These little congregations hold together with much tenacity and self-devotion. The pastors can rarely trust to their stipend or a living. 'There is no stated salary, we take what is left over, and that is not much,' says one; 'if small we put up with it and thank God; if more, we rejoice.' 'The pastor pays rather than receives,' was said of one, and might, perhaps, be said of many. Most eke out an insufficient stipend by other earnings. One we have seen was employed, probably as a clerk, in the City; another was connected with Building Societies, while a third had a business in boots, and kept his stock beneath the chapel. One and all are devoted to their cause, and each Bethel,

Ebenezer, or Zion, has its small circle of supporters; people of whom it was said by one of their own pastors that they were fifty years behind the times, and would like to think they were a hundred, but earnest God-fearing men and women to whom their religion is very real indeed, and who will come regularly even from long distances, unwilling to abandon their membership of the church to which they have become attached. . . .

[*Wesleyan Methodists*]
. . . The Wesleyan system provides all the machinery that is needed for a National Church. Partly on this account the Wesleyans approach more closely to the Establishment than do other Nonconformists. Some of their churches use a liturgy and adopt an order of morning service, differing but little from that used by the Church of England, nor is there any very marked divergence of accepted doctrine. In their buildings, too, they usually follow a style of modern gothic, similar to that commonly employed by the Church of England, the only difference being that they deliberately place the organ where the altar would stand, if there were one, and thus typify and emphasize the everlasting breach of Protestantism with the doctrines of the Mass.

It is only the upper circles of Wesleyanism that affect a liturgy, and as lower classes are reached the order of architecture changes as well as the order of the services, till we reach the plainest type of meeting-house with portico and columns as its utmost decoration, and the simple Nonconformist type of service with hymns and extempore prayers, Bible exposition and sermon.

The congregations are drawn from the same classes that support the Baptists and Congregationalists, but it is a somewhat different temperament that is appealed to,—a character more filled with religious enthusiasm than are the Congregationalists, more emotional than the Baptists, and taking a more joyous view of life than either. Mere pleasure is not regarded either as wicked or as waste of time. Wesleyans may be as deeply religious as the Baptists and as hard working as the Congregationalists, but they look for, and they find, enjoyment in all they do. This spirit finds its vent especially in music, of which much use is made. In addition to organ and full choir of male and female voices, stringed instruments are often employed, and the deep gallery behind the pulpit is filled with the orchestra thus composed.

The Wesleyans have suffered more than either Congregationalists or Baptists from chapels deserted and stranded owing to the removal of their supporters. The lack of individuality among their chapels, owing to the circuit system and the constant change of ministers, necessarily weakens the tie to any particular church. Congregationalists, even if they move to a considerable distance, will cling to their church so long as a beloved pastor occupies the pulpit, and it is the same, or even more so, with the Baptists, to whom, beyond devotion to their leader, their church is a Tabernacle or a Bethel, for the maintenance of which they are personally responsible. On the other hand, the Wesleyans profit more than the others from the flow of population into a new district; partly because we then have the reverse of the same picture, and partly because, amongst new-comers in London, there is always some proportion of those of country parentage who have been born and bred in Wesleyanism. . . .

[*Primitive and other Methodists*]
The chapels of the Primitive Methodists in London are usually quite small, but they are numerous, and widely distributed. Their members are very earnest Christians, and strongly attached. There is some interchange between them and the Salvation Army, but otherwise they rarely wander from their own religious body. Like the Wesleyans, they work on a circuit system, and being poor, have many more chapels than ministers. 'Local preachers' fill the gap, but the work of the ministers is hard, especially as regards visiting the members, who may be scattered far apart. They tell us that their churches are recruited in three ways (not indeed peculiar to this body): (1) by transfers, mostly from the country—these, it is added, are generally 'all right'; (2) by converts—brought out from the people living near; and (3) by those trained in the Sunday school and coming into communion through the Young People's Society of Christian Endeavour, these last giving the best workers.

Every chapel has its Sunday school, and the number of children coming under the influence of the denomination in this way is remarkable. The parents are rarely members, but there is no material difference in class, and no class feeling at all. There is no social gulf to bridge. 'The Primitive Methodists reach the working people; that is their glory,' says an onlooker. 'The Primitive Methodists are the only ones amongst us who touch the poor at all,' is the (perhaps hasty) verdict of a Congregationalist minister, but not very far from the truth; and other witnesses might be quoted to the same effect. It is probably the simplicity and directness of their beliefs and the democratic basis of management which attract. There is nothing sensational in their methods or imposing about the work they do. Apart from the Sunday schools, it is practically confined to the satisfaction of the religious needs of small groups of simple-minded people who were born Methodists; but some kindred souls can always be found to make good the loss the body suffers by lapse. . . .

The United Methodist Free Church seems to lie between Primitives and Wesleyans. It is an honest, earnest body of lower middle-class people with a number of churches, one or two of which exercise considerable force. Like the others, this body adopts the circuit system, and on some of the circuits the ministers are greatly pressed, says one of these hard-worked men, with 'so many chapels to manage' and 'sermons to prepare for an exacting audience apt to be censorious'. There are also a few churches belonging to the Methodist New Connexion, but these seem to have little vitality.

The Bible Christians are another offshoot of the Methodists. They are for the most part countrymen, and clannish, and have several strong congregations filled with the conviction that 'they have got the message the world wants'. Their pastors are 'content with a bare living'. . . .

[*Presbyterians, Unitarians, Society of Friends and others*]
. . . Among them the Presbyterians are by far the most important. They consist of the Presbyterian Church of England and the Scotch Presbyterians, or Church of Scotland. Their congregations are intelligent in a high degree and their ministers are men of culture and even great attainments. In both respects the level is certainly above that of most of the other Nonconformist Churches, and, I should say, above the average of the Church of England. They do not call themselves Nonconformists, and resent the name of Dissenters. . . .

The churches are handsome stone structures, almost invariably of Gothic architecture, well finished within and without, and are kept in perfect order. Like the Established Churches, they are usually named after some saint. In some cases there are buildings for a Sunday school or for mission premises, but by no means always. The church is not regarded as a local institution; the congregations come from far and wide, and there is little call for the concentration of effort on the district in which they happen to meet for public worship. Should any of them feel impelled towards collective missionary enterprise some other neighbourhood would probably be selected in which to try to 'do their duty by the poor'. . . .

Beyond such purely religious work little is attempted. There may be a literary society, but the ordinary social agencies are scarcely needed. Home life supplies everything wanted, except as regards 'young men from the country', who are often received by the minister in the church or at the 'manse' after evening service on Sunday, that he may become acquainted with them and they with each other. . . .

Unitarians, on the other hand, though impaired as religious critics by a certain narrowness of spiritual sympathy, are quite invaluable as leaders in social work. In the institution of 'Domestic Missions' they were pioneers. . . . It was not possible for the Unitarians to kindle the burning enthusiasm which Lord Shaftesbury and those who have succeeded him, have roused amongst their agents, and also in the public mind, over the carrying of the Gospel to the poor while attempting to amend the conditions of their lives. The action of the Unitarians was limited on every side: in the securing of suitable workers, as well as in obtaining sufficient money, and most of all by the discovery, early made, that every step taken to make matters better, involved some danger of making them worse. It will, perhaps, be said that they lacked the 'one thing needful'—that which Mary had and Martha had not: on this Gospel theory great experiments have been made and are yet being made, but there are none of those engaged in such attempts that might not with advantage study the work done and the experience gained by the Unitarian organisations.

As a religious body the Unitarians are small in numbers, and their numbers are still dwindling. By the orthodox their teaching is regarded, somewhat arbitrarily, as a negation, and we hear it said that 'you cannot win on a negation'; but, however regarded, it does seem as though the Unitarian view of the spiritual world in its relation to man awoke little response in the human soul, comparing in this respect unfavourably with even the most extravagant assertions of any African medicine man. Although, however, their direct corporate influence on religious thought grows less rather than greater, their doctrines may be detected working afresh elsewhere, especially among the advanced sections of the Congregationalists, and they probably hold a permanent place in religious development.

The Society of Friends is also a decreasing body, besides being less noticeable in the world than when their peculiarities of dress and speech were more strictly practised. In other ways, as well as dress, they have moved with the times, and in one case we find 'an old-fashioned Quaker meeting transformed into a militant Gospel mission'. Their great contribution to the religious life of the people has been the 'adult school', which is in fact not a school at all, but a social and religious organization of the most democratic type. But no proselytizing is involved, this being foreign altogether to the habits of this sect.

The Friends are content 'merely to welcome' such as join them. In this and in many other ways they set a wise example, and regarding one report from them my notes contain the remark that it is 'the simplest, truest and least embellished account we have had of the work of any denomination'.

And lastly, there are the 'Brethren' of both Open and Close orders, whose little places of worship are scattered throughout London and concentrated in the South-East. They may be known by the inscription to be found outside their buildings which marks the purpose: 'If the Lord will, the Gospel of the Grace of God is preached here every Lord's Day.' With the Close order, or Strict Brethren, no strangers whatever are admitted to the breaking of bread on Sunday morning. The Open Brethren admit accredited Christians to this ordinance and encourage outsiders to attend the preaching of the Gospel on Sunday evening.

In these bodies there are, properly speaking, no leaders, but in practice it always happens that two or three come to the front and lead the service; often there is one on whom everything depends. It is difficult to judge the influence of this peculiar sect upon its own people, but it is undoubtedly strong. The number of adherents is not large, but shows no signs of decrease. There is no lack of vigour. Divisions in the body may have weakened its influence on the world outside, but such are the never-failing signs of vitality in all religious sects, and it is mainly as evidence of the constant up-springing forces of primitive Christianity that the Brethren are of interest here, and there are various other small Christian sects of similar character. . . .

104   An attack on political Nonconformity, 1909

An extract from *Nonconformity and Politics* (1909), 'A Nonconformist Minister', pp. 171–2, 189–91.

The anonymous book from which this extract comes represents the opposite view to that held by Silvester Horne (see document 105). It argues the dangers of being too closely identified with one political party, for reasons similar to those advanced by R. W. Dale and Joseph Parker (see documents 95 and 83). As such it illustrates the 'spiritual' reaction against political involvement felt by an increasing number of Nonconformists, particularly after the political division of 1886.

Political Nonconformity attempts to justify itself in various ways. On the whole, however, nearly all the alleged justifications may be reckoned as variations of two which are first and chief, as re-statements of these two from slightly different points of view. The two main justifications urged in defence of Nonconformity's identification with a political party and with political work are, first, that the policy of the Liberal party is more in accord than is that of the other parties with the spirit and principles of Christianity, and, second, that inasmuch as Christianity aimed and aims at the establishment of the kingdom of God upon earth, the Church is positively called into the political field, since only through political action is the kingdom of God made to come. Even these two defences are at bottom one and the same; for to say that Christianity aims in its method and spirit at the establishment of God's kingdom upon earth, and to say then that the Liberal policy best embodies the method and spirit of Christianity, is to say in effect that the Liberal policy makes for the establishment of the kingdom of God. When one takes a look round the political field, and remembers what current politics really are, one might well suppose that any theories which led to this latter conclusion had already suffered a *reductio ad absurdum* sufficient to discredit it in the eyes of sensible men.

. . . It is one of the commonplaces forced upon the mind by observation and experience that material advance, unless accompanied by a corresponding advance in moral development, sinks the level of manhood nearer to the level of the brutes instead of elevating it nearer to the angels' rank. It is, indeed, one of the chief missions of the religious organisations in any nation to provide the antidote to this danger, and by their distinctly religious activities to create the necessary set-off against the materialising tendencies which political progress always involves. Only when this mission is faithfully discharged does political progress become progress indeed. Political Nonconformity, by its definite alliance with the definitely political forces, reverses its appointed work, and becomes a materialising force instead of the spiritualising force it ought to be. To take the 'kingdom' as signifying a perfect social order, and to work for that perfect social order in definite association with a definite political party, reduces the perfect social order (mental reservations notwithstanding) to a social order perfect only on the material side. It is a business of 'What shall we eat?' and 'What shall we drink?' and 'Wherewithal shall we be clothed?' For after all these things do the Gentiles seek; and political Nonconformity, in joining them, makes their limited aims its own, to the exclusion of its own larger aims, nominally cherished though they still may be. It cannot help itself. And the material good which under these conditions it helps to bring in may mean for many of the recipients the death of the soul.

The defence of Nonconformity's political tendencies, based upon the idea that the 'kingdom' means a perfect adjustment of man's relations with man, a perfect social and economic order, will not, therefore, hold its ground under careful examination, any more than the defence that the policy of one party is more in accord with the spirit and genius of Christianity than the policy of the rest. In making the latter defence, it is forgotten that collective action on the part of an ordinary State cannot, properly speaking, be a Christian thing at all. And in making the former, it is forgotten that 'the kingdom of God is not eating and drinking, but righteousness and peace and joy in the Holy Ghost'. This last-mentioned forgetfulness, at any rate, is surely one into which Nonconformity, with its lofty spiritual ancestry and its inspiring spiritual record, should never permit itself to fall.

105 A Nonconformist minister in Parliament, 1910

An extract from C. Silvester Horne, *Pulpit, Platform and Parliaenn* (1913), pp. 188–92, 201–3.

In 1910, the Rev. C. S. Horne, minister of Whitefield's Tabernacle in London and about to be chairman of the Congregational Union, was returned as Member of Parliament for Ipswich in the January election. Here he explains his reasons for entering Parliament, and describes how religion still lay behind many of the issues with which Parliament had to deal.

All that some of us cared for in 1910 was that the money for Pensions had been provided without taxing the poor man's necessities, and the House of Lords had rejected the proposal with contumely. The claim of the Peers to determine the financial policy of the country carried us back to the days when John Hampden broke the power of absolutism on this very question of the hereditary right to tax England apart from the consent of her representatives. No good Independent could be outside that fight. Besides, this claim by the Lords to supreme power had already meant the defeat of every proposal to give Nonconformists equal rights with Churchmen to promotion in the teaching profession; and it had meant the rejection of Licensing Reform in advocacy of which all the Christian forces of the nation had united with almost unprecedented unanimity. Now the crisis had come. . . .

There has always been a sort of unwritten law against ministers of religion being members of the House of Commons ever since the Cromwellian Parliaments of 1653 and 1654. It is not easy to see why. There are literally dozens of them in the House of Lords; and it must obviously be better that if they have a voice in Parliament they should owe it not to privilege but to the desire of the people freely expressed. More than one ex-minister of religion has attained a position of influence in the House of Commons, such as Mr Henry Richard and Mr Allanson Picton. But since the days of Praise-God Barebones I question whether any minister in charge of a Church had been returned as a member of Parliament until my own election in 1910. Yet for the life of me I cannot see that there is any difference in principle between sitting on a parish council or an education authority or a board of guardians, and sitting in the legislature that deals with national affairs on a more majestic scale. All the reforms which experience had taught me were most urgently needed if Christian righteousness was to be more than a pulpit phrase and was to become an established fact, were jeopardised by the predominance of the House of Lords in the national counsels. It seemed to me then, and it seems to me now, to be at least as much a part of my business as a democrat and a social reformer to seek to perfect the machinery through which the national conscience can express itself, as to endeavour to educate and stimulate that conscience. . . .

. . . What impressed me most of all, as a new member, was the amount of time which the House of Commons devotes to arguing religious questions. Now the historic attitude of England has to be asserted on the subject of slavery, in the Congo or on the Putumayo. Now we have to reargue the whole problem of education, into which this element of religion enters so deeply. Now we are invited to discuss ecclesiastical disorders, and to suggest a remedy. Now we are plunged into the pros and cons of the Ne Temere decree, and the relations of Church and State in respect of marriage. Now the Census Bill affords a plausible pretext for raising the question of enumerating Church adherents. Now passions are aroused over proposals to modify the King's Accession Oath; now the Regency Bill revives ancient controversies over Church Establishments. Later on comes the great Home Rule issue renewing in its crudest form the old 'No Popery' agitation. Welsh Disestablishment is accepted as the opportunity for stating the positive argument for a Free Church in a Free State. The Scotch Temperance Bill comes to us demanded by religious men on religious grounds. The Bill for suppressing the White Slave Traffic is backed by the whole force of the Churches, and nobody can expect them to be silent on the reconstruction of the Poor Law. . . . The fact of the matter is, that there is no Church meeting held in this country that is more constantly and practically concerned with living religious problems than the House of Commons. . . .

106 Epilogue: thanksgiving for victory, 1918

An extract from Sir J. Marchant, *Dr John Clifford, C.H.* (1924), p.235.

John Clifford resented the fact that the Free Churches were excluded from the National Thanksgiving Service in Westminster Abbey after the war, but rejoiced that the king and queen attended the Free Church service. This extract from his diary reflects his optimism for the future.

Saturday, November 16th—Thanksgiving Service of the Free Churches in the Albert Hall. King and Queen present. It was a great and most impressive gathering. It is the beginning of a new day in the relations of the State to 'Dissent'. It is the lifting to a slight extent of the social stigma. Of course it will not go far, but so far as it goes it is in the direction of greater freedom in religious thought and life, and may be regarded as a movement toward reality. The Free Churches are glad; but they must not forget that their strength is in their inward simplicity and faith.

Notes

1 D. Price Hughes, *The Life of Hugh Price Hughes* (London, 1904), p. 473.
2 *Congregational Year Book, 1896*, pp. 77–83.
3 *Congregational Year Book, 1896*, p. 53.
4 R. Mudie-Smith, *The Religious Life of London* (London, 1904).
5 C. F. G. Masterman, *The Condition of England* (London, 1909): edition edited by J. T. Boulton (London, 1960), pp. 207–8.
6 See letter of James Bryce to Clifford, Sir J. Marchant, *Dr John Clifford, C.H.* (London, 1924), pp. 123–4.
7 The by-election of 30 July, won by the Liberals.

Select bibliography

There is no good detailed modern history of the Free Churches in the
nineteenth century, and several of the books listed below cover
the whole or most of the period since 1662. Some of the best
modern surveys are very short. Most of the good books written
within the last twenty years are monographs on particular aspects of
the subject.

This bibliography has been selected to cover the most accessible
books. With one or two exceptions all have been published in the
twentieth century, and they are arranged in chronological order
of publication. Two categories have been omitted: articles in
journals, though there are not many which are relevant; and
biographies, because there are so many that selection is very difficult.

1   *General surveys*

H. S. SKEATS and C. S. MIALL, *History of the Free Churches of
England, 1688–1891*, London, n.d. Very much in the Nonconformist
tradition: narrative without coherent pattern for the nineteenth
century.

C. S. HORNE, *Nonconformity in the XIXth Century*, London, 1905.
A call to battle, but with much information: no footnotes.

H. W. CLARK, *History of English Nonconformity:* vol. ii, *From the
Restoration to the Close of the Nineteenth Century*, London, 1913.
Sees Nonconformist history as a decline from the original ideal.

H. LOVELL COCKS, *The Nonconformist Conscience*, London, 1943.
A short but useful critical appraisal.

W. G. ADDISON, *Religious Equality in Modern England, 1714–1914*,
London, 1944. A very useful outline.

E. A. PAYNE, *The Free Church Tradition in the Life of England*,
London, 1944. A short, but thoughtful survey.

J. W. GRANT, *Free Churchmanship in England, 1870–1940*, London,
n.d. Mainly theological and mainly about Congregationalism.

H. DAVIES, *Worship and Theology in England;* vol iii, *From Watts and Wesley to Maurice, 1690–1850*, Princeton and London, 1961; vol. iv, *From Newman to Martineau, 1850–1900*, Princeton and London, 1962. Indispensable survey of liturgical and theological trends.

2 Particular themes

B. L. MANNING, *The Protestant Dissenting Deputies*, Cambridge, 1952. Detailed survey of this influential body; less relevant for period after 1850.

W. B. GLOVER, *Evangelical Nonconformists and Higher Criticism in the Nineteenth Century*, London, 1954. Very useful and detailed.

E. R. WICKHAM, *Church and People in an Industrial City*, London, 1957. Pioneer study of Sheffield: useful for comparison with Church of England.

R. COWHERD, *The Politics of English Dissent*, London, 1959. To be used with great caution: based mainly on secondary sources and ignores conservative Dissenters.

U. R. Q. HENRIQUES, *Religious Toleration in England, 1787–1833*, London, 1961. Good background to the nineteenth century.

K. S. INGLIS, *Churches and the Working Classes in Victorian England*, London, 1963. Compulsory reading for all interested in this problem.

D. MARTIN, *A Sociology of English Religion*, London, 1967. The historical chapter contains much material not easily available elsewhere.

S. MAYOR, *The Churches and the Labour Movement*, London, 1967. A useful corrective to many assumptions about natural links between Nonconformity and the labour movement.

D. NICHOLLS, *Church and State in Britain since 1820*, London, 1967. Selection of extracts with more detail on Church and State problems than has been attempted here.

B. WILSON (ed), *Patterns of Sectarianism*, London, 1967. Mainly for sociologists, but with some interesting studies of smaller denominations.

3 Denominational histories
Baptists

A. C. UNDERWOOD, *A History of the English Baptists*, London, 1947. Standard history covering the period since the sixteenth century.

E. A. PAYNE, *The Baptist Union: A Short History*, London, 1959.
Covers the denomination as well as the Union; very good survey.

Brethren

H. H. ROWDON, *The Origins of the Brethren*, London, 1967. Covers
the period 1825–50, but gives a good general picture.

Congregationalists

A. PEEL, *These Hundred Years*, London, 1931. History of the
Congregational Union since 1831; very detailed.

R. TUDUR JONES, *Congregationalism in England, 1662–1962*, London,
1962. Broader in scope than Peel, more recent but less detailed.

Methodists

W. J. TOWNSEND, H. B. WORKMAN and G. EAYRS, *A New
History of Methodism*, 2 vols, London, 1909. Useful for a basic
narrative.

B. GREGORY, *Side Lights on the Conflicts of Methodism, 1827–52*,
London, 1898. Very valuable for Wesleyanism in the period.

H. B. KENDALL, *Origin and History of the Primitive Methodist Church*,
2 vols, London, n.d. Much local detail, especially on the origins.
Rather difficult to find things in it, but very rewarding.

H. B. KENDALL, *History of the Primitive Methodist Church*, London, 1919.
Shorter version of the *Origin*, going up to 1919. More analytical.

M. EDWARDS, *After Wesley*, London, 1935; *Methodism and England*,
London, 1943. Covers the period before and after 1850 respectively,
surveying selected themes rather than presenting a narrative. Useful.

E. R. TAYLOR, *Methodism and Politics, 1791–1851*, Cambridge, 1935.
A very important study of the neglected 'liberal' forces in
Methodism in the first half of the century.

R. F. WEARMOUTH, *Methodism and the Working-Class Movements
of England, 1800–50*, London, 1937; *Methodism and the Struggle of the
Working Classes, 1850–1900*, Leicester, 1954. Much valuable detail
which tends to obscure his failure to prove his point.

J. KENT, *The Age of Disunity*, London, 1966. Collection of essays
with important critical comments on earlier Methodist historiography.

R. CURRIE, *Methodism Divided*, London, 1968. Not a denominational history, but a valuable and controversial study of otherwise neglected aspects of Methodist history.

Presbyterians

No good general history exists.

Quakers

E. ISICHEI, *Victorian Quakers*, Oxford, 1970. A model of how to write a denominational history in the social and political context.

Salvation Army

R. SANDALL and A. R. WIGGINS, *History of the Salvation Army, 1865–1914*, 5 vols, London, 1947–68. The most detailed history, but with very few references.

Unitarians

R. V. HOLT, *The Unitarian Contribution to Social Progress in England*, London, 1938. Rather eulogistic, but a useful collection of information.

C. G. BOLAM, J. GORING, H. L. SHORT and R. THOMAS, *The English Presbyterians*, London, 1968. Covers the whole period since 1662; the most recent survey of Unitarian history.

Index